A BRIEF SYSTEMATIC THEOLOGY OF THE SYMBOL

T&T Clark Studies in Systematic Theology

Edited by
Ian A. McFarland
Ivor Davidson
Philip G. Ziegler
John Webster†

Volume 39

A BRIEF SYSTEMATIC THEOLOGY OF THE SYMBOL

Joshua Mobley

LONDON • NEW YORK • OXFORD • NEW DELHI • SYDNEY

T&T CLARK
Bloomsbury Publishing Plc
50 Bedford Square, London, WC1B 3DP, UK
1385 Broadway, New York, NY 10018, USA
29 Earlsfort Terrace, Dublin 2, Ireland

BLOOMSBURY, T&T CLARK and the T&T Clark logo are trademarks of Bloomsbury Publishing Plc

First published in Great Britain 2022
Paperback edition published 2023

Copyright © Joshua Mobley, 2022

Joshua Mobley has asserted his right under the Copyright,
Designs and Patents Act, 1988, to be identified as Author of this work.

For legal purposes the Acknowledgments on p. vii and Statement of Copyright on p. viii constitute an extension of this copyright page.

All rights reserved. No part of this publication may be reproduced or transmitted in any form or by any means, electronic or mechanical, including photocopying, recording, or any information storage or retrieval system, without prior permission in writing from the publishers.

Bloomsbury Publishing Plc does not have any control over, or responsibility for, any third-party websites referred to or in this book. All internet addresses given in this book were correct at the time of going to press. The author and publisher regret any inconvenience caused if addresses have changed or sites have ceased to exist, but can accept no responsibility for any such changes.

A catalogue record for this book is available from the British Library.

Library of Congress Cataloging-in-Publication Data
Names: Mobley, Joshua, author.
Title: A brief systematic theology of the symbol / Joshua Mobley.
Description: London ; New York : T&T Clark, 2021. | Series: T&T Clark studies in systematic theology ; volume 39 | Includes bibliographical references and index. |
Identifiers: LCCN 2021018909 (print) | LCCN 2021018910 (ebook) | ISBN 9780567702500 (hb) | ISBN 9780567702517 (paperback) | ISBN 9780567702524 (epdf) | ISBN 9780567702531 (ebook)
Subjects: LCSH: Christian art and symbolism | Trinity–History of doctrines.
Classification: LCC BV150 .M63 2021 (print) | LCC BV150 (ebook) | DDC 231/.044–dc23
LC record available at https://lccn.loc.gov/2021018909
LC ebook record available at https://lccn.loc.gov/2021018910

ISBN:	HB:	978-0-5677-0250-0
	PB:	978-0-5677-0251-7
	ePDF:	978-0-5677-0252-4
	eBook:	978-0-5677-0253-1

Series: T&T Clark Studies in Systematic Theology, volume 39

Typeset by Integra Software Services Pvt. Ltd.

To find out more about our authors and books visit www.bloomsbury.com and sign up for our newsletters.

CONTENTS

Acknowledgments	vii
Statement of Copyright	viii
Introduction	1
Background	1
The Argument	11
Outline	14
Chapter 1	
THE TRINITY	19
Introduction	19
Augustine, Signs, and the Trinity	21
Karl Rahner's Symbolized and Symbol	30
De Lubac's Sacramental Pneumatology	39
Conclusion	49
Chapter 2	
CREATION	53
Introduction	53
Two Trinitarian Models	56
Aquinas on Creation	56
Duns Scotus	72
Conclusion	88
Chapter 3	
ANTHROPOLOGY	91
Introduction	91
Nature and Grace	93
Anthropology and Fourfold Exegesis	103
Mary the Exegete	116
Chapter 4	
ECCLESIOLOGY	123
Introduction	123
Symbolism and Ecclesiology	124
A Few Critiques	140
Conclusion	154

Chapter 5
TOWARD MYSTICAL REASON 157
    Introduction 157
    From Mysteries to Mystery 160
    From Mystery to Mysticism 170
    From Mysticism to Mystical Reason 185

Conclusion 193
    Symbolism: A Reprise 193
    Evil, the Symbol, and the Cross 196

Bibliography 206
Index 215

ACKNOWLEDGMENTS

I would like to thank the Reverend Professor Simon Oliver and Professor Karen Kilby for their patience and insight as I developed this project as a PhD at Durham University. While any deficiencies are my own, this project owes its conception and completion to these exemplary scholars.

I have had the privilege of doing theology among friends and family. Dr. Benjamin Crace, Dr. Jameson Ross, Hannah Lucas, and the fellowship of the Dun Cow have all been key conversation partners and friends. The Centre for Catholic Studies at Durham University has also been immensely supportive. For my parents, who first taught me to believe and think together, for my siblings and their families, and the rest of our family, I am indebted. Our children have been delightful and patient (my daughter once equated me finishing this project with the eschaton!).

Finally for Caitlyn, the gratitude offered here is wholly inadequate to the grace received.

STATEMENT OF COPYRIGHT

The copyright of this book rests with the author. No quotation from it should be published without the author's prior written consent and information derived from it should be acknowledged.

INTRODUCTION

Background

This book is a speculative systematic theology that attempts to provide a dogmatic outline for the recovery of a traditional theological practice and rationale. It arises from the problematic posed by the great *ressourcement* theologian, Henri de Lubac.[1] De Lubac sought to recover a mode of theology that he called "symbolism," a patristic mode of thought that assumed a real unity-in-distinction between symbolized and symbol, sustaining a thoroughly sacramental vision.[2] It indicates an entire theological paradigm in which symbols ontologically participate in what they symbolize, and all things ultimately symbolize God. To put it somewhat simplistically, a symbol is a sign that mediates the presence of the symbolized,[3] and "reading" symbols is a work of spiritual exegesis, a holistic

---

1. For an excellent and accessible volume outlining the broad concerns of the *ressourcement* movement, see Gabriel Flynn and Paul D. Murray, eds., *Ressourcement: A Movement for Renewal in Twentieth-Century Catholic Theology* (Oxford: Oxford University Press, 2012); see also Jürgen Mettepenningen, *Nouvelle Théologie – New Theology* (Edinburgh: T&T Clark, 2010). For an overview de Lubac's work and its reception, see Jordan Hillebert, ed., *The T&T Clark Companion to Henri de Lubac* (London: Bloomsbury T&T Clark, 2017). Other important works include Hans Urs von Balthasar, *The Theology of Henri de Lubac: An Overview*, trans. Joseph Fressio and Michael Waldstein (San Francisco, CA: Ignatius, 1991); John Milbank, *The Suspended Middle*, 2nd edition (Grand Rapids, MI: Eerdmans, 2005); Susan K. Wood, *Spiritual Exegesis and the Church in the Theology of Henri de Lubac* (Edinburgh: T&T Clark, 1998); Hans Boersma, *Nouvelle Théologie and Sacramental Ontology: A Return to Mystery* (Oxford: Oxford University Press, 2009); for a biography, see Rudolf Voderholzer, *Meet Henri de Lubac: His Life and Work* (San Francisco, CA: Ignatius Press, 2008).
2. Henri De Lubac, *Corpus Mysticum*, 2nd ed., trans. Gemma Simmonds et al. (London: SCM Press, 2006), 221–48.
3. Peter Struck, *Birth of the Symbol: Ancient Readers and the Limits of Their Texts* (Princeton, NJ: Princeton University Press, 2004), 262.

engagement in and through symbols with their hidden source. Such reading involves understanding the symbol itself, encountering God in and through the symbol, and being personally and corporately transformed into a clearer symbol through the encounter. This was a vision at once mystical and rational, thoroughly scriptural and profoundly philosophical, and through and through was *theological*, that is, it sought to understand God in all things and all things in God. De Lubac traces the various dissolutions of modernity—the severing of faith from reason, mysticism from rationality, biblical exegesis from theology, etc.—to the demise of this theological framework.[4] Recovering such a theology, de Lubac thinks, is not just an exercise in nostalgia, but offers a vision that can nurture forms of Christian life fit for the challenges of the present.

Yet de Lubac is characteristically coy about how such a theology might be recovered, or what such a recovery might require. What would symbolism, systematically developed in a contemporary idiom, entail and accomplish? This book proposes an answer to this question. I take up de Lubac's important but fragmentary reflections on symbolism and develop them systematically in order to address a number of crucial issues in contemporary theology. Beginning with God, I explore the ways the language of symbols can furnish an appropriate analogy for the Trinity. In brief, Father–Son–Spirit can be described as symbolized–symbol–symbolism; the Son is the symbol of the Father, and the Spirit is the personal agent of unity between symbol and symbolized. Creatures then participate analogically in these relations, so that symbolized–symbol–symbolism analogically corresponds to God–creation–church: creation is a symbol of God, and the church is symbolism, the unity of creation with creator. To anticipate what will be gained from such a theology, I will argue that symbolism, thus developed, resists modernity's "ontotheological" temptation, refuses both a "Barthian" flattening of nature *and* a neo-Thomist reification of pure nature, and recovers a sense of theology as an ecclesial discipline of mystical reason. But those are end results of a rather long road, which I have now to narrate.

Beginning in the late 1930s, Henri de Lubac helped to initiate the movement known as *ressourcement*, a return to the sources of Christian theology in scripture, tradition, and the liturgy.[5] De Lubac advocated the retrieval of patristic texts as a way of regaining the dynamic spirit of Christian theology. This implied a critique of the then-dominant neo-Scholastic theological manuals, an implication verified when, in *Surnaturel*, de Lubac explicitly called into question the spiritual and theological adequacy of the neo-scholastic theory of pure nature. Such a theory, de Lubac argued, leaves nature untouched by grace save in the most extrinsic fashion, creating the conditions for modern secularism and atheism. His argument hinged

---

4. De Lubac, *Corpus*, 221–48.

5. Much of this section is taken from my "Symbolism after Dialectics: de Lubac, Rahner and Symbolic Theology," *The International Journal of Systematic Theology* 20, no. 4 (October 2018), 537–53. For background information on de Lubac, see Jordan Hillebert, "Introducing Henri de Lubac" in *Companion*, 3–28.

on a re-reading of Thomas in light of patristic tradition, arguing that the weight of tradition lay on the paradoxical position that humans have a natural desire for the supernatural that can nonetheless only be fulfilled by grace. While the argument was by no means new, de Lubac's articulation of it was explosive, earning him an apparent censure from the papacy.[6] And yet, by the Second Vatican Council, the theological tide shifted and de Lubac's stock rose precipitously: he was invited to assist as a theological expert at the council and was subsequently made a cardinal.

While his work on nature and grace remains controversial, his advocacy of patristic retrieval is nearly universally lauded.[7] But what did de Lubac see in tradition that he thought worth reclaiming? De Lubac refers to the style of patristic theology he sought to retrieve as "symbolism," in contrast to a later style he calls "dialectics." *Corpus Mysticum* is de Lubac's book-length treatment of the theme, showing how the shift from symbolism to dialectics was the crucial driver of the evolution of eucharistic theology. The details of sacramental semantics will be addressed in Chapter 4, so I will focus here on the changing theological paradigms that underwrote those shifts. "Symbolism" is de Lubac's word for a broadly Augustinian approach to theology which "consisted in the consideration of 'signs' and 'things.'"[8] While never precisely defined, symbolism is, for de Lubac, a sacramental outlook in which symbols truly make present that which they symbolize. The universe is a theophanic network of symbols that disclose the mystery of their creator, a reality seen most especially in the church and the eucharist.[9] Those symbols are in turn open to exploration by the faculty of reason. The discovery of the symbolized in the symbol requires a union of mysticism and rationality, for the symbolized "is itself radiant with a secret intelligibility."[10]

A set of vocabulary swirls around de Lubac's concept of symbolism. Hans Boersma has variously called this de Lubac's "participatory ontology," "sacramental ontology," or simply, a return to "mystery."[11] De Lubac himself strings together interrelated phrases to describe the symbolic outlook:

---

6. Pope Pius XII, *Humani generis*, available at http://www.vatican.va/content/pius-xii/en/encyclicals/documents/hf_p-xii_enc_12081950_humani-generis.html. De Lubac's defenders and de Lubac himself claim that he was not the target of this encyclical. That his own theology, rightly understood, does not conflict with *humani generis* is clear, but it seems equally clear that he was indeed its intended target.

7. I say "nearly" because neo-Thomists still bristle at the idea that patristic tradition can be understood by anything other than commentarial Thomism. See Steven A. Long, *Natura Pura* (New York: Fordham University Press, 2010), 108.

8. De Lubac, *Corpus*, 274. Citing Augustine, *On Christian Teaching* 1.4, trans. R.P.H. Green (Oxford: Oxford University Press, 1997), 8 (the translator has chosen an uncommon numbering system for this work. For consistency I follow his system and include a page number).

9. De Lubac, "Internal Causes of the Weakening and Disappearance of the Sense of the Sacred," in *Theology in History* (San Francisco, CA: Ignatius Press, 1996), 231.

10. De Lubac, *Corpus*, 231.

11. Boersma, *Nouvelle*, 290.

If we could for a moment translate Augustine's thought into our own language, we would say that for him any mystery, that is to say any revealed truth, is a sacrament, that is to say a sign, and that on the other hand any sacrament, that is to say any sacred rite, is itself a mystery, that is to say broadly a truth to be understood.[12]

Symbolism indicates a sacramental created order that contains mysteries to be understood by reason guided by faith. If de Lubac's description lacks systematic clarity, it is intended to convey the spirit in which symbolic theology was conducted. The symbolic structure of reality was a ubiquitous assumption, a paradigm that influenced the entire patristic theological outlook in ways never fully articulated. Augustine is only one exemplar of this approach; all the Fathers were "geniuses of ontological symbolism."[13]

Symbolism, for de Lubac, thus names an ontology of the real presence of the symbolized in the symbol. A symbol is not merely an "imitation" or "resemblance" of the symbolized. Because they carry within them the "ontological trace" of their source, as Peter Struck summarizes, "representations are not phantoms but manifestations."[14] Symbols manifest in their very being what they symbolize. Contemplation of symbols, therefore, has "the anagogic power to lift us up" to the symbolized itself.[15] To ascend through a symbol to what it symbolizes is indeed a mode of rationality, for it is to grasp the inherent logic of a thing, but it is a rationality that is inherently mystical, for the logic of a symbol is a meaningful *presence*. To understand a symbol is to encounter what it symbolizes. Yet the symbol is not the symbolized. It remains other, so that what is symbolized remains hidden,

---

12. De Lubac, *Corpus*, 231.

13. De Lubac, *Corpus*, 226. By including Augustine and all the Fathers, de Lubac's word "symbolism" names more than the specific theological sub-discipline called "symbolism" by Dionysius and developed in the Middle Ages. Symbols, for Dionysius, mediated the divine presence precisely because of their *unlikeness* to God—symbolism was the extreme end of an apophatic mysticism. This would be transformed in the West until symbols were reduced to metaphors and relegated to an inferior theological discipline. See Olivier Boulnois, "*La théologie symbolique face à la théologie comme science*," Revue des sciences philosophiques et théologiques 95 (2011–12), 217–50. De Lubac's use of the word includes these shifts, but also seeks to name a broader sacramental instinct among the Fathers. His usage is more synthetic and theological than exactingly historical. On the theological rationale for such historiography, see Kevin Hughes, "The 'Fourfold Sense': De Lubac, Blondel and Contemporary Theology," Heythrop Journal XLII (2001), 451–62. For an opposite account that *contrasts* rather than synthesizes Augustine and Dionysius, see Marie Dominic Chenu, *Nature, Man, and Society in the Twelfth Century*, ed. and trans. Jerome Taylor and Lester K Little (Toronto: Toronto University Press, 1998), ch. 3.

14. Struck, *Symbol*, 262. This quote is specifically in relation to Dionysius, but it well represents de Lubac's vision.

15. Struck, *Symbol*, 262.

glimpsed only in its absence.[16] This rather bold Neoplatonism was embraced, but significantly qualified in ancient Christianity. Augustine, especially in *De trinitate*, will emphasize the human *inability* to meet God in this way.[17] Humans are made in the image of God, but this image is marred by sin, and our ability to read the image is also broken. We thus need a new image and new vision, a new Adam and a new Spirit. But this does not alter the fundamental structure: it rather means that all ascent through symbols must now be conducted in and through Christ, which means in communion with his body the Church and in reflection on scripture. And this means that the right reading of symbols, and the encounter it engenders, can only be received as a gift of grace, the generous bestowal of vision from Christ in the Spirit.

According to de Lubac, symbolic theology dominated Christian thought until approximately the high Middle Ages and allowed theologians to hold together as symbol and symbolized the threefold body of Christ. The historical body of Christ, born of the Virgin and ascended into Heaven, is symbolized in the eucharistic church, truly made present by it.[18] This presence-in-symbol does not, however, collapse the distinction between the two terms. Symbolism sees unity-in-distinction, structured after intra-Trinitarian relations. To call the eucharistic church the body of Christ is not merely an "elegant comparison"; its symbolic substructure makes it an expression of the highest realism.[19]

This symbolic architecture was slowly reconfigured into a dialectical form of theology, which came to view symbolic vocabulary with suspicion.[20] Under a dialectical impulse the terms "mystical" and "spiritual" came to be viewed in *contrast* to "real" and "true": "all the symbolic inclusions were transformed into dialectical antitheses."[21] The old formulas needed to be rethought under new semantic orientations. De Lubac argues that this dialectical shift began in earnest with Berengar of Tours (d. 1088) but can also be seen in theologians of unimpeachable orthodoxy. St. Anselm is emblematic of this shift, and Aquinas is implicated as well.[22] For de Lubac, Anselm's mode of faith seeking understanding

---

16. While this language is very Heideggerian, as Peter Struck shows, it is actually ancient and Neoplatonic.

17. See John Cavadini, *Visioning Augustine* (Oxford: Wiley Blackwell, 2019), 1–22.

18. De Lubac does not specifically formulate "the church makes the eucharist" in *Corpus Mysticum*. That formula comes much later in Henri De Lubac, *The Splendor of the Church*, trans. Michael Mason (San Francisco, CA: Ignatius, 1986), 106.

19. De Lubac, *Corpus*, 245.

20. While this was a new development in Christianity, it had ancient roots. Aristotle had already questioned the allegorism that was to become symbolism. Aristotle redefines an enigma in a text, so central to allegorical reading, as a *flaw*, favoring instead discursive clarity. Struck's summary could just as well apply to early modern scholasticism as to ancient poetry: "where others see murky riddles hinting at profound truths Aristotle sees murky nonsense." Struck, Symbol, 24.

21. De Lubac, *Corpus*, 226.

22. De Lubac, *Corpus*, 236–8, 242.

remained broadly Augustinian, but his concept of understanding consisted less in participation than in *demonstration*. While by no means a "rationalist," Anselm helped inaugurate a Christian rationalism which "could no longer envisage the understanding of mysteries outside [its] *demonstration*."[23] This tendency rapidly developed in the Barengarian controversy. De Lubac argues that eucharistic terminology became a flashpoint in the evolution of theological method, with the rise of dialectical rationalism' displacing an older symbolism that sought understanding as both reason and mystical participation. Underwriting the shifts in eucharistic terminology, and driven by the requirements of that debate, a new era of dialectical Christian theology was born, an era with an ominous trajectory: dialectics became Christian rationalism, which became secular rationalism, eventually occluding Christianity altogether.

De Lubac does not have an entirely negative view of dialectical theology. Its development "was normal and therefore good."[24] Eucharistic realism had to be defended; de Lubac has no desire to forget the dialectical age. The theologian can no less abandon dialectical theology than abandon Anselm and Aquinas. So with discernable frustration de Lubac asks, "Could eucharistic realism not have been safeguarded without the virtually total abandonment of symbolism?"[25] De Lubac's call to recover symbolism is thus not a call to nostalgic forgetfulness, but to a new synthesis. De Lubac prescribes what would become his own program of *ressourcement* as a means of regaining such symbolic theology: the theologian should be steeped in patristic theology.[26] This retrieval of patristic symbolism informs three major pillars of his oeuvre: scripture, creation and ecclesiology.[27]

If the demise of symbolism is bound up with eucharistic controversy, symbolism itself is found in its most concentrated form in spiritual exegesis. The literal sense of scripture is the symbol of the spiritual, and reading is a matter of discovering Christ, and thereby being ecclesially and morally formed toward an eschatological fulfillment.[28] Because symbols truly mediate the symbolized, Christ can truly be found in the literal sense, and the reader truly raised up to life in God. As with eucharistic ecclesiology, fourfold exegesis would decline with the

---

23. De Lubac, *Corpus*, 238. Italics added. Fideism is the also linked to this shift: "The mystery to be understood gave way before the miracle to be believed," De Lubac, *Corpus*, 240.

24. De Lubac, *Corpus*, p. xxiv. Anselm is also seen as the great defenders of the Augustinian outlook in Henri De Lubac, *Medieval Exegesis*, vol. I (Grand Rapids, MI: Eerdmans, 1998), 62, 67.

25. De Lubac, *Corpus*, 259.

26. De Lubac, *Corpus*, 260.

27. Henri De Lubac, *Catholicism: Christ and Common Destiny of Man*, trans. Lancelot Sheppard and Sr Elizabeth EnglundOcd (San Francisco, CA: Ignatius, 1988), 99, ch. 6.

28. De Lubac, *Catholicism*, ch. 6; *Medieval Exegesis*, 3 vols. (Grand Rapids, MI: Eerdmans, 1998–2009), *passim*; De Lubac, *Surnaturel: Etudes Historique* (Aubier: Editions Montaigne, 1946), 25.

rise of dialectics.²⁹ While the fourfold sense was formally maintained, dialectical theology eroded the links between exegesis, theology and life: "This doctrine, once its strength had been sapped, survived too long outside the pale of living exegesis, not to mention living theology and spirituality."³⁰ While fourfold exegesis persisted beyond the patristic era, it did so as the flower of a patristic paradigm blooming beyond the paradigm itself. The flower too would eventually decay.

The controversial *Surnaturel* explores what it means for humanity to be a symbol of God. For de Lubac, humanity has a natural desire for the supernatural, a desire borne of its ontological link to God as both source and end. Though marred by the fall, the human soul is *"par ses propriétés naturelles, par son essence même, au moin inchoativement l'image de Dieu."* Consequently, the soul *"n'est vraiment 'formée' que lorsqu'elle est devenue 'déiforme'."*³¹ The formation of the soul consists of being conformed to the image of God, symbolizing the divine life more and more truly (though never, of course, fully). There is no such thing as pure nature, for human nature is a symbol, always already desirous of its divine source and end. Yet this divine end can only be received as a gratuitous gift. The human symbol, then, inhabits the now (in)famous "suspended middle."³² The fulfillment of its nature lies in participating in the divine life, but the divine life can only be received, never demanded. Yet ontological symbolism does not thereby imply the destruction of the integrity of the natural by the supernatural. The natural desire for the supernatural is the paradox of human nature, and by extension, the entire natural world, as a symbol of the divine.³³ The demise of symbolism led to the imposition of a dialectical either/or: either human nature was autonomous in its own realm, or nature was overrun by grace. On de Lubac's account, human nature thus came to be isolated from its supernatural destiny in all but the most extrinsic fashion, opening the door to secularism and atheism.

Taken together, *Corpus Mysticum* and *Catholicism* evidence a thoroughly symbolic ecclesiology. The church is the symbol of Christ, his real presence on earth by the unifying work of the eucharist. De Lubac summarizes his symbolic approach in sacramental terms in his celebrated phrase: "If Christ is the sacrament of God, the church is for us the sacrament of Christ; she represents him, in the full and ancient meaning of the term; she really makes him present."³⁴ Here too the loss of symbolism heralds an ominous future: eucharistic theology collapsed into individualistic piety, and the church became more and more identified with its bureaucratic and juridical structures. The symbolic heart of ecclesiology was slowly lost in the dialectical era.³⁵

---

29. De Lubac, *Medieval I*, 53–74.
30. De Lubac, *Medieval I*, 74.
31. De Lubac, *Surnatural*, 31.
32. Balthasar, *De Lubac*, 15. Milbank, *Suspended*, passim.
33. See Chapters 3 and 5 for expanded discussions.
34. De Lubac, *Catholicism*, 76.
35. See Chapter 4 for an extended discussion.

These three doctrines then are all immediately concerned with de Lubac's appeal to symbolism. In each of these doctrines the decay of symbolism is disastrous: scriptural interpretation is reduced to an historical discipline, pure nature opens the way to secularism, and the church devolves into individualistic piety internally and juridical authority externally. Whether in scripture, human nature, or ecclesiology, the story is the same: patristic assumption gets dissected by dialectics, dismembered by rationalism, and buried by modernity. The logic of de Lubac's case is that any attempt to reclaim any one of these patristic doctrines in isolation will treat a symptom of the demise of symbolism, without treating the underlying cause. Neither the spiritual interpretation of scripture, nor the transcendent calling of the human person, nor the mutual constitution of church and eucharist can be adequately secured apart from a reclaiming of theological symbolism. It must be reclaimed as a whole, as a unified theological vision, if these various sub-topics are also to be secured. De Lubac himself never attempts such a holistic account. To fulfill de Lubac's *ressourcement* vision, therefore, what is needed is a systematic framework for symbolism, however lightly sketched, in which symbolism might be recovered in contemporary terms.

One prerequisite for such a framework would be a reconstruction of the requisite theologies of the Fathers. Symbolism, on de Lubac's account, was less of a specific subject matter in theology than a general habit of thought characteristic of the patristic era, and any recovery of it will require a broad and clear account of patristic theology itself. This is an important work, and one that has proceeded apace for some time.[36] This work has been key, not least because de Lubac's own account often lacked nuance and detail, at his own admission.[37] The shift from symbolism to dialectics was not so uniform as his early account in *Corpus Mysticum* might seem to suggest, as his own late work on Pico della Mirandola and Nicholas of Cusa shows.[38] But reconstruction is not the whole of the *ressourcement* project for the simple reason that we cannot nostalgically leap across a millennium-and-a-half of Christian thought and practice as though it never happened. Assuming that patristic theology ought to enrich our own, we will need to know why our minds do not naturally turn in patterns of symbolism; why do patristic habits of

---

36. I have relied especially on Lewis Ayres, *Augustine and the Trinity* (Cambridge: Cambridge University Press, 2010); Rowan Williams, *On Augustine* (London: Bloomsbury, 2016); John C. Cavadini, *Visioning Augustine* (Hoboken, NJ: Wiley Blackwell, 2019); Gilles Emery, *Trinity in Aquinas* (Naples, FL: Sapientia Press, 2003); Rik Van Nieuwenhove and Joseph Wawrykow, eds., *The Theology of Thomas Aquinas* (Notre Dame, IN: University of Notre Dame Press, 2005).

37. See Bernhard Blankenhorn's critique in a review of Boersma's *Heavenly Participation: The Weaving of a Sacramental Tapestry* in *The Thomist* 78, no. 3 (July 2014), 477. De Lubac called it a naïve book in *Mémoire sur l'occasion de mes éctrits* (Namur, Belgium: Culture et Vérité, 1989), 28; cited in Laurence Paul Hemming, "Henri de Lubac: Reading *Corpus Mysticum*," *New Blackfriars* 90, no. 1029 (September 2009), 521.

38. Henri De Lubac, *Pic de la Mirandole* (Paris: Aubier Montaigne, 1974).

thought appear not only uncomfortable to us, but even positively wrong-headed? A judicious narration is therefore also required, an understanding of the road from there to here. This project, too, has proceeded apace. Many genealogies of modernity have contributed to understanding how patristic assumptions became so highly suspicious in the modern era.[39] This book seeks to draw on both of these *ressourcement* projects. I will draw heavily on the reconstructive efforts directed toward Augustine, Aquinas, and others. Key portions of the work will also follow the trajectories of certain genealogies of modernity. For instance, I will explore the much-debated Thomas-Scotus difference in a chapter on creation. To the reader of contemporary theology, neither my reconstructions nor my genealogy will be new or surprising.

What remains to be done after reconstruction and genealogy is a fresh synthesis into a new and living whole. While there are numerous excellent studies of de Lubac's work, three systematicians in particular have made de Lubac's theology central to their own synthetic projects. Hans Boersma leans heavily on the work of de Lubac to advocate a return to a "sacramental ontology."[40] Boersma rightly points out that at the core of de Lubac's project (and *ressourcement* more generally) is an ontology that is sacramental and participatory. Building on the analogy of being, Boersma argues that because creation exists by participation in God, creation is inherently sacramental, i.e., that it mediates the presence of its creator. I am generally in agreement with Boersma, and "sacramental ontology" is certainly a synonym for symbolism. However, Boersma's account needs a more stable dogmatic grounding: his sacramental ontology remains almost entirely Christological, and I am not convinced that this is sufficient. Any account of analogical participation assumes a doctrine of creation, and that doctrine must be, as it is for Augustine and Aquinas, fully trinitarian if it is to be fully Christian.[41] Boersma's emphasis on Christ as the source and end of creation is not misplaced, but it is incomplete: the Father creates in Christ by the Spirit. The divine life symbolized in creation is the life of the Father, Son, and Spirit, and this reality must structure any dogmatic

---

39. For example, Conor Cunningham, *Genealogy of Nihilism: Philosophies of Nothing and the Difference of Theology* (London: Routledge, 2002); portions of John Milbank, *Theology and Social Theory: Beyond Secular Theory*, 2nd ed. (Oxford: Blackwell, 2006); Amos Funkenstein, *Theology and the Scientific Imagination*, 2nd ed. (Princeton, NJ: Princeton University Press, 1986); Alain De Libera, *La philosophie médiévale*, 3rd ed. (Paris: Presses Universitaires de France, 1998).

40. Hans Boersma, *Nouvelle*, introduction and ch. 3; *Heavenly Participation: The Weaving of a Sacramental Tapestry* (Grand Rapids, MI: Eerdmans, 2011). Due to coronavirus restrictions, I was only able to obtain this on Kindle. I have provided a chapter number and Kindle location to aid referencing.

41. Boersma does in fact state this in relation to Gregory of Nyssa's trinitarian theology, but this brief appeal serves mostly as an example of Nyssa's critical appropriation of Platonism, rather than a structuring principle for theology. Boersma, *Sacramental*, ch. 2, Loc. 595.

account of analogical participation. Beyond Boersma, this systematic theology is a performance of the claim that only a robust trinitarian theology can sustain a sacramental ontology. The validity of that claim will need to be judged by the success of this project as a whole.

John Milbank, the theologian perhaps most closely associated with de Lubac, builds off de Lubac's account of the natural desire for the supernatural to pursue his own highly original ends. Milbank's engagement with de Lubac stems from a conviction that de Lubac more than any other twentieth-century theologian identified in the paradox of nature and grace the key to "a renewal of speculative theology in a new mode that would restore its closeness to the exegetical, mystical, and liturgical reading of revealed signs."[42] Such a reading more closely unites philosophy and theology and creates space within dogmatic theology for history, politics, and event. Where Milbank radicalizes de Lubac's thesis and expands it into the realm of political theology and social theory, I attempt to integrate it (beyond de Lubac's own account) into trinitarian theology. For instance, throughout the book I will point to the importance of pneumatology for the engagement of theology with history, for as both Augustine and Aquinas insist, creation is spoken in the Word, but it is set in *motion* by the life of the Spirit.[43] My own project therefore moves from de Lubac's account of symbolism in a different direction than Milbank's: where Milbank moves "out" to politics, my project moves "in" toward a trinitarian core. Of course, neither Christology (Boersma) nor politics (Milbank) can be separated from trinitarian theology, so this account is not in competition with theirs. Indeed, both Boersma's Christology and Milbank's political theology are moments "within" trinitarian theology, and this makes it all the more important to specify the trinitarian structure of symbolism more clearly.

Perhaps the most holistic, and certainly the most sustained, attempt to renew symbolism for today is that of Hans Urs von Balthasar, whose sweeping work seeks, among many other things, to reintegrate all of theology into a trinitarian paradigm.[44] In many ways his appeal for a return to aesthetics and drama in light of trinitarian theology goes a long way toward providing an account of symbolism. But in one crucial area, indeed, *the* crucial area, it is deficient. Symbolism, as I will argue, is indeed held together by a trinitarian logic, but Balthasar's Trinity turns

---

42. Milbank, *Suspended*, 2.

43. Augustine, *The Literal Meaning of Genesis*, I.36, trans. John Hammond Taylor, *Ancient Christian Writers* 41 (New York: Newman Press, 1982), 41; Thomas Aquinas, *Summa Theologiae* Ia.45.6.ad. 2, All quotations from Laurence Shapcote, O.P., trans., *Latin/English Edition of the Works of St. Thomas Aquinas* (Lander, WY: The Aquinas Institute for the Study of Sacred Doctrine, 2012).

44. Hans Urs von Balthasar, *The Glory of the Lord*, 7 vols. (San Francisco, CA: Ignatius Press, 1982–9); *Theo-Drama: Theological Dramatic Theory*, 5 vols. (San Francisco, CA: Ignatius Press, 1988–98); *Theo-Logic*, 4 vols. (San Francisco, CA: Ignatius Press, 2000–2005); *Mysterium Paschale* (San Francisco, CA: Ignatius Press, 2000), and many more.

on a logic of *distance*, or at least threatens to do so.⁴⁵ That logic of distance risks what John Milbank, with characteristic verve, has called "a gnostic hypostasization of the violence of the cross."⁴⁶ While it is not clear that Balthasar has actually instantiated such a gnosticism, it is undoubtedly risked by his notion of infinite distance between the trinitarian persons and his theology of Holy Saturday. A logic of symbols, however, avoids such a temptation altogether, while nonetheless embracing the many gains that Balthasar's work affords. It does so by insisting with Balthasar, but more consistently than Balthasar, that the Spirit is the ground of difference and freedom within the Trinity, rendering talk of *distance* or an *abyss* wholly superfluous. But that argument requires a clear sense of what a logic of symbols entails, and so I defer that discussion to the conclusion where I will argue both for and against Balthasar. It remains, then, for symbolism to be adequately systematically accounted for, a goal this work seeks to fulfill.

This book is therefore a speculative systematic theology that attempts to articulate a traditional theological practice and rationale in a contemporary mode: it is an attempt to provide a dogmatic outline for what symbolism might mean today. It will, of course, only be an outline, but as I will argue, there is real value in glimpsing the whole as a whole, however lightly sketched. Indeed, where prior engagements have been somewhat fragmentary, one contribution of this book will be its attention to the whole context in which a theology of the symbol must be understood.

The Argument

The road to such a dogmatic outline runs through a particular way of conceiving and employing trinitarian theology. In the tradition of Augustine's *De trinitate*, I develop two triads by which to understand the Trinity and all things in relation to the Trinity. I first offer what I argue is an appropriate analogy for trinitarian relations: to Father–Son–Spirit corresponds symbolized–symbol–symbolism. The Father is symbolized in the Son, who is the symbol of the Father, the Father's replete self-expression. The Spirit is the fully personal agent of unity and love of the Father and Son. Thus, if the Father is the symbolized, the Son the symbol, then the Spirit is symbolism, the dynamic and personal union of symbolized and symbol. This is not so much to understand the Trinity by overlaying it with a predetermined logic of symbols. Rather, it is to begin with trinitarian faith and attempt to shape an analogy around that faith, in this case, to understand symbols in a trinitarian pattern.⁴⁷

---

45. See Karen Kilby, "Hans Urs von Balthasar on the Trinity," in Peter C. Phan, (ed.), *The Cambridge Companion to the Trinity* (Cambridge: Cambridge University Press, 2011), 208–22; *Balthasar: A (Very) Critical Introduction* (Grand Rapids, MI: Eerdmans, 2012), ch. 5.
46. Milbank, *Suspended*, 81.
47. Chapter 5 will detail the necessary circularity of this kind of protocol.

The great value of construing symbols in this trinitarian way is that it allows us to see more clearly how *created* symbols mediate God's presence. Created symbols, I will argue, analogically participate in these triune relations. As the Father is eternally symbolized in the Son as the hidden source of divinity, so by analogy God is symbolized in creation, ever hidden within and beyond it. As the Son is the symbol of the Father, so, analogically, creation is a symbol of God. This is true because of the role of the Logos in creation. Creation is, as Nicholas of Cusa says, the unfolding of the Logos through time, and is thus wholly *significant*, for it symbolizes God in its very being.[48] And this unfolding is destined to be re-enfolded in God, to return to its hidden source in grace. As the Spirit is the fully personal union of Father and Son, so the church, understood as the *totus Christus*, is the unity, the movement of love and desire between God and creation. The church, then, is symbolism, a finite participation in the work of the Spirit, the world reconciled.

Thus we have three triads:

1) Father   Son   Spirit
2) Symbolized   Symbol   Symbolism
3) God   Creation   Church

The first triad grounds the others. It is an understanding of the Trinity in an Augustinian-Thomist mode that provides the basic structure of what follows. The second triad describes the first, seeking to articulate trinitarian relations in the language of symbols. The final triad is the creaturely correlate to the triune mystery. Its relations are analogical reflections of the primordial relations of the Trinity. Thus, God is temporally symbolized in creation, as the Father is eternally symbolized in the Son. Creation is the temporal symbol of God as the Son is the eternal symbol of the Father. And the church is the union of symbol with symbolized, creation and God, just as the Spirit is the fully personal agent of unity between Father and Son. While much detail, nuance, and qualification will be added, these three triads are the basic structure of this systematic theology.

All of this has significant and salutary consequences for contemporary theology. Thinking in this way allows us to see how it is that God is always hidden in creation, never an object over and against which I might stand as a subject. This resituates a Heideggerian complaint about the ontotheological drift of Western philosophy and theology into firmly trinitarian territory: God is hidden as the Father is hidden, the mysterious fount and source who may only be encountered through the symbol. God is never objectified within creation, only symbolized. It indicates, further, that creation cannot be conceived as a mere "vacuole" for

---

48. Nicholas of Cusa, *De Dato Patris Luminum* 4.110, in Jasper Hopkins, *Complete Philosophical and Theological Treatises of Nicholas of Cusa*, Vol. 1 (Minneapolis, MN: Arthur J. Banning Press, 2001), 381.

grace, a passive recipient of divine revelation, as in certain strands of Barthianism (though not all).[49] Barth's famous triad, revealer–revelation–revealedness risks bypassing the doctrine of creation in favor of a wholly determinative "God-from-outside."[50] While Barth has tools for overcoming this christologically, Barthianism has not always been successful in deploying those tools. Because creation is the unfolding of the eternal Word in the Spirit it is truly a symbol of God, and therefore a "thick" reality. If creation cannot be evacuated of integral reality, nor can it be reified by a concept of pure nature. As a symbol, creation is always in a movement of desire toward God. As a symbol it is always *more* than natural, for it is always in motion back toward its hidden source, always also symbolism. It is this dynamic that de Lubac's natural desire for the supernatural seeks to describe. And this finally sustains theology as intrinsically mystical. If a hidden God speaks in time through symbols, then theology is the discipline of learning the language of these symbols that God might be rightly known and loved. Theology, at its core, is therefore the extension of the spiritual interpretation of scripture into all creation: the search for Christ hidden within and beyond the literal sense of everything. This movement from the literal to the spiritual sense of creation is one way of uniting the symbol with symbolized, for to "read" creation in this way is to return it to God in praise and right living. Theology is therefore a form of symbolism, the exercise of rationality *in the Spirit*; it is mystical reason.[51] Thus, my configuration of triads avoids an ontotheological reduction of God, a "Barthian" flattening of nature and a neo-Thomist reification of pure nature, and finally recovers theology's intrinsic mysticism.

I should make clear that triads two and three are entirely my own. They will not be found in this particular arrangement in any of my sources. It is thus this particular conceptuality and its attendant benefits that constitutes the unique contribution of this book. It is not, however, entirely foreign to my sources. It is, as will be shown, deeply rooted in Augustinian and Thomist theologies of the inner word, of creation ex nihilo, of the church as the *totus Christus*, of the desire, love and unity of the Spirit. I have drawn the logic of these themes together in a way that highlights their inner unity, their mutual internality to each other. In short, trinitarian discourse has the potential to reunite what has been pulled apart. It is this very traditional notion—God and all things in relation to God—that I have sought to give new articulation. This is not, therefore, a precise repetition of patristic symbolism: it is newly articulated in a dogmatic outline of what symbolism might mean for us today.

---

49. Steven A. Long coined this term as a critique of de Lubac and Balthasar's view of nature. This is possibly a good descriptor of Barth's view, but not de Lubac's. Long, *Natura*, ch. 2.

50. Karl Barth, *Church Dogmatics I/1* (Edinburgh: T&T Clark, 1956), 363.

51. My focus on the discipline of theology is not intended to downplay the myriad of other ways the symbolism of creation is instantiated. Theology is an act of love in service of the whole Body of Christ, who will of course exhibit other forms of this love.

The grand conceptualities of this work risk a certain shallowness with both its sources and its themes as I attempt to articulate them together in such a limited space. But central to my argument is not merely the relations between the three terms in the triads, but their fundamental *unity*. One cannot understand a symbol without some notion of what it symbolizes, and a correlative understanding of its intrinsic motion of symbolism. An attempt must be made, therefore, however minimally sketched, to understand all three together. The triad symbolized–symbol–symbolism names a structure of relations, and these relations only function as a whole. They must, therefore, like the Trinity, be grasped together or not at all. What I offer, then, is a *brief* systematics of the symbol which could no doubt fill volumes, but which offers an overarching dogmatic framework in which to place much recent research in the ressourcement tradition of Christian theology.

Further, the language of symbols here developed risks being read as a totalizing program for understanding God, one that effectively flattens the complex accounts of Father, Son and Spirit, God, creation, and church given in scripture and tradition.[52] However, while the language does seek to draw together diverse strands of Christian reflection, it does so as an illuminative exploration, not a definitive description. As Lewis Ayres describes Augustine's trinitarian theology, "Augustine seems to see this way of exploring the divine life as a way of bringing together a variety of scriptural (and philosophical) resources and dynamics, not as a 'model' which can simply carry the field."[53] It is in this spirit that I offer this systematics of the symbol. Like all creaturely attempts at knowledge of God, it breaks down at certain points. But these limits, I will argue, do not impose themselves because the language is wrong, but rather because it is insufficient. And the theological vocation is in part to discover ways of continuing to speak about God in the face of this pervasive insufficiency. Moreover, it is precisely these limitations, as Chapter 5 will argue, that force rational reflection to become love and worship. Toward that greater end, then, I offer this systematic theology of the symbol.

Outline

Chapter 1 establishes the trinitarian foundation of such a theology. I first explore Augustine's trinitarian account of signs and knowledge, outlining the role of the inner word rightly guided by love in understanding trinitarian relations. I then follow Karl Rahner in expanding this logic throughout the theological spectrum. Rahner follows Thomas and Augustine's doctrines of the inner word to argue that all of being is symbolic, meaning that it comes into being by expression in a symbol: Father in Son, church in sacrament, soul in body, etc. The Son, as the Inner Word of the Father, is the Father's symbol, the fullness of the Father

---

52. I am thankful to Lewis Ayres for pointing out this weakness.
53. Ayres, *Trinity*, 325.

expressed in another. In dialogue with de Lubac, I then argue that the Spirit is symbolism, the dynamic movement of unity between Father and Son. The Spirit, moreover, secures the *difference* between the Father and Son, as the Father desires and loves the Son as the other, and the Son the Father. The Spirit is therefore the fully personal agent of unity-in-distinction within the godhead. Moreover, while I maintain the controversial *filioque* of the Western tradition, I emphasize the paradox of Son and Spirit. The Spirit proceeds from the Father *per filioque* but is also the gift the Father gives the Son in generation, and so is paradoxically "prepresent" in the Son's begetting. This paradox will ground every other paradox touched on in this work.[54] Symbolized–Symbol–Symbolism thus describes the aboriginal triad of Father–Son–Spirit. Everything that exists is given its own share in this triune pattern.

Chapter 2 explores how the Father, Son, and Spirit create in a single unified act that is nonetheless accomplished according to the trinitarian *taxis* and paradox. I explore this in relation to Thomas Aquinas's account of creation. The Father speaks creation in the speaking of the Word, and that divine speech is set in motion through time by the movement of the Spirit. Thus, creation is a symbol of the Trinity, a temporal unfolding of the Word in motion back toward the Father in the Spirit. This account is not the only one available, however: Duns Scotus provides an alternative account of creation on the basis of a different account of the Trinity, one that emphasizes a logic of productive power over a logic of symbols. Scotus modifies the Franciscan tradition to prioritize the productive powers of the divine essence over the relations of the persons, and this turns his doctrine of creation into an account not principally of trinitarian relations in act, but of divine causal power. Once the distinction between God's absolute and ordained power was centralized by Scotus's successors, creation came to be seen as so exhaustively threatened by God's absolute power that it could no longer be trusted to symbolize God. The desacralization of creation ensues. My argument is that this change is rooted in trinitarian theology, and a recovery of a trinitarian theology of symbols can help recover the sacral value of creation as symbol of the triune God.

Chapter 3 extends this reflection on creation by turning to anthropology. Creation is destined to return to God in humanity, specifically in the humanity of Christ. Humanity thus forms the hinge between creation and redemption. As the hinge, it is marked by a natural desire for the supernatural: naturally desirous of God as source and end but requiring grace for the fulfillment of that desire. Rather than rehash that debate at length, I will instead draw attention to the isomorphism between scripture and anthropology. Under a trinitarian logic of symbols, the shape of scripture is the shape of the human, with Christ standing at the middle of both. Both scripture and humanity are symbols, stories authored by God to be read by a spiritual creature capable of reading symbols. In particular, the structure of nature

---

54. On de Lubac and paradox, see Rowan Williams, "A Paradoxical Humanism" in Hillebert, *Companion*, xiv–xix.

and grace mirrors the structure of the Old and New Testaments.[55] Just as Christ is only intelligible as *Israel*'s messiah, as the fulfillment of Israel's founding promises, so grace assumes and perfects but does not destroy nature. But just as there is no aspect of Israel's scripture in which the eternal Logos is not always-already present and working, so there is no pure nature not always-already marked by grace. Nonetheless, in spite of the "pre-presence" of Christ in the Old Testament and the undeniable continuity of Christ's life and work with Old Testament messianic promises, Christ comes in a manner completely beyond Israel's expectations, a fulfillment at once longed for and yet unforeseeable. So too is nature "suspended," caught up in a destiny at once constitutive of it and yet beyond it. This paradox is summed up in Mary's *fiat* and *Magnificat*, where constitutive desires are fulfilled by a surpassing grace. To be a human symbol is to be like Israel, desirous by nature for a destiny that can only be gratuitously given.

If humanity is suspended between created nature and divine grace, it is in Christ's body that the consummation of nature in the supernatural is attained. Chapter 4 thus focuses on ecclesiology and proceeds in two stages. I first argue that the *totus Christus* can be conceived along the same triad: Christ is symbolized in the church by the symbolism of the eucharist. This is a rescription of de Lubac's work in *Corpus Mysticum*. The church is the body of Christ, his living symbol in the world, alive by the dynamic movement of desire and love instantiated in the eucharist. Thus, the eucharist makes the church, and all three are the *totus Christus*. The second stage considers the *totus Christus*—the eucharistic church in union with its head—in relation to creation and God. If creation is a symbol of God, then the *totus Christus* is symbolism, creation in motion back toward the Father. The church in its life and especially its sacraments returns creation to God in praise, not as a contrast to creation, but as the revelation of its deepest life. In this way we can understand de Lubac's assertion that the church is a sacrament. It is creation united to God, symbol to symbolized. The church is a finite participation in the eternal work of the Spirit, i.e., symbolism.

Chapter 5 then makes a final appeal for symbolism by drawing attention to the relation of symbolism to mystery. This secures three particular gains which must be held together to be held at all. First, it avoids an "ontotheological" reduction of God by maintaining absolute divine transcendence: God is only ever symbolized in the world, as the Father is eternally symbolized in the Son. It then secures the mystical quality of creation by refusing either a "Barthian" flattening of nature or a neo-Thomist reification of pure nature. Creation is the temporal unfolding of the life of God in time, as the Son is the symbol of the Father, and is thus neither mere vacuole, nor a self-enclosed perfection. And this finally reclaims theology as a discipline of mystical reason, as the discipline of reading mystical signs in the Spirit.

---

55. I say mirrors because the relationship is by no means identical. The Old Testament is the story of God's grace at work! But its structural relation to Christ is shaped by the same logic of symbols as nature and grace.

An entire theological program is thus enfolded in a trinitarian vision. While these gains are present in other theologies, a systematic theology of the symbol gathers them together under one trinitarian paradigm. Only such an account, or something very much like it, can accomplish de Lubac's vision of a reclaimed theological symbolism. I have undertaken this project because de Lubac's call to symbolism has yet to be sufficiently accounted for in systematic terms. I account for it with a trinitarian theology of the symbol, a way of understanding and loving God and all things in relation to God. If, then, we are to continue de Lubac's program of *ressourcement*, symbolism must be systematically reclaimed. The next chapter begins such a systematic theology with the doctrine of the Trinity.

Chapter 1

THE TRINITY

Introduction

As we have seen, Henri de Lubac calls the patristic theology he hoped to recover "symbolism," a mode of theology that assumed a real union-in-distinction between symbols and what they symbolize. But de Lubac nowhere develops this idea systematically. The goal of this chapter is to begin such a systematic account by setting out the trinitarian structure of symbols. In the end, I will argue that the Trinity can be understood as symbolized–symbol–symbolism: the Father is symbolized in the Son, who is the Father's replete self-expression in another. The Son, as the eternal Word, is thus the symbol of the Father, receiving the fullness of the Father's being. The Spirit is symbolism, the fully personal agent of love and unity of symbol and symbolized. To arrive at this account, I engage three theologians: Augustine's trinitarian doctrine of signs, Karl Rahner's Christology of the symbol, and de Lubac's pneumatological sacramentology.

De Lubac's account of symbolism claims to arise from Augustine's theology of signs: "Augustinian theology consisted in the consideration of 'signs' and 'things.'"[1] I turn to Augustine, therefore, to begin this systematic theology of the symbol. Augustine's early *De magistro* builds off an analysis of human learning to argue that only Christ can teach us the truth.[2] Christ is the origin both of all experience as creator and of all knowledge as illuminator, and so all experiences within creation are only finally meaningful in Christ. Yet this account remains abstract from the life, teachings, death, and resurrection of Christ. In later works, Augustine will emphasize that it is specifically in the incarnation, death, and resurrection

---

1. Henri De Lubac, *Corpus Mysticum*, 2nd edn., trans. Gemma Simmonds et al. (London: SCM Press, 2006), 274; Augustine, *De doctrina christiana*, 1.4, trans. R. P. H. Green (Oxford: Oxford University Press, 1997), 8.

2. Augustine, *The Teacher* in *The Teacher; The Free Choice of the Will; Grace and Free Will*, trans. Russel P. Robert (Washington, DC: Catholic University of America Press, 1968). Due to coronavirus restrictions, I did not have access to the book I originally used in this chapter. I have the numbering system used by the translator, but not exact page numbers.

of Christ that creaturely symbols are finally meaningful. In the incarnation the eternal Word becomes a creaturely symbol, and this renders all creation a symbol of God. The incarnation is intended to shape not only our concepts about God, but our desire and love for God. This is borne out in Augustine's doctrine of the inner word. The inner word is the capacity of the mind for self-understanding and self-expression. But in order to be true, it must be begotten in right love. This inner word begotten in love is, Augustine thinks, an apt analogy for the Trinity. The Son can thus be conceived as a sign (for a word is a sign) that bears the fullness of the Father's presence and is thus the *symbol* par excellence. The Spirit, then, is the fully personal agent of love and unity between symbolized and symbol. I will call this pneumatological dynamic, symbolism. Thus we could summarize Augustine's Trinity with the triad, symbolized–symbol–symbolism, an apt analogy for Father–Son–Spirit.

I will then turn to Karl Rahner who expands Augustinian symbolism into a great chain of symbols: Father in the Son, the divinity of Christ in his humanity, Christ in church, church in sacrament, soul in body.[3] The theology of the symbol, in Rahner's hands, is given maximum theological scope, touching on everything that is. But Rahner's theology of the symbol remains entirely dyadic—neglecting the role of the Holy Spirit. To reclaim a trinitarian theology of the symbol, we will need a pneumatology of signs.

To unfold the place of the Spirit in symbolic theology, I will turn finally to de Lubac's theology of those two paradigmatic signs and things: sacraments and mysteries. De Lubac discovers three nuances between patristic usages of the words "mystery" and "sacrament." Each nuance points toward the Spirit in a firmly Augustinian mode. First, mysteries are hidden within sacraments, as symbolized within symbol, giving rise to desire and love. Secondly, a mystery is the self-donation that makes a sacrament a sacrament, a gift from symbolized to symbol. Finally, a mystery is the nuptial union between sacraments and what they signify, so that symbol and symbolized are known together. Desire, gift, and unity, then, are the animating centers of de Lubac's sacramentology, and while he rarely draws this link, are firmly Augustinian understandings of the Spirit. The Spirit is the active and personal agent of unity, internal to both Father and Son, Symbolized and Symbol, and wholly personal and hypostatic. This pneumatology then ensures that symbols are not arbitrarily related to the symbolized, for the Spirit is wholly internal to both symbolized and symbol. Between symbolized and symbol breathes the Spirit, the wholly personal and active agent of desire, gift, and union: symbolism itself. Creatures then participate in the Spirit by reading the symbols, uniting symbols to the divine symbolized, knowing God in all things and returning creation to God in praise. Beginning with Augustine's Trinity, taking on the ontological and theological implications of Rahner's Christology of the symbol and de Lubac's pneumatology of symbolism, we arrive at the trinitarian

---

3. Karl Rahner, "The Theology of the Symbol," in *Theological Investigations*, vol. 4 (New York: Seabury, 1974), 221–52.

triad: symbolized–symbol–symbolism. In the next chapter we will consider the implications of this for the created order, and this discussion of the Trinity will be deepened there as well, but I begin here to establish the basic trinitarian structure of symbols.

Augustine, Signs, and the Trinity

Augustine's semiotics is a first on two accounts. He is the first to make a theory of signs coextensive with a theory of language, and he is the first to account for the role of a receiving subject or interpreter of the sign.[4] Prior accounts, notably in sustained debate between Stoics and Epicureans, never tied a sign-theory so closely to a theory of language, and never recognized that the interpretive act is a key component of signification. These two insights make Augustine a seminal figure in the development of the philosophy of semiotics.[5] In Augustine's classic definition, "A sign is a thing which of itself makes some other thing come to mind."[6] Three poles: a *sign* signifies *something* to *someone*. This tripartite structure is most obviously the case in human language, but in contemporary times has been applied to all life and even all physical existence.[7] Augustine's two breakthroughs set the stage for a full-fledged "semiotic point of view."[8]

But Augustine's point is never the sign theory. Semiotics is always a servant of his theology. So much is to be expected. But the more important point of Augustine's theory of signs is that signification itself is a symbol, and therefore contemplation of the creaturely process of communication becomes a pathway of ascent into God. Semiotics itself must be "referred" to love of God and neighbor. It is the eternal source for which the structure of signification is a symbol that Augustine is after. Semiotics, in Augustine's thought, modulates into a higher key, becoming a tool of anagogical ascent. Such modulations are not, however, the end of his semiotic discourse. Rather, semiotics is universalized, coextensive with creation, and rooted in eternal generation and procession. If the extensiveness of

---

4. The literature on this subject is vast. See R. A. Markus, "St. Augustine on Signs," *Phronesis* 2, no. 1 (1957), 60–83; Gerard Watson, "St Augustine and the Inner Word: Philosophical Background," *Irish Theological Quarterly* 54, no. 2 (1988), 81–92; Edward Morgan, *The Incarnation of the Word: The Theology of Language of Augustine of Hippo* (London: T&T Clark, 2010); Lewis Ayres, *Augustine and the Trinity* (Cambridge: Cambridge University Press, 2010), 82–92, 193–8; Susannah Ticciati, *A New Apophaticism: Augustine and the Redemption of Signs* (Leiden: Brill, 2013).

5. Cf. John Deely, *Four Ages of Understanding* (Toronto: University of Toronto Press, 2001), ch. 6. See also, Markus, "Signs," Appendix A, for a helpful, though dated, delineation of terminology.

6. Augustine, *de doctr.*, 30.

7. Cf. John Deely, *Basics of Semiotics* (Bloomington: Indiana University Press, 1990).

8. Cf. Deely, *Understanding*, 221.

Augustine's semiotics is a breakthrough, which it certainly is, then it is theology that enables such an extension. This accounts for the difficulty of extracting from Augustine a sign-theory for its own sake. It simply does not exist for its own sake. Indeed, Augustine would argue that to stop at a semiotics *qua* semiotics would be to fail to go where semiotics itself leads: "It is a miserable kind of spiritual slavery to interpret signs as things."[9] A philosophy of signs, Augustine would say, should lead us into the divine life in which all signification analogically participates. I will therefore follow Augustine in ascent from an analysis of signs and signification, to the precondition of external signs in inner words begotten in love, to the eternal life of God. Humans beget inner words in love; the Father speaks the Word in the Spirit. Reflection on the former will lead to greater participation in the latter.

From Him …

How may we understand the Trinity if it is so utterly beyond all creaturely reality? We are temporal creatures, and all our knowledge arises through processes of signification. We require signs to understand. But how then can we know the triune God who is ineffably beyond our signifying capacity? Augustine consistently returns to this difficulty in different forms, and while his position is refined throughout his career, his answer consistently turns on a logic of presence. We come know God through signs because signification itself is a finite participation in the eternal speaking of the Word. It is the *presence* of eternal truth itself to both the mind and that which the mind seeks to understand that renders signification possible and revelatory.[10] Signs are thus always more than "mere" signs, for they can only be recognized as signs by their participation in God.

This insight is developed in an early treatment of language and signs. In *De magistro* Augustine reflects in dialogue with his son on the problem of learning.[11] Two axioms arise from his discussion: every*thing* we learn, we learn by signs, but we only know the meanings of signs by the things they signify. An experience of things without signs would be an undifferentiated pile of sensation; an experience of signs without things would be nothing but empty noise. But how then do we learn, if we can know neither signs without things nor things without signs? Which comes first? Augustine solves this aporia christologically. Christ, as the source of all that is, operates on both sides of the sign–thing distinction: he is the creative source of each thing, and the illumination that makes signs meaningful. Christ is the Inner Teacher in whom the simultaneous knowledge of signs and things arises.[12] Thus, for Augustine, neither human teachers of signs, nor the accumulated effects of experience, can ever teach anything to the human mind unless joined together by Christ; we have no other teacher.

---

9. Augustine, *De doctr.*, 3.21 (Green: 72).
10. See, for instance, Augustine, *De trin.* 9.11 (Hill: 277).
11. Augustine, *De magistro*, 10.30 and 10.33.
12. Augustine, *De magistro*, 11.38.

Robert Markus argues that this solution "short-circuits" the development of Augustine's semiotics.[13] Augustine, according to Markus, is on the cusp of realizing that our experiences and the language we use to narrate and understand them arise together and are co-constitutive, but Augustine stops short to pursue his own christological purposes. The concern of *De Magistro* is christological, so Markus does not fault him for making his theory of signs auxiliary to Christology. But had Augustine not reached so quickly for christological resolution, Markus argues, he might have seen that sign-systems themselves coordinate signs and *significata*, without requiring christic mediation. Augustine has almost, but not entirely "broken through the barrier between signs and *significata,* the mutual externality to each other of language and experience."[14] Indeed, Augustine does not make this breakthrough. But Markus's observation (it is not quite, for Markus, a critique) risks missing the point. Markus is right that there is no mutual externality of language and experience, but neither is there, for Augustine, any mutual externality of Christ the Interior Teacher and the human mind, and therefore no mutual externality of Christology and semiotics. Markus is attempting to reconstruct Augustine's semiotics independent of christological concerns, a goal that he acknowledges is not really possible.[15] In building an Augustinian semiotics *qua* semiotics, he methodically ignores Augustine's point that semiotics is christological, and his christological solution is no less semiotic for its Christology. Christology is not an alien solution to a native semiotic problem, so that invoking the former interrupts the latter.

This would be an alien solution to a semiotic problem if Christ were alien to the human mind and the created order, since he would be performing a function in place of the mind, competitively replacing its native (in)capacities. But christic illumination is not extrinsic to the human capacity to learn. Christology is woven into the very fabric of anthropology, so that the union of sign and thing in Christ is what sustains their union in the human mind. Yet the intellect does not end where christic illumination begins. The paradox is that this christic dynamism is both wholly the work of Christ *and* natural to the human mind; because Christ is both creator and illuminator, all functions of the human mind are finite participations in his eternal reality as Logos. His ongoing work is wholly *interior* to the mind, so that there is no competition between Christ's work of illumination and the human act of understanding. To think is to be ontologically related to the Logos in this human way. This means that Augustine's christological resolution is not thereby *not* semiotic resolution. It is fully semiotic because fully human. Signs and things are unified in Christ and therefore arise in a single act of human understanding.

---

13. Markus, "Signs," 70. This is repeated by Deely, *Ages*, 218. The term "semiotics" arises "after Locke and Peirce," and is a theory of signs. The medievals called it *doctrina signorum*. Augustine had no name for it. Deely, *Ages*, 362.
14. Markus, "Signs," 70.
15. Markus, "Signs," 70.

Thus, it is not quite true that language and experience remain mutually external to one another in *De magistro*. Augustine's negative claim that neither experience nor signs teach is a claim about origins and ends: knowledge, the union of signs and things in the mind, neither arises from, nor is consummated in, signs or things. Their simultaneity disallows any claims to priority. Christ, as the power and wisdom of God, the creator and illuminator of all things,[16] is prior to and the proper end of both experience and significance, and therefore the one in whom the two cohere.[17] The mind's unified act of understanding is dependent upon this prior and teleological unity of sign and thing in Christ. Christic illumination thus places all meaning within a narrative of procession and return, a doctrine of creation in which intelligibility is an analogical expression of eternal intelligibility *en se*. The upshot is that all our sensory experience is grounded in Christ's knowledge of his creation, and all our linguistic expression arises from the higher functions of rationality which are a participation in Christ's own illuminative nature as *Logos*. To make any sense of anything at all is to do something profoundly christological, for it is to unite experience and illumination in an irreducibly singular way. Markus is surely right that Augustine does not press the semiotic analysis far enough, but even if he had recognized that language systems themselves are capable of coordinating signs and *significata*, this would still be but a finite reflection of Christ's work. It is not going far beyond Augustine to say that it is because there is one Christ who is both wisdom and power that there is one unified language-experience event.

This fully human and yet Christic account of learning begins to articulate a symbolic account of humanity. It is because all experience and all signs participate in the power and wisdom of Christ that experience is significant. Thus read, the human mind is itself symbol, for it mediates the *presence* of Christ. This symbolic logic then ensures that there is no "dialectical antithesis" between Christology and semiotics.[18] The two form a "symbolic inclusion" in which the latter is contained within, illuminated and sustained by the former. The process of signification, it turns out, is a vestigial presence of Christ in the mundane exchanges of daily life. The mind's ability to synthesize signs and things with an irreducible and seemingly impossible spontaneity is a symbol of Christ in his dual work of power and wisdom—creation and signification. The symbolic relation allows Augustine to modulate from one paradox to a higher one present within it and beyond it, but not in competition with it. In this case, the paradox of learning points to the paradox of Christ at once constitutively "in" and yet not "of" the human mind.[19]

---

16. *De magistro*, 9.38. Quoting 1 Cor. 1:23.
17. Cf. *De trinitate* 4.25, trans. Edmund Hill, O.P. (New York: New City Press, 1991), 171.
18. De Lubac, *Corpus*, 226.
19. Not accidentally, there are echoes here of the natural desire for the supernatural: it is "in" us, but not "of" us. Henri De Lubac, *Theology in History* (San Francisco, CA: Ignatius, 1996), 129.

Yet for all its christological emphasis, *De magistro* remains at a distance from the history of Christ himself. It simply is not clear what role the incarnation, death and resurrection of Christ makes to this scheme, or what role sin plays in distorting our knowledge. In short, this Christianized Neoplatonism fails to fully integrate the Christian gospel, a shortcoming Augustine will rectify in his later years.[20]

Through Him …

Augustine will revisit the theme of Christ's role in human knowledge often, but with increasing emphasis on the concrete life of Christ. Christ is still the foundation of all knowledge and experience, but this is now centered on his life and death. Sin deforms created symbols, making ascent to God through created symbols impossible. We need a new symbol and a new vision. If *De magistro* emphasizes that all things are *from* Christ, later works like *De doctrina christiana* and especially *De trinitate* will emphasize that all things must pass *through* Christ. In Rowan Williams' words, in the incarnation "God has 'placed himself in the order of signs' (in de la Taille's famous phrase), and so brought to light the nature of all signs in respect of his own nature as uniquely *res*."[21] The incarnation reveals that all signs point to God:

> *Everything* that has taken place in time in "originated" matters which have been produced from the eternal and reduced back to the eternal, and has been designed to elicit the faith we must be purified by in order to contemplate the truth, has either been testimony to this mission or has been the actual mission of the Son of God. Some testimonies foretold that he was going to come, some testified that he had come. It was only fitting that when he through whom every creature was made became a creature himself, *all creation* should bear witness to him.[22]

All creation is a sign of Christ, and in him a sign of God. Moreover, Christ is a sign of God by being the very presence of God on earth. If a symbol is a sign that mediates presence, then Christ is the symbol *par excellence*. And this reveals all creation to be a symbol of God *in Christ*. The incarnation reveals discourse about "signs and things" to be discourse about "symbols and symbolized." All creation is now seen to carry within it the ontological trace of the divine, for it is created in Christ and for Christ. This is not to say that creation just is God, nor that there is

---

20. Hence, John Cavadini will compare the Christ of *De magistro* to the far more tactile *blood* of Christ that is so pivotal in *De trinitate*. Cf. *Visioning Augustine* (Hoboken, NJ: Wiley Blackwell, 2019), 52.
21. Rowan Williams, *On Augustine* (London: Bloomsbury, 2016), 148.
22. *De trin.* 4.25 (Hill: 171).

not a second work of redemption and elevation needed to see God. I will discuss these issues in chapters two and three. The point here is that Christ is the symbol of God, and all creation now joins with him in symbolizing the Father.

That all creation is now a symbol of God renders the Christian faith truly catholic: all that is good, beautiful, and true now has a place in the faith, even if that place can only be discerned by a contentious testing. Entire modes of discourse, then, are to be embraced and then modulated into a higher key ("used," in Augustine's words). Languages, history, science, and rhetoric, whether of pagan or heretical origin, are to be learned and directed toward love of God and neighbor.[23] Of course, love of God and neighbor will require modification of many discourses, but Augustine is happy to affirm the aims of all endeavors of human culture, because all things are symbols—contain the ontological trace of Christ—and no true thing is a dialectical contrast to the final "Thing." If all things are a symbol of God in Christ, then nothing dialectically opposes God. Indeed, because the symbol-symbolized relation is universalized, even sin is not a dialectical antithesis to the true "Thing." Apart from God there is no-thing. The failure to symbolize God is a pure lack, an unspeakable contradiction.[24] Strictly speaking, there are no dialectical antitheses, only degrees of symbolic inclusion.[25]

The Christian life, then, consists in making these kinds of modulations from symbols to symbolized. Doing so is a process of purification: not escaping from the world of created things, but embracing created things according to their eternal source and end. That embrace is made possible, for Augustine, only in the incarnation. If in *De magistro* the human intellect is a symbol because of the presence of Christ the creator and illuminator, in later works all creation is a symbol because God became human and raised creation to God through Christ.

To Him ...

Learning to read created symbols, especially the incarnation, is intended to shape the formation of what Augustine calls the "inner word." When a mind comes to know something, it generates an inner word, a "word of the heart."[26] John Cavadini describes it thus: "it is an eternally valid precultural reality focused on a capacity for self-awareness and self-expression which is productive of culture—of

---

23. *doctr.*, 2.102 (Green: 54). On Augustine's engagement with rhetoric, see Ayres, *Augustine and the Trinity*, 132.

24. See discussion of *privatio boni* in the conclusion.

25. I am aware that this touches on very sensitive questions about power and privilege: who gets to decide what degree of symbolic inclusion a thing inherently has, and what modifications it requires in order to be embraced? But the disposition of openness I describe here must be instantiated as a true listening openness. I envision catholicity that is not hegemonic precisely because it is universal, and so none can claim a total vision of the whole.

26. *De trin.* 14.10 (Hill: 378), 15.19 (Hill: 409).

signs and sign-systems—but not reducible to any particular cultural expression."[27] When the human mind comes to know something it "begets" an inner word that can then be "incarnated" in language and culture. It is wholly interior to the mind, and is thus one with the mind itself, and yet it is also a word, so it is a *kind* of sign. It is the mind fully expressed in another—the mind's self-symbol. An inner word that is wholly true is impossible in this life, for our perspective always remains fragmentary and clouded by sin. The journey to eternity is thus one of learning to know God and ourselves rightly and instantiating that right knowledge in culture.

But the quality or truthfulness of an inner word is not merely constituted by the correctness of its perceptions or its comprehension of facts. An inner word is true according to the quality of the love in which it is begotten. As we currently live, our desires and loves are too deformed and disordered to know either God or ourselves rightly, and the cultures instituted by the incarnations of our inner words are likewise deformed. If we are to reach our eschatological destiny, we will need a newly aligned will. This is one reason the incarnation is necessary. The incarnation is not merely the gift of new information about what God is like, or even a substitution of our broken symbols for his whole one on the cross. The incarnation is also intended to present our wills with a moving picture of eternity that we might learn to desire and love it rightly.[28] It is by contemplating the life of Christ that we learn to desire and love God rightly, as Christ works to entice us into meeting the Father in himself. As I will argue in the third section of this chapter, the symbol works by *concealing* the symbolized, so that the allure of a treasure hidden in a field might entice us to sell all to acquire it.[29] The incarnation, then, is an erotic symbol, a drawing toward the secret trace of the symbolized hidden within.

This language of desire and love puts us firmly in the territory of the Holy Spirit. The point of love's necessity for the begetting of true inner words is that the eternal Son is never without the Spirit. If Christ is the eternal Word of the Father and therefore the analogical source of all knowledge, the Spirit is the fully personal agent of love between Father and Son and therefore the analogical source of all love and desire. The union of symbols with the symbolized is therefore a work of the Spirit. I will expand this pneumatology of the symbol in the last section, but the point here is that humanity is a symbol of God not just by participation in the eternal Word but also by participation in the Spirit. And thus encountering God in symbols is as much a matter of desire and love as of right knowledge, for to know the hidden Father is to know the Son in the Spirit.

Right love and a true inner word are eternal realities: our fragmentary inner words and partially aligned loves are echoes of the presence of the eternal Word and eternal Spirit. For Augustine:

---

27. Cavadini, *Augustine*, 47.
28. Cavadini, *Visioning*, 51.
29. Mt. 13:44.

In that eternal truth according to which all temporal things were made we observe with the eye of the mind the form according to which we are and according to which we do anything with true and right reason, either in ourselves or in bodies. And by this form we conceive true knowledge of things, which we have with us as a kind of word that we beget by uttering inwardly.[30]

The reason we have any knowledge at all, or any love of what we know, is that we bear within ourselves the presence of the eternal Logos and the eternal Spirit. Only against this eternal backdrop can we recognize or love anything at all. But this presence is not to say that we *possess* the Word and Spirit as something we own and control. The presence of the eternal remains ever beyond, outside our grasp. In reflecting on the difference between goodness instantiated in a particular thing and goodness itself, Augustine says, "we should seek the good of the soul, not the good it can hover over in judgment but the good it can cling to in love, and what is this but God?"[31] The presence of God in signs can only be recognized and known as it is loved; it can never be positively possessed. A symbolic presence is thus something like a presence-in-absence, the transcendence *hidden* within symbols.

For this reason, Markus rightly refers to Augustine's concept of the inner word as "persistently close to an eschatological perspective."[32] A true inner word, begotten in right love, is something only possible in the beatific vision: "This is a perfection of the image that lies some time in the future."[33] While all temporal knowledge and love presupposes the trace of the eternal Word and Spirit, only in eternity will knowledge and love be perfected by a perfect presence. When we finally see the Father in his Word by the Spirit, our own inner words will finally be true and our loves pure. The reason for this is that our inner word will be a perception of the eternal Word, and our love a reception of eternal Love. When both of these are present in a way undistorted by sin, our own knowledge and love will be eternally satisfied, having returned to their original source.

And here we have the most profound implication of Augustine's analysis. God is symbolized in creation because God is first symbolized in God. A symbol is a sign that mediates presence. An inner word is a wholly interior symbol: inasmuch as it is a word, it is a sign,[34] and inasmuch as it is wholly equal to the mind it is the mind's self-presence. The inner word of the Father, the eternal Son, is the symbol par excellence, the sign that *is* the Father's presence expressed in another. And this replete self-expression is only possible because of the agent of unity who actively unites symbol and symbolized, being wholly of the Father and the Son, the Spirit. The Spirit could thus be conceived as the eternal reception and interpretation of the eternal symbol, "interpreting" the Word as wholly reflective of the Father,

---

30. *De trin.* 9.12 (Hill: 277–8).
31. *De trin.* 8.4 (Hill: 244).
32. Markus, "Signs," 80.
33. *De trin.* 15.20 (Hill: 409–10).
34. *doctr.*, 1.9 (Green: 9).

and therefore the love generated by its reception.[35] And because the Son is the symbol—the sign that mediates presence—then the Spirit's act of interpretation is likewise an interpretive *presence*. Like the Son, then, the Spirit is *wholly personal* love and wholly divine unity, receiving the presence of the Father by the Son and returning Son to Father in and "interpretive" act of love. I will return to this somewhat contentious pneumatology below.

Thus, the language of symbols, to borrow a principle of Thomas, is more appropriately said of God than of us.[36] Our inner words formed in love are temporal symbols of God because the Father is eternally symbolized in the Son by the Spirit. Symbols are a trinitarian reality first, and only by analogy a creaturely reality. In generation, the Father is present in a sign, i.e., in a symbol. In spiration this symbol is "interpreted" and united to the Father as love. We are called to participate in this same process—to know the Father in the Son by the Spirit—only because the Father eternally *is* in the Son by the Spirit. Augustine's Trinity is symbolic, the mediation of presence in a rightly loved symbol.

This brief sketch has followed Augustine upward. From Christ protologically, through Christ in the incarnation, and to Christ the eternal Word in the Spirit, Augustine has directed our gaze toward the eternal life of God. Humans learn through signs, but such learning is only possible because all knowledge and experience arise from Christ's own work as creator and illuminator, power and wisdom. Augustine will come to center this analysis more firmly on the life of Christ: Christ is the sign that fully mediates God's presence, i.e., the replete symbol of God. Thereafter, all creation is a symbol *in Christ*, mediating the presence of God by its inclusion in Christ's humanity. In contemplating Christ's life, humans learn to form right inner words in rightly ordered love, and this, Augustine thinks, is an apt analogy for the Trinity. The Father begets the Son in the Spirit, as an inner Word in Love. The Son is the symbol of the Father, the Spirit the union of love between symbolized and symbol. All creaturely symbols exist by participation in this eternal source. Of course, inasmuch as creaturely signification is a multi-phase process, God is nothing like this. There is not first a Father, then a Son, then a Spirit. Rather, the three subsist as symbolic relations.

Thus, we might summarize this account of the Trinity with the triad, symbolized–symbol–symbolism. The Father is the eternal source, symbolized in the Son, the eternal symbol, by the symbolism of the Spirit. Symbolism, on this account, is the active, personal movement of love and unity between the symbol and the symbolized. As we will see, this has the benefit of opening all of reality to a trinitarian logic. If all things are symbols by the incarnation, then they participate in this process of symbolism, and learning to narrate that process will be part of the theological task. To move toward such an account, I turn to an essay by Karl

---

35. Cf. John Milbank, *The Word Made Strange* (Oxford: Blackwell, 1997), 187.
36. Thomas Aquinas, *Summa Theologiae* 1a.13.5, Laurence Shapcote, O.P., trans., *Latin/English Edition of the Works of St. Thomas Aquinas* (Lander, WY: The Aquinas Institute for the Study of Sacred Doctrine, 2012).

Rahner, who has sought to narrate the entire theological spectrum as a theology of symbols. In the process of narrating all things in relation to God, here and especially in the next chapter, more detail and nuance will be added to this brief account of the Trinity.

Karl Rahner's Symbolized and Symbol[37]

The systematic possibilities of the symbolized–symbol relation are explored and expanded in the middle of the twentieth century by Karl Rahner. Augustine's story of ascent is recast by Rahner as a chain of symbolic inclusions cascading down from God. His story moves from the Trinity, through Christology, to ecclesiology and anthropology, before returning again to christological devotion. Yet Rahner fails to consistently apply his theology of the symbol and neglects the role of the Spirit. Nonetheless, his systematic analysis of the symbolized–symbol relation opens significant theological possibilities.

The Theology of the Symbol

Rahner's essay, "The Theology of the Symbol" follows a scheme of *exitus* and *reditus* similar to Augustine's account, but with clearer systematic focus.[38] Rahner receives Augustine's Christology of the symbol through Aquinas, and thematizes it. For Rahner, all being is symbolic, meaning "a being comes to itself by expression" in a symbol.[39] Being, then, is self-realizing, and the symbol is this self-realization in self-representation: "The symbol, strictly speaking (symbolic reality) is the self-realization of a being in the other, which is constitutive of its essence."[40] A true symbol is not an arbitrary sign because it is intrinsic to the being that it symbolizes. This is founded, Rahner tells us, on trinitarian logic. Within the Trinity the Father has his being inasmuch as he is symbolized in the Son.[41] That the Son is the image of the Father is an expression of the strongest and most foundational unity. The entire created order then shares analogically in this symbolism, albeit in a creaturely and refracted form. Rahner's symbolism thus reverberates throughout the theological spectrum, pointing toward a fully symbolic ontology. From the symbolism of Father in Son, Rahner moves to Christology, ecclesiology, sacramental theology, anthropology, and finally back

---

37. Much of this section is taken from my "Symbolism after Dialectics: de Lubac, Rahner and Symbolic Theology," *The International Journal of Systematic Theology* 20, no. 4 (October, 2018), 537–53.
38. Rahner, "Symbol," *passim*.
39. Rahner, "Symbol," 230.
40. Rahner, "Symbol," 234.
41. To take one example, *De trinitate*, 15.12 (Hill: 403): "The Son is understanding, begotten from the understanding of the Father, which is the Father."

again to his initial concern, the sacred heart of Jesus. Christ is the symbol of God, Christ's humanity the symbol of his divinity, the church the symbol of Christ, the sacraments symbols of grace and the church, the body symbol of the soul, the sacred heart of Jesus the symbol of his whole.[42]

Rahner's *ressourcement* of symbolism involves a synthesis of patristic, Thomist, and neo-Thomist theology, with some significant borrowings from modern philosophy. He follows Augustine and Aquinas in arguing that the Word is the self-expression of the Father: The Father "speaks" his essence as the Logos, in such a way that the Father only is inasmuch as he is expressed in the Son.[43] The Thomist doctrine of analogy then provides Rahner with a link between the symbolism of divine being and that of creaturely being.[44] Creatures participate in the eternal symbolization of the Father in the Son analogically, becoming themselves analogical symbols. Christ is the highpoint of this creaturely symbolization, being both creaturely symbol and divine symbol, the Realsymbol of God, as Rahner puts it.[45]

Creaturely participation in symbolic reality is then reflected in Thomist metaphysics and sacramental theology. Substances are truly present in their accidents, and accidents are the symbols of their substances. In eucharistic theology, this means the eucharistic elements become the body of Christ by being his symbol. Symbolizing Christ means making him really present. For humanity this means that the body is the symbol of the soul—the body is the self-realization of the soul in a symbol; neither exists, properly speaking, without the other.[46] Rahner thereby returns to his initial concern that in worshiping the sacred heart of Jesus, worshipers are not worshiping a part of Jesus but his integral whole. His sacred heart is the symbol of his entire being, as the body is to the soul, an accident to its substance, Christ to God. Therefore, debates about what exactly is worshiped in the Sacred Heart are transcended by reclaiming a patristic assumption along medieval theological lines. Christ's sacred heart symbolically is his entire person. The worshiper need not worry whether it is Christ's love, Christ's humanity, or Christ's body being worshiped, for there is only one Christ, one Realsymbol of God.

The role of modern philosophy in Rahner's discussion, as with much of Rahner's work, is complex and subterranean. Stephen Fields argues that "Rahner develops Realsymbol by interpreting Thomism in light of the tradition of Kant to Heidegger."[47] This initially means that Rahner deploys Heidegger's "hermeneutics

---

42. Cf. Annice Callahan, "Karl Rahner's Theology of the Symbol," *Irish Theological Quarterly* 49, no. 3 (September, 1982), 195–205.
43. Rahner, "Symbol," 236.
44. Rahner, "Symbol," 232.
45. Rahner, "Symbol," 238.
46. Cf. Aquinas, ST 1a.93.3.
47. Stephen Fields, *Being as Symbol* (Washington, DC: Georgetown University Press, 2007), 20.

of retrieval" which "seeks creatively to interpret a text in order to release its hidden or implicit intelligibility," posing questions to a historical text "that arise from a contemporary problematic."[48] Fields then subdivides Rahner's retrieval of symbolism into four "predicates," each with its own precedents and history, situating Rahner within a broader history of ideas. Rahner's view of the symbolic nature of reality is analogous (rooted in Neo-Thomism, Blondel, Marérechal), sacramental (Thomism), self-perfecting (Goethe, Hegel), and linguistic (Möhler, Goethe, Kant, Hegel and Heidegger).[49] In each of these, Rahner takes an idea and refashions it into a new synthesis. Because Rahner rarely cites such sources, Fields discerns these links on the basis of broad correlations; his interpretation is self-admittedly speculative.[50]

This method is helpful for locating Rahner within a wider field of view but can obscure the organic unity of Rahner's own thought in favor of a compelling history of ideas. Hence, Fields suggests that Rahner is too philosophical in his symbolism, and that the future of symbolic theology will be in more thoroughly theological and religious reflection.[51] This is curious, since Rahner explicitly develops a theology of the symbol as a reflection on Christian worship. Fields first abstracts philosophical principles from Rahner's theological reflections, situates Rahner within them, and then accuses Rahner of being too philosophical! In contrast, we should see Rahner's theology of the symbol as an explication of Christian worship, in creative and traditional terms, and in critical dialogue with modern philosophy.[52] Rahner's theology of the symbol is an assimilation and transformation of a broad spectrum of theological and philosophical resources that begins with the generation of the Son and ends with the adoration of the Sacred Heart.

Christological Trajectories

Rahner's account is therefore bookended by christological concerns. An initial concern for intra-trinitarian symbolization ultimately leads to a reflection on the unity of the incarnate Christ—a unity so profound as to guarantee that the human heart of Christ is the symbol of God. The Cyriline shape of this should not be missed. Whatever we make of Rahner's remark that if given the choice between being an "orthodox Monophysite" and an "orthodox Nestorian," he would choose to be an "orthodox Nestorian," we should not see him as thereby denying or

48. Fields, *Being*, 2. Of course, this is true of de Lubac as well.
49. Field's point about language is that language, for Rahner, is "embodied thought"—the coming-into-being of thought itself. Cf. Fields, *Being*, ch. 5.
50. Fields, *Being*, 5.
51. Fields, *Being*, 104. Field's archetype for this possibility is von Balthasar.
52. Fields has shown persuasively that Rahner is not an uncritical modernist. For a coordination of theology and philosophy in Rahner, see Karen Kilby, "Philosophy, Theology and Foundationalism in the Thought of Karl Rahner," *Scottish Journal of Theology* 55, no. 2 (2002), 127–40.

minimizing a firmly Cyriline Christology of unity.[53] Rahner's point is precisely that in the incarnation God is born a man, as his Marian and Sacred Heart theologies affirm. In symbolic theology, there is no distance between the human and divine natures of Christ, for the one makes the other truly present in a single unified person. There is only one divine Son, one Christ who, in being the Realsymbol of God, makes God fully present.

Rahner's "orthodox Nestorianism" expresses his concern to guard the integrity of the authentic humanity of Christ *as* the symbol of the Divine. Christ symbolizes God as a human—his humanity is irreducible, for it is only in his humanity that we meet his divinity. Indeed, "orthodox Nestorianism" is a very unfortunate phrase, since it is actually Nestorius who jeopardizes the symbolic value of the humanity of Christ. Nestorius's concern to guard against God suffering makes it very difficult for him to see how God can be born. If God is born, Nestorius worries, God dies—better to minimize such language. Mary, therefore, cannot be the mother of God. But in making this move, a break is implied between the human and divine natures of Christ, since the Virgin birth, for Nestorius, is not quite the birth of God. The crucial link between symbolized and symbol is interrupted, an interruption that at least threatens to be more than a distinction.[54] For Rahner, by contrast, the incarnation reveals that all reality points to God not just as cause, but as "his substantial determination or as his own proper environment."[55] The humanity of Christ is not an arbitrary sign; it is the symbol—the only possible symbol—that discloses the reality of God. It is only *as* a human that Christ symbolizes God. This is possible because of the divine image in which humanity is created. The incarnation reveals the dramatic extent of humanity's image-bearing capacity: from the incarnation onward, God has a human heart which can be worshiped without any fear of idolatry. The grammar of the *theotokos* and the grammar of the sacred heart are the grammar of the Realsymbol.

This symbolic structure can also accommodate Cyril's concept of the enhypostatic union. Because the movement between symbolized and symbol first describes the procession of the Son from the Father, it retains a certain "processional priority" for the symbolized. In terms of the Trinity *ad intra*, this

---

53. Karl Rahner, *Karl Rahner in Dialogue: Conversations and Interviews 1965–1982*, trans. and ed. H. Biallowons, et al. (New York: Crossroad 1986), 127. For the accusation of quasi-Nestorianism, see Aaron Riches, *Ecce Homo* (Grand Rapids, MI: Eerdmans, 2016), 9. Riches's is an extraordinary work, but he misses the ways Rahner's symbolism unites divinity and humanity in Christ, balancing Rahner's avowal of "orthodox Nestorianism." See Joseph Wong, "Karl Rahner's Theology of Symbol and Three Models of Christology," *Heythrop Journal* 27, no 1 (1986), 6–7.

54. Cf. Riches, *Ecce Homo*, ch. 1. For a similar analysis, see Rowan Williams, *Christ the Heart of Creation* (London: Bloomsbury, 2018), ch. 2. The extent to which this was a genuine division between the natures of Christ is debated. Cf. Richard A. Norris Jr ed., *The Christological Controversy* (Philadelphia, PA: Fortress Press, 1980).

55. Rahner, "Symbol," 235.

means the Son proceeds *from the Father*. In Lewis Ayres's description of Augustine's trinitarian theology, "Divine communion [is] constituted by the intra-divine acts of the divine three, in an order established by the Father."[56] There is a "direction of travel" in the Trinity and in the created order. The symbol proceeds from the symbolized. This processional priority is altogether magnified when elements of the created world symbolize the divine. The divine is in no way reliant on its created symbols, in the way that the Father is "mutually determinative" with the Son, but sustains them entirely in relation to its own self-sufficiency.[57] God does not need to be symbolized in creation in order to be God, so a created symbol symbolizes God asymmetrically. Within creation, the "processional" priority of the symbolized is a structure of ontological difference, a one-way dependence. Since, therefore, the human nature of Christ is the symbol of his divinity, the divine nature retains ontological—"processional"—priority. The human nature of Christ is entirely founded upon, sustained within, his divine nature. This does not imply any diminution of the human nature of Christ, since the created symbol is neither arbitrary nor elidable. Rather, it sustains the fundamental ontological difference between God and creation, while guaranteeing the identity of God and Christ, the Realsymbol. In Christ, symbolized and symbol meet in one divine man.

While God does not need created symbols, God is not thereby only arbitrarily related to them. Recall that for Rahner a true symbol is intrinsic to that which it symbolizes—it is its necessary self-expression. Creaturely symbols are, we might say, *un*necessary divine self-expression. They are unnecessary because the divine is not co-constitutive with them. But they are nonetheless divine self-expressions. In what Aquinas calls a "mixed relation," the creature expresses the divine life without being necessary to that divine life.[58] What is unnecessarily expressed is the divine life in another key. The incarnation is the baffling extremity of this symbolic structure where created symbol perfectly coincides with uncreated Symbol—no longer by participation but by nature. Since the human symbol cannot be arbitrary, the incarnation reveals that humanity is God's "own proper environment." Simply put, this human, Jesus Christ, is what the life of God looks like in time. Christ is the symbol of God, as the Word, and the symbol of humanity, as the replete human life. This makes him, in turn, the symbol of the entire created order, so that symbolic relations obtain all the way down. From Father to Son, Son to Christ's humanity, Christ to Church, Church to world and all creation, all are enmeshed in symbolic relations: in the Symbol we live and move and have our being. Rahner therefore confidently declares that a theology of symbols is "the basic structure of all Christianity."[59] From Rahner's analysis of the relation

---

56. Ayres, *Augustine*, 258.
57. Simon Oliver, *Creation: A Guide for the Perplexed* (London: Bloomsbury, 2017), 52.
58. Aquinas calls this dynamic "mixed relations." Cf. Oliver, *Creation*, 48–53.
59. Rahner, "Symbol," 252. Of course, Rahner's theology of the symbol is also complicatedly philosophical. See Fields, *Being as Symbol*.

between symbolized and symbol, an entire symbolic ontology begins to emerge, and Rahner's accomplishment is to see the expansive possibilities this affords.

The Hiddenness of the Symbolized

This relation between symbolized and symbol should also be read in the other direction, for mediation in a symbol implies the hiddenness of the symbolized. Eternally, this means the Father is only known through the Son—the Father is the hidden source and mysterious fount of divinity. The Father remains "hidden" in the Son by the Spirit as the unoriginated one. And this has analogical consequences in creatures, for whom God remains hidden within and beyond created symbols. We cannot step out of our creaturely status to see God—we must seek God through the symbols of life in time, a way definitively opened by Christ the Realsymbol. To see God in Christ is to see the Father hidden in the Son and is thus the temporal refraction of the eternal hiddenness of the Father in the Son. Indeed, this funds the entire theology of the symbol outlined by Rahner. We *must* ascend through the chain of symbols to meet God; anything less than this would make a theology of symbols an idle and otiose speculation. But if the Father is eternally known in an eternal symbol, then we as creatures are bound to come to know God through temporal symbols. A systematic account of the nature of symbols thus becomes an important theological task.

In Chapter 5, I will develop this crucial point in more detail in conversation with a different essay of Rahner's. To anticipate the argument there, acknowledging God as only ever symbolized in creation helps resist the "ontotheological" temptation to reduce God to one being among others. If God is present in symbols, God is absent as an *object* for evaluation. God can never be objectified, only symbolized. And this means that God is present in creation precisely in God's absence. I will, however, defer that analysis to Chapter 5, for it requires a stronger sense of what it means for creation to be a symbol (Chapter 2), and the work of the Spirit in the church as symbolism (Chapter 3). I flag it here because it relates first and foremost to the person of the Father, whose personhood *is* his hiddenness in the Son. The two sides of the symbolized–symbol relation correspond to Father and Son, to hiddenness and manifestation, a relation that holds true in creaturely relations to God as well. What is needed, then, is a systematic theology of the symbol by which to understand these relations in greater depth and richness.

Roads Untaken

For its expansive gains, Rahner's theology of the symbol remains inconsistent. Rahner sees his theology of the symbol everywhere in Christian theology: it is "the basic structure of all Christianity."[60] But the theology of the symbol is not quite the basic structure of all of Rahner's theology. It remains an underdeveloped theme. A

---

60. Rahner, "Symbol," 252.

few have located symbolism as the hermeneutical key for understanding Rahner,[61] but in the ocean of secondary literature on his work, these appeals are rare. It may be that symbolism represents an overlooked cornerstone of Rahner's thought, but it seems more likely that symbolism is one stone among many. Studies elucidating symbolism's role in Rahner's wider thought are welcome and helpful, but the fact remains that while symbolism sits comfortably in Rahner's work, it does not have the level of ubiquity he suggests it should. Rahner has produced an insightful theology of the symbol, but he has not quite produced a symbolic theology.

The under-deployment of Rahner's theology of the symbol can be seen in a number of common criticisms of his work. A more consistent deployment of this theme could mitigate the impact of these critiques. George Lindbeck accuses Rahner of building his theology on a foundation of common human experience, thereby flattening the particular forms of life that constitute the diverse actualities of religion.[62] A common "transcendental" experience is the foundation from which specifically Christian, i.e., "categorical," experience is understood. Similarly, Johann Baptist Metz argues that Rahner ahistoricizes Christianity by his transcendental method, giving Christianity a "transcendental omnipresence."[63] This transcendental omnipresence obviates the need for Christians to "run the race" of seeking justice and loving mercy because the church is "always already" there. John Milbank argues that Rahner is unsuccessful at banishing an extrinsic view of grace. Because Rahner maintains a formal reality for pure nature, he ends up repeating the two-tiered metaphysics of neo-Scholasticism. Rahner's metaphysics of subjectivity, according to Milbank, leaves Christian revelation as simply making explicit a preexisting orientation toward transcendence which is not itself grace. Thus, Rahner "naturalizes the supernatural," that is, he makes the supernatural merely the explication of a natural orientation already present. Therefore:

> The historical events, the human acts and images which can alone be the site of supernatural difference, are here reduced to mere signs of a perfect inward self-transcendence, always humanly available.[64]

---

61. For instance, Stephen Fields: "It is generally acknowledged that the Realsymbol lies at the core of Rahner's thought." Fields, *Being*, 2. See also Callahan, "Rahner's Theology," 195–205; Maria Elisabeth Motzko, "Karl Rahner's Theology: A Theology of the Symbol" (PhD diss., Fordham University, 1976); For Joseph Wong Christology is central and symbology central to Christology: Joseph Wong, *Logos-Symbol in the Christology of Karl Rahner* (Rome: Libreria Ateneo Salesiano, 1984).

62. George Lindbeck, *The Nature of Doctrine: Religion and Doctrine in a Postliberal Age* (Philadelphia, PA: Westminster Press, 1984), 24, 31.

63. Johann Baptiste Metz, *Faith in History and Society*, trans. David Smith (New York: Seabury Press, 1980), 161.

64. John Milbank, *Theology and Social Theory*, 2nd ed. (Oxford: Blackwell, 2006), 224.

Though every critic has their distinctive concerns, the common consequence of these perceived weaknesses is that Rahner's ontology overruns or overlooks concrete human existence. The particular is drowned in a tide of foundationalism, transcendental methodology, and extrinsic grace.

Rahner is not without fault in relation to these criticisms. His style and method certainly lend themselves to the sense that he proceeds ahistorically, moving from general ontology toward Christian particularity. Even his "Theology of the Symbol" begins with a general ontological analysis and only then acknowledges that he is actually developing a christological ontology. His method and his insistence on a formal category of pure nature make the criticisms seem warranted. But a more consistent symbolism could have at least blunted the consequences these critics see in those moves. In Rahner's symbolic ontology, being only is as it represents itself outwardly. In response to Lindbeck, Rahner could say that the Incarnation, in which the humanity of *this* person, Jesus, is revealed to be the non-arbitrary symbol of the Father, guarantees the irreducible value and particularity of every human. The incarnational symbol here is not an arbitrary "any" human, or a vague anthropological principle. It is *the* expression of God's nature in time, revealing all individual human natures to be derivative symbols of the divine. Thereafter, every particular can be seen as a symbol of God only in its particularity. There is no such thing as a general symbol. For Metz, Rahner could respond that symbolizing the divine is not an absolute given—it requires active participation in becoming. So the race is not already run. Rather, God has revealed in the incarnation that only in the running of each particular race is the symbol revealed to signify its creator.

This suggests a partial response to Milbank. If Rahner is guilty of maintaining extrinsic grace and therefore, as Milbank puts it, "naturalizing the supernatural," it is also true, for Rahner as for de Lubac, that symbolism flows in the opposite direction. Symbolism supernaturalizes the natural by making concrete human existence the site of divine signification. This signification is an intrinsic signification, otherwise the symbol would be arbitrary. We could further ask the question whether it is pure nature or graced nature that symbolizes the divine. Rahner is clear that symbolic reality is concrete reality, and since pure nature never in fact exists, it is graced human nature that symbolizes the divine. This is obvious since for Rahner grace is the gift of God himself, so to make God present as his symbol is to have already received the gift of God's self. So all the granular details of human existence become potential sites of supernatural difference. Alleged extrinsicism in regard to grace can be mitigated by intrinsicism in regard to the symbol.

This does not solve the disagreement with Milbank, since Rahner retains a "remainder concept" of pure nature to secure the gratuity of grace. Milbank locates the gratuity of grace in the act of creation ex nihilo and sees the notion of pure nature as unnecessary and dangerous.[65] For my part, I agree with Milbank about the risky superfluity of a theoretically pure nature, since that would seem

---

65. Milbank, *Theology*, 220–2.

to imply a human nature that was not already, at least inchoately, a symbol of the divine. Rahner's symbolism does not solve this disagreement with Milbank or the inheritors of de Lubac's *Surnaturel* thesis.⁶⁶ What I am suggesting is that Rahner's intrincism in regard to the symbol mitigates the consequences risked by his metaphysics. The case is the same for postliberal, liberationist, and intrinsicist critiques: Rahner's theology of the symbol could help him avoid departicularizing and dehistoricizing the human experience of the divine.

But these are responses we must supply. The conceptual tools to blunt these critiques are there, but Rahner has not made the most of them. The symbolic nature of reality is certainly "there" in his theology, but had he applied his ontological symbolism more ubiquitously, he could have escaped at least some of his later critics. Rahner himself expresses the incompleteness of his theology of the symbol and points toward needed development.⁶⁷ Yet Rahner does not quite reclaim the ubiquity of symbolic theology. Nonetheless, Rahner's account is expansive and suggestive and deserves to be engaged. Where Augustine ascends the chain of symbolic inclusions from the temporal to the eternal, Rahner descends from divine life, down through Christology into the entire created order, developing with extraordinary clarity a Christological and thereby symbolic ontology.

The Vanishing Ghost

Yet the account of symbols I have offered so far, for all its expansive possibilities, is significantly aporetic, for it fails to make the Spirit necessary for the symbol–symbolized relation. For Rahner, the symbolized only is inasmuch as it is self-symbolized in the symbol: being is self-realizing. But this way of stating it risks leaving little if any "necessity" or "rationale" for the Spirit. The Spirit becomes quite literally an afterthought—thought only after the primal differentiated unity between Father and Son has been established. It then becomes difficult to see why the Spirit is necessary to the already-established symbol–symbolized relation, and if unnecessary, how the Spirit is not simply an arbitrary datum of Christian faith.⁶⁸ If the theology of the symbol is "the basic structure of all Christianity," then the question of the relation of the Spirit to the symbol–symbolized dyad becomes all the more pressing. Is the Spirit not essential to the basic structure of Christianity? It should be impossible to give an account of the basic structure of Christianity without accounting for the Spirit. How might we account for the Spirit in a way that neither reduces it to a *datum* of faith to be fideistically affirmed nor to a sub-personal union between symbol and symbolized? It will not do to say that I have been developing a Christology, and thereby excuse myself for neglecting the Spirit, for, again, to establish a relation between Father and Son independent of a

---

66. Milbank's position should be distinguished from de Lubac's, since de Lubac is prepared to allow a minimal role for hypothetical pure nature.
67. Rahner, "Symbol," 242–3.
68. This is the problem posed by Milbank, *Strange*, 171–93.

pneumatology is already to relegate the Spirit to an after-thought, crippling the entire trinitarian program from the outset.[69]

In fact, embedded in the contours of the discussion so far are the tools to "see" the Spirit. The structures of symbolic presence demand a third term: a closer look at the play of symbolized and symbol in the sacraments will reveal this ineludible third person. To discern the shape of that person we turn to Henri de Lubac. De Lubac is of course not the *ressourcement* theologian known for pneumatology. That title certainly belongs to Yves Congar. Yet de Lubac's theology of the sacraments, those archetypal signs and things, reveals a significant pneumatological character. Engaging him rather than Congar's more direct discussions of the Spirit allows me to stay within the arc of an Augustinian theology of "signs and things." Between symbolized and symbol is symbolism, the necessary and irreducible movement of the Holy Spirit. Yet de Lubac fails to fully extract the pneumatological implications of his own thought. There is some digging left to be done.

De Lubac's Sacramental Pneumatology

If Karl Rahner develops the symbolized–symbol relation, I will argue that de Lubac gives us symbolism—the union of symbolized and symbol, the eternal Holy Spirit and the creaturely act of interpretation. Symbolism, as we will see, is the union of symbolized and symbol, the life of the symbolized–symbol relation. In every place de Lubac speaks of this dynamic it is obvious that it can only be the Holy Spirit. Nevertheless, de Lubac rarely makes the connection. The systematic possibilities of this remain a road untaken. What follows is an attempt to take a few steps down that road. Symbolism is the Spirit and, analogically, the spiritual life, including those spheres so dear to de Lubac: spiritual theology, spiritual exegesis, and the human spirit as such. In what follow I reason with de Lubac from the sacraments toward the Spirit. The relation between two words in particular, "mystery" and "sacrament" point toward a pneumatology of the symbol.

Desire

The word "mystery" takes us right to the heart of de Lubac's concept of symbolism. Generally speaking, de Lubac argues, mystery and sacrament are used interchangeably in patristic theology. Often enough, an author will substitute one word for the other just to avoid verbal repetition.[70] Yet de Lubac discerns three basic nuances between the two terms. First, a mystery is often that which is hidden

---

69. This is a problem endemic to Christologies, even ones by otherwise careful authors; Rowan Williams's *Christ the Heart of Creation*, for example, barely mentions the role the Spirit might play in Christology.

70. De Lubac, *Corpus*, 45, 49. Jerome translates the Greek *mysterion* as *sacramentum* in Eph 5:32.

beneath the sacrament, which is to say, the symbolized contained within the symbol:

> The *sacramentum* would therefore play the role of container, or envelope, with regard to the *mysterium* hidden within it. In this way, according to Paschasius Radbertus, the purple cloak in which the soldiers clothed Jesus is the mystery of which the scarlet thread of Rahab was the sign. The ordained series of the different *sacramenta* leads us as if by so many stages right to the ultimate mysteries, which are no longer sacraments at all: the "mysteries of the Godhead."[71]

So far this is nothing more than the Augustinian sense of signs and things outlined above. Signs spiral upward to their ultimate source in God; signs are the pedagogy of eternity, and sacraments are those special signs that orient the pilgrim's use of all other signs, leading the learner upward.[72]

But the word mystery draws out an often-unnoticed function of symbols: that they also conceal.[73] The point of this concealing is multifaceted. On the one hand there is the basic fact that none can see God and live: God adapts godself to temporal signs so that the divine presence can be mediated to us without our annihilation. Symbols conceal God's glory. The second reason is connected to the first, namely, that struggling through symbols to discover things produces the humility necessary for the vision of God. The journey to eternal vision is a journey through symbols, and gaining that final vision is requisite upon acquiring the virtues developed in the arduous processes of learning to read. Hiddenness in symbols accomplishes this.

But symbols also conceal for the joy of discovering things hidden in symbols. Concealment gives rise to the desire for revelation and the delight of discovery. Augustine offers the example of hearing straightforwardly of how saints, originally living in sin, are born again by the Spirit in the waters of baptism to love God and neighbor. How much more joyous is it, he asks, to learn this lesson by way of a mystical exegesis of Song of Songs 4:2, where the beloved is the church whose "teeth" tear people away from sin, baptizing them like "ewes" coming from washing, who bear the "twins" of love of God and neighbor?[74] What is enjoyable about learning through signs is the erotic pull and fulfillment of desire. Because our growth in virtue requires, for Augustine, the realignment of our desires, God speaks to us through mysteries hidden in signs as a lover playfully teasing the beloved into

---

71. De Lubac, *Corpus*, 47. Citing numerous examples including Ambrose (PL, 15, 1605 B, 1663 C, 1770 A).

72. The connection between the sign-value of all things and the specific signification of sacraments is discussed by Augustine. Our inability to read the signs of creation owing to the fall necessitated an entire sacramental framework to teach us to read again. *doctr.*, 3.22-32 (Green: 72–5).

73. Neither Markus nor Deely recognize this.

74. Augustine, *doctr.*, 2.10-15 (Green: 32–3).

deeper intimacy. The concealing work of signs releases the power of *eros*: it is the erotic pull of a faintly perceived yet hidden presence. In de Lubac's words, "the mystery is itself radiant with a secret intelligibility."[75] The play of hiddenness and manifestation between signs and things calls forth desire; sacraments conceal mysteries that desire might have its day.

This whole dynamic is closely associated with Augustine's pneumatology. Indeed, Augustine finds it to be an apt analogy for the Spirit. In *de Trinitate* IX.18, Augustine asks why the Spirit—love, in his triad memory–understanding–love/will—is not begotten. He appeals to the processes of learning. Obtaining knowledge, Augustine's analogy for the begetting of the Word, is preceded by inquisitiveness, a desire to know. Knowledge is therefore begotten by both the mind and the mind's desire for knowledge. Once knowledge is realized, desire to know becomes love of what is known, so that desire and love "are something of the same kind."[76] Desire, then, is a kind of down payment, a "deposit guaranteeing an inheritance" in love. Desire–love is the dynamic in which knowledge is born. It is therefore improper to say that the love of knowledge is begotten alongside knowledge, for knowledge is begotten *in* desire, which is an anticipatory participation in love. This, Augustine argues, is an analogy for why the Spirit is not begotten: as the desire–love between Father and Son, the generation of the Son occurs in the Spirit.[77] This is an important clarification in Augustine's trinitarian theology. His affirmation of the *filioque* has been held up as evidence that the Spirit is really just an afterthought for him—thought after the initial unity of Father and Son. On the contrary, that the Spirit is of the Father and the Son does not mean the Spirit is parasitic upon a prior unity, for the Spirit *is* that unity. The Spirit is the desire in which the Son is begotten and the love the Son returns to the Father, and is thus, paradoxically "pre-present" in the filiation by which it is spirated.

To say that the Son is begotten *in* the Spirit does not suggest that the Son has a relation of origin to the Spirit. To say that the Spirit is active on "both sides" of filiation—desire of Father, love of Son—is not to say that the Spirit has no relation of origin to the Son. The Son, as Aquinas would later argue, is the subsistent relation of Son from Father and only the Father.[78] The Spirit, then, is the subsistent relation of the Father by the Son. But this does not make the Spirit superfluous to the Father and Son, for to use any of the classical terms for Spirit—desire, gift, unity, love—is to suggest that "the Father and Son can only be Father and Son in the act of spiration."[79] This means that while the Spirit proceeds from the Father *per filioque*, the Spirit is paradoxically necessary to the Father–Son relation.

We can see this pneumatological paradox in the created order in the natural desire for the supernatural.[80] For de Lubac, following a reading of Thomas in

---

75. De Lubac, *Corpus*, 231.
76. Augustine, *De trin*. 9.18.
77. Cf. Ayres, *Augustine and the Trinity*, 265–6.
78. Aquinas, ST 1a.36.3.
79. Milbank, *Strange*, 173.
80. Henri de Lubac, *Surnaturel*, 488 and elsewhere.

line with Patristic tradition, humans have a natural desire for the vision of God. However, in spite of being a *natural* desire, the desire can only be fulfilled by grace. From a neo-Scholastic perspective, this is seen as problematic, for a natural desire, according to the Aristotelian principle of proportionality, must be naturally attainable. A natural desire that can only be fulfilled by grace is simply a contradiction.[81] But de Lubac is convinced, and his reading of tradition on this is convincing, that humans are not subject to the law of proportionality in this way, that humans are constituted by a paradoxical natural desire for the supernatural. I will expound on this in Chapter 3, but here I want to point out this paradox has an eternal precedent in the Spirit. The *desiderium naturale* and its fulfillment in grace is the Spirit both "before" and "after," a kind of "pre-participation" and an active participation in grace. Desire is an anticipatory participation in the fullness of love, and because it is a symbolic inclusion and not a dialectical contrast, it is at once fully natural and fully supernatural.

This "pre-participatory" dynamic can be clarified by returning to Augustine's signs and things. The hiddenness of a mystery beneath a sign is not an absolute opacity. If it were, it would not be enticing, for we would have no way of recognizing or pre-apprehending its intrinsic desirability or even recognizing the symbol as a symbol. Only if we have some down-payment or deposit in the eternal goodness of God can we recognize its goodness as such. Only if we already participate in the Spirit can we desire the Spirit. In other words grace must be erotic. It must elicit a desire that is not purely elicited, but naturally embedded in the human spirit. It is this very desire, de Lubac argues, that makes the human *spiritual*.[82] And human spirituality, the natural desire for the supernatural, is a finite participation in eternal "spirituality," the desire and love of Father for Son and Son for Father moving for all eternity in a dance of *eros* and fulfillment. This should not be surprising. If the Spirit is the unity of Father and Son, then the Spirit's work in time is to unite us to God—a union anticipated by erotic desire, fulfilled in love, and through and through a work of the Spirit. The natural desire for the supernatural will be discussed in more detail in Chapter 3. For now the point is that sacramental mysteries conceal in order to provoke desire, and that desire is a natural and supernatural participation in eternal spiration.

But there is more to be said about the Spirit as desire. The language of desire is the language of difference. In the grammar of symbols, desire arises in the concealment of the symbolized in the symbol, which is only possible on the basis of the difference between them. A symbol cannot simply be the symbolized, otherwise it would not be a symbol. If symbols did not conceal, they would simply be identical to the things they symbolize. But what might this constellation of terms—"desire," "concealment," "difference"—involve when speaking of the Trinity? We should be careful not to indulge too deeply in *curiositas*, but the

---

81. Cf. Lawrence Feingold, *The Natural Desire to See God According to St Thomas Aquinas and His Interpreters* (Naples, FL: Sapientia Press, 2010), xxix.

82. Cf. De Lubac, *Surnaturel*, 484.

question cannot be avoided. Von Balthasar's reflections on Holy Saturday and divine difference are perhaps the most obvious place to turn. There is much to retain here, especially his insistence that the difference between the Father and Son is the ground of the possibility of creation as what is analogically different. Unfortunately, as Karen Kilby points out, for Balthasar the gift from the Father to the Son involves something like the risk of loss, and in the infinite distance between Father and Son lies the possibility of sin.[83] In consequence, Holy Saturday risks becoming, in John Milbank's words, "an abandonment of the metaphysics of cosmic harmony in favor of a gnostic hypostasization of the violence of the cross."[84] By seeing an abyss in the difference between Father and Son, Balthasar founds the possibility of sin in the godhead, and hints at "the shadow of rupture between the Father and the Son."[85] We must, with Balthasar, speak of the eternal value of the difference between Father and Son—a difference which will become especially important in the next chapter on creation. But unlike Balthasar, we must ground this difference in a logic of symbols, not a logic of distance. I will expound this in more detail in the conclusion, but to anticipate, Balthasar speaks of the Spirit as sustaining the unity-in-difference between Father and Son as love and desire. If this is already provided by the Spirit, why does he need an "abyss" between Father and Son to sustain their loving difference? I will argue in the conclusion that Balthasar has all he needs in the Spirit without positing an infinite abyss between the persons. In this way, divine difference is *in the Spirit*, the first place as desire, in the second as love. The Father already loves the Son in his desire, which is to say he knows the Son and the Son's return gift even in his begetting of the Son. This is why the Spirit must be fully personal and not some quasi-personal go-between. Otherwise, the distance between God and God would be an empty space. On the contrary, the distance between God and God is God, the fully personal Holy Spirit, in whom the Father begets the Son.

Gift

The desire consequent upon concealment leads to the second nuance de Lubac discovers between mysteries and sacraments. A mystery is often more of an act or accomplishment than a static reality: "While the *sacramentum* is 'confected',

---

83. Cf. Karen Kilby, "Hans Urs von Balthasar on the Trinity," in *The Cambridge Companion to Hans Urs von Balthasar* (Cambridge: Cambridge University Press, 2004), 211.
84. John Milbank, *The Suspended Middle*, 2nd edn. (Cambridge: Eerdmans, 2005), 80.
85. Milbank, *Suspended,* 80. See, for instance, Hans Urs von Balthasar, *Mysterium Paschale* (San Francisco, CA: Ignatius, 1990), preface, Kindle Loc. 66, and elsewhere. Hereafter, *MP*. Due to Coronavirus restrictions, I was not able to obtain a physical copy of this book and have relied on the Kindle edition. I have cited the chapter number and Kindle location to aid referencing.

carried, deposed, kept, divided, broken, distributed, received, absorbed, eaten and drunk, the *mysterium* itself is 'done', worked, celebrated, offered, completed, interrupted, re-started, frequented."[86] In this sense the mystery is not only the thing the sacrament conceals, but the dynamic making of the sacrament. A mystery is a sacrament enacted, a sacrament accomplished. In accomplishing the sacrament, the mystery makes the sacrament sacramental. And so we "adore the sacrament," but we "celebrate the mysteries."[87] In this case, the host is made the body of Christ by the transubstantiating mystery. It is this motion, this dynamic "making" of the sacrament, that is the mystery.

The direction of the trinitarian *taxis* is key here. Recall that for Augustine's trinitarian theology and Rahner's theology of the symbol, the symbolized maintains a "processional priority." The symbol proceeds from the symbolized. So in sacramental terms, the sacrament is made a sacrament by the mystery. But in trinitarian terms, this "making" cannot be a kind of creation ex nihilo of the Son. To avoid any hint of subordinationism, it must be the complete self-donation of the Father to the Son, so that the Son is entirely from the Father and of the Father's own Spirit. For Augustine, this self-constituting self-donation is the fully personal Holy Spirit.

The Spirit is the "active agent of unity"[88] between Father and Son. The union of Father and Son, while made under the *arche* of the Father, is accomplished in the Spirit. The full and active personhood of the Spirit is irreducibly important—and in no way diminished by being "of the Father and of the Son"—in a trinitarian symbolism. This is made clear again in the ways the Spirit is active in the generation of the Son. When the Father begets the Son, he does so by donating his entire Spirit to the Son. This donation, this gift of self, is constitutive of filiation, so that it is in the giving of the Spirit that the Son is begotten.[89] The Spirit is therefore properly called gift. The Son returns the gift of love to the Father, a love that is the Son's entire being, and most properly called the Spirit. So the Spirit, in being of the Father and of the Son, both gift and love, sits on both sides of filiation— "constituting" the symbol as a symbol of the Father who alone is *arche*. If the Spirit as desire indicates the difference between Father and Son, the constituting Spirit-as-gift is the realization of the presence of the Father in the Son.

Here, then, is another symbolic inclusion. The sacrament is accomplished, as filiation is "accomplished," in the Spirit. Sacraments come alive—become sacraments—in the Spirit who, as the eternal and active agent of unity and love, accomplishes the presence of the symbolized in the symbol. What "makes" the sacrament a sacrament is the self-giving of the mystery. The mystery gives itself to the sacrament, becoming truly present within it. This act of donation is what constitutes both the mystery as a mystery in relation to a sacrament, and the sacrament as a sacrament. Without the donation, the mystery would not be a

---

86. De Lubac, *Corpus*, 49–50.
87. De Lubac, *Corpus*, 49–50.
88. Ayres, *Augustine*, 257.
89. Ayres, *Augustine*, 266.

sacramental mystery, just an unknown and unknowable fact, which, from a human perspective, might as well not exist. The sacrament would then not be a sacrament, just some base material that may or may not bear metaphorical similarity to the mystery. The gift of the mystery to the sacrament establishes both in a mutual relationship. When de Lubac draws our attention to the activating sense of the word mystery, he draws us into the realm of the Spirit. The Spirit is the activating gift of real presence.

Unity

This active sense of mystery immediately implies the third nuance de Lubac discovers between sacraments and mysteries. If a mystery is the accomplishment of a sacrament, then it necessarily includes both sacrament and that which is symbolized by the sacrament: it is the nuptial union between the two. The word "mystery" "focuses less on the apparent sign, or rather the hidden reality, than on both at the same time: on their mutual relationship, union and implications, on the way in which one passes into the other, or is penetrated by the other."[90] A mystery, in this sense, is the penetration of the symbol by the symbolized, the "transfer of attributes," the "communication of idioms" between them.[91] Both symbol and symbolized are implicated in the mystery, for a mystery is the union of the two. In the Eucharist, the presence of Christ in the host, the union of his body with the eucharistic body is the mystery—the way the one and the other come together in a differentiated unity.

Once again, de Lubac's account of mystery leads us into the realm of the Spirit. As the union between Father and Son, the Spirit is fully *of* them both. The Spirit is the Spirit of the Father and the Spirit of the Son, the replete gift of the Father and the replete love the Son, establishing the Trinity as a union-in-distinction. *The Spirit is the original symbolic inclusion*, the fully personal and active agent of unity in whom all symbols are joined to the symbolized. In Lewis Ayres's words, "The Spirit gives himself as the Father's gift and as the Son's gift. Father and Son are one because the Spirit gives himself in the begetting of the Son and gives himself as the Son's love for the Father."[92] And here the trinitarian paradox comes into its own: the Spirit is wholly internal to both Father and Son and yet wholly personal and hypostatic. Here in spiration we have the eternal movement in which every other symbolic inclusion is a participatory refraction.

Roads Untaken

The irony is that de Lubac seems oblivious to the pneumatological implications of this sacramentology. His concern is sacramentality as such, the dynamics of

---

90. De Lubac, *Corpus*, 51.
91. De Lubac, *Corpus*, 53.
92. Ayres, *Augustine*, 254. Emphasis mine.

presence, and, most importantly, the "spirit" of the fathers, the animating mode of their theological discourse. And these three nuances recover just that. While there is a touch of equivocity in these uses of the word mystery, it is not a sheer difference. De Lubac has in fact unearthed three irreducible requirements of a systematic theology of symbolism. The entire conceptual framework in which signs and things, sacraments, and mysteries function requires these nuances of meaning. (1) Without the concealing work of signs, the symbol–symbolized relation risks falling into an undifferentiated identity in which the sign simply is the thing. If symbols did not conceal and reveal, there would be no distinction between symbol and symbolized, and no room for the movement of *eros* in between. (2) Without the actualizing movement of the Spirit, signs would lose all organic and living links to things, being reduced to either brute facts of revelation or clever metaphors; the former resulting in sacramental fideism, the latter in Zwinglianism. And (3) if a mystery is not the coinherence of symbol and symbolized, their mutual union and exchange of idioms, then the entire landscape of symbolic inclusions collapses for want of an eternal source and abiding rationale. It is the Spirit as fully personal unity who overcomes all apparent dialectical antitheses. Without this final nuance, any hope of a sacramental or symbolic ontology is lost; the dissolutions of modernity win the day.

In trinitarian terms, each of these nuances necessitates the Spirit. Whether the eros of the Father and Son, the self-gift of the Father to the Son, or the unity of Father and Son, the entire construct breathes the life of the Spirit. Without the Spirit, in other words, it would be impossible to distinguish Father from Son, see the Father in the Son, or know the Father and Son together as one. Only the Spirit fully and finally banishes the specter of the arbitrary from a trinitarian theology of signs and things, for only the Spirit can secure a link between Father and Son that distinguishes and unites and is entirely intrinsic to both.

But these are implications we must draw. The fact that all three of these nuances can be mined from patristic usage of a single word underscores the extent to which their thought, never fully systematized, turned upon a pneumatological logic. De Lubac has indeed uncovered the patristic vision. The word mystery is simply the focal point of a systematic theology built on the axiom "unify to distinguish." Its three nuances are necessary facets of what unity-in-distinction requires. And that living unity-in-distinction is the Holy Spirit. The Holy Spirit, in other words, is the eternal source in which all symbolic inclusions participate. The "spirit of the Fathers," it turns out, is the Holy Spirit, which must be the most obvious statement de Lubac never wrote.

The Slant of Light

And this finally returns us to Augustine's tripartite definition of signs and things. Signs reveal something to someone. Signification terminates in interpretation, so that the third term forms the consummate moment in every act of communication. This interpretive moment, I want to suggest, is eternally the Holy Spirit, who unites symbolized and symbol in an overflowing act of interpretation. De Lubac hints at this possibility in his theology of Scripture.

For de Lubac, scripture is the "distending" through time of the Word spoken eternally in the heart of the Father:

> *Semel locutus est Deus: God has spoken once*: God pronounces only one word [*Parole*], not only in himself, in his unchanging eternity, in the immovable act by which he engenders his Word [*Verbe*], as Saint Augustine recalled, but also, just as Saint Ambrose already taught, in time, and among human beings, in the act by which he sent his Word to dwell in our earth.[93]

The one Word of the Father is the word spoken in the pages of scripture. The Incarnation reveals this identity:

> A twofold recapitulation, that of the Word [Parole] eternally pronounced in the breast of the Father and that of the Word addressed to men in the sequence of the ages, the first being there to permit the second, and the second also to reveal the first.[94]

And just as the Word is spoken in eternity in the desire, gift and unity of the Spirit, so the Word is spoken in the Old Testament in the Spirit:

> What was given in the Old Testament "was under another form", but it was already under the action of the same Spirit. The Word of God had been truly sent to them, just as it was to be truly sent to Mary, and God has no other word [*parole*] than his Word [*Verbe*], his only Son.[95]

As the Logos is joined to the Father in the Spirit, so the Logos is joined to humanity in the womb of Mary in the Spirit. In the same way, the Spirit incarnates the Word in the Old Testament, so that Christ is everywhere the "Spirit" of the letter. Thereafter, reading the Old Testament will be a matter of spiritual exegesis. Reading in the Spirit, then, will be a matter of desire becoming love in the discovery of the eternal Word, receiving the gift of God's presence in the sacrament of his Word, and uniting all disparate symbols to that which they symbolize: Christ, the Symbol of the Father. All the nuances mined in the previous section come to bear in spiritual exegesis.

The union of the Word in eternity and time establishes the possibility of spiritual exegesis, for recognizing and "reading the word" is the work proper to the Spirit. The meaning of the text is secured by the Spirit, for the Spirit unites scriptural symbol with eternal symbolized:

---

93. Henri De Lubac, *Medieval Exegesis*, Vol. 3 (Grand Rapids, MI: Eerdmans, 2009), 142.
94. De Lubac, *ME* III, 142.
95. De Lubac, *ME* III, 141.

The words of the revelation uncover their unity by accepting their final sense in the Spirit. By that very fact, they receive their final permanence. Indeed, just as the eternally uttered Word [Parole] is unique, so now is its human hearing, for time and eternity are joined in the Word made flesh.[96]

But spiritual exegesis expands beyond the book of Scripture, so that the entire book of nature becomes a site of divine signification. Recall that all signification is from, through, and to Christ; now we are in a position to specify that the final referent of all symbols is only known under the action of the Holy Spirit. If the Spirit is the union of Symbolized and Symbol, then uniting symbolized and symbol in creaturely understanding is a kind of spiritual interpretation. Ascending through symbolic inclusions requires learning to interpret symbols, or, in Augustine's terms, to refer all signs to the ultimate *res*. All things symbolize God, and learning to read God in all things is the work of spiritual exegesis.

But creaturely symbols are entirely inadequate to the divine symbolized, and so there is always a surplus of meaning. And this immediately calls into question our ability to exhaustively map creaturely symbols onto the divine. God's infinite nature means that when creatures symbolize God, they do so in indeterminate and multivalent ways. Every symbol admits of multiple "readings," a pattern exemplified in the fourfold interpretation of scripture. Divine abundance forbids any rigid taxonomy of symbols, so that any given event in scripture (roughly, the literal sense) might correspond in various ways to Christ and his Church (the analogical sense), to moral living (the tropological sense) and eschatological promise (the anagogical sense). The movement between these categories is persistently more aesthetic than discursive. The infinite perfection of God ensures that uniting creaturely symbols to Symbolized requires aesthetic judgments of fittingness.

If spiritual exegesis is an aesthetic discipline, it is not thereby un-rational. The mystery of God does not silence reason; it entices it higher. For de Lubac as for Augustine, reason is always already circumscribed in mystery and thus always mystical: "The more mystery there is, the more reason."[97] This aesthetic mysticism takes the form of right living, so that reading the symbols is the process of becoming a truthful symbol. Spiritual exegesis is not forming noetic or conceptual comparisons between God and the World; it is participating in the perfections of God in the pluriform contexts of life in time.[98] Spiritual interpretation is lived interpretation. So finite participation in the work of the Spirit is an aesthetic, mystical (which symbolically includes rational) and ethical interpretive endeavor, for it is nothing other than to know and understand the Word, spoken from all eternity, in all the contingent moments of human existence. It is an ascent—

---

96. De Lubac, *ME* III, 141.
97. De Lubac, *Corpus*, 232.
98. Cf. Milbank, *Strange*, ch. 1.

aesthetic, mystical, ethical—through spiraling symbolic inclusions into the life of God.

When de Lubac advocates Augustine's "signs and things" as the framework for overcoming all the dissolutions of modernity, he is advocating a return to the Spirit, a pneumatology of symbolic inclusions. As the Spirit is of the Father and the Son, so semiotics might be semiotic and christological, Christ might be divine and human, reason might be rational and mystical, and on and on. In every symbolic inclusion the symbol is united to the symbolized in an analogical "non-identical repetition."[99] Any movement from a creaturely paradox to a divine one, from a structure in creation to a "structure" in God, in short, any ascent from symbol to symbolized is a movement in the Spirit. For the Spirit is symbolism.

Denigrating the Spirit?

Does this pneumatology denigrate the Spirit? Is it not problematic to make the Spirit something between the other two? I do not think so. Rather, in conceiving the Spirit as desire/love, gift and unity, Augustine elevates those terms to the level of hypostasis. The fact that our culture finds union or desire or gift to be less "personal" says more about our own failure than Augustine's. The proper upshot of an Augustinian pneumatology is that desire, love, gift, and union are all equally important to (and indeed co-constitutive of) word, reason, and origin. That we have historically elevated one over the other is no indictment of Augustine. For the word, power and reason of God can only arise in love, gift, and unity. To call the Spirit these things is not to denigrate the Spirit, but to elevate the mode of existence that draws together the life of symbols as lives worth living. Recognizing this would go a long way toward better understanding Augustine, to say nothing of the apostle Paul.

Conclusion

Augustine offers us a vision of theology in which we ascend through symbols to the eternal life of God. He accomplishes this by dramatically expanding the scope of the sign-thing relation, so that all things are a sign of their creator. But this sign is not a mere pointer, for it contains the "ontological trace," and thus the *presence* of the signified. I use the term "symbol" to mark this difference: a symbol is a sign that mediates presence. For Augustine, the incarnation renders all creation a symbol, it reveals the presence of Christ at the heart of everything that is. Our pilgrimage toward the heavenly city is one of learning to read these symbols and refer them to their divine *res*. That process is intended to shape our own inner words in right love, that we might know and love God rightly. In the

---

99. Cf. Catherine Pickstock, *After Writing* (Oxford: Blackwell, 1998), 25.

end, all our inner words and loves will be perfected in the immediate presence of the first Word and first love: we will know God even as we are known. And this, Augustine thinks, is where an ascent through signs leads us. From Christ the creator, through Christ the redeemer, to the triune life of God: the Father who speaks an inner Word in Love, Father–Son–Spirit. The inner Word of the Father is the symbol of the Father, the sign that bears the fullness of the Father's being. Unlike created symbols, the eternal Word and the Father are one, there is no hiatus between Father and Son. The Spirit, then, is the active agent of love and unity of Father and Son. The Spirit is fully personal, and yet mutually internal to both Father and Son, and so "paradoxically pre-present" in the generation of the Son. Thus, Augustine's Father–Son–Spirit could be described as symbolized–symbol–symbolism.

This trinitarian account of the symbols is developed by Karl Rahner's theology of the symbol. Where Augustine moves from temporal signs to heavenly reality, Rahner moves from heavenly reality down through the chain of symbolic inclusions. The Father is symbolized in the Son, divinity in the humanity of Jesus, substance in accident, soul in body, Christ in his sacred heart. This analogy of symbols, or great chain of symbols, opens the possibility of describing all things according to a symbolic logic. It moves us toward an ontology of the symbol founded upon the relation of Father and Son.

Henri de Lubac's sacramental pneumatology closes the circuit. While de Lubac does not draw the connections clearly, his sacramentology foregrounds the Spirit. The Spirit is the desire of Father for Son and love of Son for Father, maintaining the distinction between Father and Son. The Spirit is the active gift of the Father and the Son, the one in whom the presence of the Father in the Son is established. And the Spirit is the union of Father and Son, the active and personal agent of divine unity and love. While filling out an account of the Spirit, it also points the way toward understanding more deeply how symbols function. There must be a dynamic movement between symbol and symbolized, a gift of presence donated from symbolized to symbol, and received and returned in love. The unity of symbolized and symbol is not a static thing, but a constant movement, a real presence. This pneumatology will have significant consequences in future chapters for our understanding of created symbols. The Spirit is symbolism, the personal movement of love, gift, and unity between Father and Son. All of this finally yields the triad, symbolized–symbol–symbolism as an apt analogy for Father–Son–Spirit.

This triad offers a number of benefits. It draws together a number of themes in trinitarian theology in a useful shorthand. It marks the Father as the hidden source: hidden because only ever known in the Son, and source as the overflowing fount of divinity. It indicates the nature of the Son as begotten Word, consubstantial with and yet non-identical to the Father, avoiding both an Arian diminution of the Son and a modalist flattening of difference between Son and Father. It indicates the irreducibility of the Spirit, the Spirit's paradoxical "pre-presence" in the begetting of the Son, and the Spirit's mutual internality to both Father and Son.[100]

If this triad draws together a number of helpful themes in understanding the Trinity, it performs an enormous amount of work in understanding triune action in time. Because God's being and God's act are one, the relations of the Trinity structure the shape of God's works, most especially creation and redemption. In what follows I argue that the triad symbolized–symbol–symbolism corresponds, analogically, to God–creation–church. Like Father to Son, God is the hidden source of creation who can only be known through created symbols. As both Augustine and Thomas argue, creation is spoken in the speaking of the Word, and this makes creation the "unfolding" of the Logos through time. Creation is thus a participation in the Son as a symbol of God. This is by no means to suggest that creation just *is* the Son, only that it exists by participation in the relation of Son to Father.[101] The church, then, is the union of God with creation, symbol with symbolized, and is thus symbolism, a finite participation in the work of the Spirit. At each stage, the structure of relations I have named from the Trinity illuminates the hidden structures of reality, the ontological trace of God's presence in the world. I turn now to creation, the temporal symbol of this eternal Trinity.

---

100. The triad, however, also has its limits. One might ask, for instance, "To whom does the Father symbolize himself in the Son?" This kind of question, however, presumes some kind of a mythological process that cannot exist within God. We can no more ask this than ask "to whom does the Father speak the Word?" Thus, while the language of symbols helps draw together these various strands of classical trinitarian theology, it does not serve as *more* descriptive than Word, Wisdom, or Image as names for the Son. It rather seeks to specify the relation of these to the other key features of trinitarian thought, and systematic theology as a whole.

101. There are pneumatological dimensions to creation as well, but that will be unfolded in the next chapter.

Chapter 2

CREATION

Introduction

In the previous chapter I sketched a view of trinitarian theology that, following de Lubac, I call symbolism. It arises from an Augustinian account of the Son as the inner Word of the Father, and the Spirit as the union or love between them. I summarized this account with the triad symbolized–symbol–symbolism as a fitting analogy for Father–Son–Spirit. In formulating this triad, I focused on Henri de Lubac's term, "symbolic inclusion" to describe the ways various theological topics are enfolded within this trinitarian paradigm. Symbols carry all the way down, so that what we encounter in the world symbolizes the life of God: symbols mediate the presence of the symbolized. This means that lower things are symbolically included in higher things, and the Augustinian shape of theology is to ascend through the chain of symbolic inclusions to the Trinitarian life of God.

In this chapter I turn to the doctrine of creation, but in doing this I do not leave the doctrine of the Trinity. Indeed, more detail will be added to the discussion of the Trinity from Chapter 1. This is because creation is first of all a doctrine about God, and secondly a doctrine about creatures.[1] As Thomas Aquinas says, "the processions of the divine persons are the cause of creation,"[2] therefore knowledge of the divine processions is "necessary for the right idea of creation."[3] To know the universe we inhabit, we must know the Father, Son, and Spirit.

But this is not to say that theology is an entirely top-down affair. For God is known to us only in the created effects of temporal reality, that is, through God's symbols. These symbols have been given that we might come to know the divine through them. And so I have formulated a second triad, symbolically included

---

1. Cf. John Webster, "Trinity and Creation" in *The International Journal of Systematic Theology* 12, no. 1 (January 2010), 5.
2. *ST* 1a.45.6.ad 1.
3. *ST* 1a.32.1.ad 3.

in the first. As Father–Son–Spirit can be described as symbolized–symbol–symbolism, so can God–creation–church. The latter triad is analogically related to the prior two. Creation is a symbol of God, God's gift of participation in being. The fact that we only come to know God through the material elements of life in time follows this same symbolic logic: The Father is only known in the Son, God is only known by creatures through created analogies. This is the heart of Thomas's doctrine of analogy, and his use of Augustine's psychological analogy for the Trinity. God is present to us in creation by analogy, and theology is disciplined reflection on the analogical symbols of God. Meditation on the structures of life in time—not least the human mind—is not a way to furnish data for theological science to dissect, but a means of ascent, a symbolic inclusion through which we might glimpse God.

This account of creation as a symbol seeks to ground a doctrine of analogy in the Trinity itself. Analogical participation in God is possible because the Son symbolizes the Father in the Spirit; analogical participation is the creaturely correlate to intra-divine symbolism. In this way, the shape of the Trinity is also the shape of participation in the Trinity. Only if the analogy of being is first a doctrine about God and secondly a doctrine about the relations between God and creation can it avoid the Barthian critique that it opens the way to a deracinated natural theology. Symbolism is an attempt to express just such a trinitarian doctrine of analogy.

I will develop a trinitarian doctrine of creation with reference to two thirteenth-century theologians. Thomas Aquinas, as representative of a Dominican school of theology, places a premium on the relations of the divine persons, seeing in their inner-relatedness the foundation of a theology of creation. Duns Scotus, representative of a Franciscan strand of theology, prioritizes the productive powers of the divine essence over the relations of the persons.[4] This prioritization of production over relation, I will argue, fractures the symbolic value of creation, making it the product of sheer divine power irrespective of the persons. The specter of pure nature then arises from this particular trinitarian theology, since creation finally adverts only to the causal powers of the divine intellect and will which are formally prior to the persons: Creation is a symbol of power, not persons, and this devolves over the centuries to two-tier theology of pure nature (under the rubric of divine power) and grace (under the rubric of the persons).

---

4. For an accessible and neutral overview of these two schools, see Russell Friedman, "Medieval Trinitarian Theology from the Late Thirteenth to the Fifteenth Centuries," in *The Oxford Handbook of the Trinity* eds. Gilles Emery O.P. and Matthew Levering. (Oxford: Oxford University Press, 2011), 197–209. For a more aggressive account, see Catherine Pickstock, "Duns Scotus: His Historical and Contemporary Significance," *Modern Theology* 12, no. 4 (October 2005), 566.

I pursue this now-common comparison between Aquinas and Scotus because it is germane to a systematic theology of the symbol.[5] A differently conceived doctrine of the Trinity generates a different concept of creation. Once Scotus prioritizes productive power over persons, the world is no longer a symbol of divine life, but of divine power. Scotus is only representative in these moves—he is a part of a theological school, and by no means the only person who holds these theological commitments. But he is this school's most influential thinker, and so it is helpful to focus on his theology as indicative of broader trends. In restricting my focus to the theological question of symbolism, I hope the reader will forgive my treading a well-worn road. I will indicate in a few brief paragraphs the Scotist legacy in early modern thought, because Scotus's abandonment of symbolism was to have significant consequences which must be named, even if every consequence was not already fully and explicitly present in Scotus.

I will conclude with a reflection on Thomas and Scotus's respective uses of Augustine's psychological analogy. When Thomas adapts Augustine's "psychological analogy" for the Trinity, he does so in a way broadly consistent with Augustine's usage: a created structure that participates in, but is not univocally attributable to, the divine life. Scotus, by contrast, follows a general trend in medieval Franciscan theology to reify the analogy, making divine intellect and will *literally* the producers of the divine persons.[6] For Scotus, intellect and will are not analogical symbols of divine life; they are the productive principles of the divine life. Aquinas, I argue, follows Augustine in using the analogy as a means to glimpse God; Scotus uses the analogy to prove God. In the latter case, theology ceases to be a mysticism, concerned only with the formalities of logic irrespective of the theologian's own analogical participation. Thus, the decline of symbolism in theological content corresponds to a decline of symbolism in theological method, a method in which naming God is coextensive with becoming like God, becoming a truer symbol.

---

5. This kind of comparison between Scotus and Aquinas has become a common and controverted move in contemporary theology. See Daniel Horan, *Postmodernity and Univocity: A Critical Account of Radical Orthodoxy and John Duns Scotus* (Minneapolis, MN: Fortress Press, 2014), 3. As Horan's subtitle demonstrates, this critique of Scotus is commonly associated with Radical Orthodoxy, though, as he notes but fails to respond to, the story that Scotus lies at or near the birthplace of modernity shares far broader support than this one Anglo-American theological movement. Cf. John Milbank, *Theology and Social Theory*, 2nd edn. (Oxford: Blackwell, 2006), 305. The primary point of contention is whether Scotus's theory of univocity is ontological or merely conceptual. See Richard Cross, *Duns Scotus* (Oxford: Oxford University Press, 1999), ch. 3.

6. This is well documented. See Russell Friedman, *Medieval Trinitarian Thought from Aquinas to Ockham* (Cambridge: Cambridge University Press, 2010), ch. 2.

Two Trinitarian Models

In the thirteenth and fourteenth centuries two distinct models of the Trinity are discernable. A predominately Dominican model, represented by Thomas Aquinas, prioritizes the mutual relations of the persons.[7] The persons subsist as their relations of origin. For the Franciscans this was worrisome, for how could a person be defined by a relation without in some way preceding that relation? On what basis could a relation obtain without a logically prior person? Bonaventure therefore formulates an account of the persons founded on emanation: the emanation of the Son must logically precede the Son's relation to the Father, since integral personhood precedes relation.[8] For Bonaventure, this is entirely within the realm of our conceptualization of the Trinity, a way of speaking necessary to the inadequacies of our capacities. But the Franciscan tradition will quickly set about reifying Bonaventure's emanationist account: "for [the Franciscan tradition], then, emanation or origin is the actual and not merely the conceptual source of the distinction between the persons."[9] What for Bonaventure had been a fruitful analogy for the "how" of processions became a quasi-mechanical description of how emanation actually occurs and therefore how the integrity of the persons is actually secured.[10] Eventually, Scotus will embrace this reification of concepts of the processions and combine it with Augustine's psychological analogy: the Son and Spirit are products of the divine essence, literally the inner Word and Love proceeding from the intellect and will. These two accounts of the Trinity result in two accounts of creation, a difference whose consequences I will attempt to show.

Aquinas on Creation

Processions

In the *Summa Theologiae*, Thomas begins his discourse on the Trinity with the question of whether there are processions in God.[11] The crux of the question is the phrase "in God." For Arius, Aquinas argues, the Father is the cause of the Son, who is an effect as the Father's first creature. The Spirit is then the creature of both

---

7. Cf. Russell Friedman, *Medieval*, chs. 1–2.
8. Bonaventure, I *Sent.*, d. 27, *pars* I, a. un., q. 2, *solutio*. See discussion in Friedman, *Medieval*, 23.
9. Friedman, *Medieval*, 31.
10. To this extent, Bonaventure remains within the tradition of symbolic theology. See Joseph Wawrykow, "Franciscan and Dominican Trinitarian Theology (Thirteenth Century): Bonaventure and Aquinas," in Gilles Emery O.P. and Matthew Levering (eds.), *The Oxford Handbook of the Trinity* (Oxford: Oxford University Press, 2011), 182–96. For this reason, I rather draw the contrast between Scotus and Aquinas, where it is more decisive.
11. *ST* 1a.27.1.

the Father and Son. In this way, Arius places the processions of the Son and Spirit *outside* of God. Similarly, Aquinas argues, Sabelius maintained that the Father, Son, and Spirit are only so in their relations to the world. Yet again, the processions are determined by something external to God. But how are we to understand two processions—of the Son and the Spirit—that remain entirely internal to God?

Thomas appeals to two powers he explored in the previous sections of the Summa. The divine intellect and will, he argues, are where we should look for two wholly internal and self-constitutive processions in God. Since God has acted outwardly in creation, and God's being and God's act are one, Thomas argues there must also be "an inward procession corresponding to the act remaining within the agent,"[12] which is the principle of the outward act. In other words, the twin affirmations that God is simple and that God has created *require* that God's simplicity be processional. If God establishes creation as something other than God, there must be a prior differentiation *within* God to ground this external difference.[13] An undifferentiated monad could not create something external to itself and maintain its simplicity. An inner procession is required, so that God's outer action might conform to God's inner being. The inner procession of the Word is thus the ground of the external procession of creatures.

Thomas argues:

> This [internal procession] applies most conspicuously to the intellect, the action of which remains in the intelligent agent. For whenever we understand, by the very fact of understanding there proceeds something within us, which is a conception of the object understood, a conception issuing from our intellectual power and proceeding from our knowledge of that object. This conception is signified by the spoken word; and it is called the word of the heart signified by the word of the voice.[14]

Aquinas follows Augustine in appealing to the "inner word" as an analogy of the eternal Word. When we understand something, our intellect understands it in producing an interior "likeness" or "word." This inner word is the completion of the act of knowing, so that all knowledge is a kind of emanation from the self. For the divine intellect, what is known is, in the first place, the divine essence, so that the procession of the inner word is a procession of self-knowledge.[15] Since God is pure and perfect intellect, then this procession must be constitutive of who God is: God is irreducibly and eternally processional. The divine intellect then corresponds to the eternal Word, now conceived as the inner word proceeding

---

12. *ST*. Ia.27.1.
13. See Simon Oliver, "Trinity, Motion and Creation ex Nihilo," in David Burrell (ed.), *Creation and the God of Abraham* (Cambridge: Cambridge University Press, 2010), 133–51.
14. *ST* Ia.27.1.
15. *ST* Ia.14.2.

from the Father[16]: *in the beginning was the Word, and the Word was with God, and the Word was God.*

The will is the other—the only other—procession that remains entirely internal to the agent.[17] The logic is similar. To the procession of the inner word in the intellect, there corresponds the procession of love in the will:

> The operation of the will within ourselves involves another procession, that of love, whereby the object loved is in the lover; as, by the conception of the word, the object spoken of or understood is in the intelligent agent.[18]

Where the inner word is an emanation that makes the known present in the knower by its intellect, love proceeding from the will is the emanation that makes the beloved present to the lover. In God, this emanation of the will remains entirely internal, for what is loved is God's own self: the Son by the Father and the Father by the Son. This mode of operation as the love between the Father and Son is the reason the divine will corresponds to the Spirit.

This correlation of intellect and will to Son and Spirit is not a literal identification. Thomas's trinitarian theology is a spiritual "'exercise' carried out by means of 'reasons.'"[19] By examining the structures of life in time, Thomas intends to train the mind toward knowledge of God. The training had by consideration of creation leads us to God because all of creation is analogically related to God. Because God is pure act, God is God's intellect and will; God is pure intellection and pure willing. Human (and Angelic) intellects and wills participate in the original intellect and will that God eternally is. Thomas is therefore free to seek in the functioning of intellect and will an appropriate analogy for the Son and Spirit. But in calling this an "appropriate analogy," I am not suggesting that it is a weakly correlated similarity or thin metaphor. This is precisely the critique that Scotus will make.[20] Scotus claims that in the Dominican tradition, the inner word and love

---

16. Cf. *ST* 1a.27.2: "So in this manner the procession of the Word in God is generation; for He proceeds by way of intelligible action, which is a vital operation:—from a conjoined principle (as above described):—by way of similitude, inasmuch as the concept of the intellect is a likeness of the object conceived:—and exists in the same nature, because in God the act of understanding and His existence are the same, as shown above (1a.14.4). Hence the procession of the Word in God is called generation; and the Word Himself proceeding is called the Son."

17. *ST* 1a.27.5. Aquinas examines goodness and power as alternate candidates for processions, but rejects them as common to the divine essence, not to one of the three persons.

18. *ST* 1a.27.3.

19. Gilles Emery, "Trinitarian Theology as Spiritual Exercise in Augustine and Aquinas," in *Trinity, Church and the Human Person* (Naples, FL: Sapientia Press, 2007), 71; citing Thomas Aquinas, *Summa Contra Gentiles* I, ch. 8 (#49–50); *De potentia* q. 9, a. 5 and others.

20. Scotus, I *Ord.* 13, nn. 21, 23.

bear only an "extraneous likeness" to the Son and Spirit.[21] For some Dominicans, this charge is not unwarranted, notably Durand of Pourçain, for whom the name "Word" is only appropriated to the Son, not properly predicated. But Durand notwithstanding, Scotus's accusation of metaphorical equivocation does not stand for the following reasons.

The Son is not literally the product of the divine intellect coming to know the divine essence, and yet the Son is properly called Word, as the Spirit is properly called love. The reason for this is that "Word" and "Love" are analogical terms—they apply more appropriately to God than to creatures. It is not, in fact, our understanding of the Trinity that is crafted around the concept of the inner word, but the concept of an inner word is modified to fit the Trinity. For Thomas, "Word" refers most properly to emanation: "'Word', according as we use the term strictly of God, signifies something proceeding from another."[22] The word "Word," considered in its most primordial meaning ("first and chiefly") is nothing other than emanation.[23] The inner word of the Father is the Father's understanding of all that is, so that God's knowledge is always begotten in a kind of "speaking": "thus the whole Trinity is 'spoken' in the Word; and likewise all of creatures."[24] From a perspective of symbols, this last statement is extraordinary. It implies that because the relation of Father to Son is that of symbolized to symbol, then *everything* that exists, exists because the Father is not without the symbol. The emanation of the symbol from the Father underwrites everything. When Aquinas affirms that the Son is properly called "Word," he is invoking an entire symbolic ontology, of which the Son is the primordial type. Thereafter, every inner word is a faint participation in this original unity of symbolized and symbol. It is for this reason that the contemplation of similitudes is "a foretaste of what [believers] hope to see in the beatific vision."[25] Every act of knowledge is the emanation of another from within, an inner word ultimately derived from the primordial word, the Word most properly speaking. So central is the analogy that Emery states, Thomas's "whole Trinitarian theology depends upon [its] validity."[26] The production of an inner word in the intellect and of love in the will are, Thomas thinks, the highest created image of the divine life. Creaturely intellection and willing are participation in the divine processions of Son and Spirit and are therefore key links in the chain of symbols leading us into knowledge of God. The psychological analogy is not a "thin metaphor"; it is the affirmation that God is more truly Word and Love than our words and our love, which is to say that all of being is symbolic.

---

21. Scotus, I *Ord.* 13, nn. 21, 23. See discussion and translation in Friedman, *Medieval*, 74–5.
22. ST Ia.34.1.
23. ST Ia.34.1. Cf. Gilles Emery, O.P., *Trinity in Aquinas* (Naples, FL: Sapientia Press, 2003), 148–53.
24. *ST* Ia.34.1.ad 3.
25. Emery, *Trinity*, 128.
26. Emery, *Trinity*, 256.

Distinctions must be made between the Son–Word and Spirit–Love. The Spirit does not proceed in the same way as the Son, which is reflected in differences between intellection and willing. Thomas says in an earlier section of the *Summa* that "knowledge is of things as they exist in the knower; but the will is directed to things as they exist in themselves."[27] Intellectual procession, Aquinas tells us, operates by likeness.[28] The inner word is a similitude or image of the thing known, so that likeness mediates presence. A thing is present to the intellect by its image. I know something, in other words, because of the unity that exists between the thing and my mind, the extent to which the thing is "in" my mind by its likeness. This is not, however, the facile "representation" of cartesian cognition. For Thomas, the relationship between the world "outside" and the world "inside" is not a simple dualism. Rather, the intellect actually makes the "outside" world present "inside," by the dual processes of the migration of the form into the mind, and the production of an inner word.[29] For the divine intellect, what is known is the divine essence, so that by the speaking of the Word, the divine essence is made present to the Father. This means that, to translate into my terminology, for Aquinas the Father only is inasmuch as he is symbolized in the Son. The Word is the eternal image, the symbol by which the Father knows and is God.

The procession of the Will, on the other hand, proceeds not by likeness, but by inclination or movement.[30] Love, which is to the will what the inner word is to the intellect, is a directedness toward another. Thus, while the intellect speaks of divine likeness, the will speaks of divine desire-in-difference: the Father in himself and the Son in himself, *as their mutual movement toward each other.* Because the Father is not the Son, and the Son not the Father, there is a mutual motion of desire and love between them, and this movement is called the Spirit. While the classic description of the Spirit as the unity of Father and Son might seem to place it in the role of the intellect, focusing on the exactness of the representation of the Father by the Son, for Aquinas, the Spirit-as-will emphasizes the unity of the Father and the Son as a term that maintains their distinct integrity as divine persons while uniting them in mutual movement toward one another. The Spirit secures the eternal distinction between Father and Son by uniting them as Father and Son, and so not collapsing them into a single person. As the previous chapter argued, the Spirit *is* union-in-distinction, the original "symbolic inclusion" in which all others participate.

Indeed, without the Spirit, it would be impossible to maintain any meaningful distinction between the Father and Son, since a word must itself be received, or "interpreted" as meaningful. For Augustine and Aquinas, the Spirit is the love in

---

27. *ST* 1a.19.3.ad 6.
28. *ST* 1a.27.4.
29. Cf. John Milbank and Catherine Pickstock, *Truth in Aquinas* (New York: Routledge, 2001), ch. 1.
30. *ST* 1a.27.4.

which the divine knower knows its knowledge.[31] To love what is known by an inner word is to make an interpretive judgment about its value or worth. It is to recognize the representative value of the Word as truly shining forth the fullness of the Father and responding to this depiction with pleasure and desire. If there were no such "interpretive moment" in the Trinity, the speaking of the Word would merely be a blunt self-assertion without reciprocity. In this situation, even the Word would fail to be a hypostasis, since it would lack any reciprocal act of love with which to return to the Father. It would be merely a pulsar in a vacuum, a burst of light never seen or reflected or truly known. An inner word without either desire or love fails even to be an inner word, becoming instead a product of the Father's capricious self-expression. When Christocentrism eclipses pneumatology, divine self-communication is reduced to sheer imposition without the appropriate reciprocity required by relations of love. If the Spirit is not an authentic "second difference" from the Father, then neither the Son nor the Spirit (and therefore neither the Father) can maintain any hypostatic integrity.[32] To the emanation of the inner word corresponds the emanation of love, necessarily.

These emanations have a distinct "direction of travel." The *one* indivisible divine essence is received according to a particular *taxis*: "the Son receives it from the Father, and the Holy Ghost from both."[33] In receiving the divine nature from the Father, the Son is the symbol of the Father. The Spirit, in being of the Father and the Son is the mutual love and unity between them. This distinction of order maintains for intellect and will: "the procession of love occurs in due order as regards the procession of the Word; since nothing can be loved by the will unless it is conceived by the intellect."[34] So the inner word proceeds from the intellect, and love proceeds from the will after the intellect.

The Son and Spirit therefore share equally in the divine essence but do so in different ways. This is the heart of Thomas's argument for the *filioque*. Unless the Son and Spirit proceed in different ways from the Father, then they would be impossible to distinguish eternally, since they are only distinguishable by their relations.[35] If the Spirit proceeds directly from the Father, as does the Son, the Spirit shares the same relation of origin as the Son, making the Son and Spirit indistinguishable.[36] What procession *per filium* offers is a second procession in a mode distinct from the Son's, a "second difference" from the Father that is

---

31. Augustine, *De trinitate* 4.19, trans. and ed. Edmund Hill Op (New York: New City Press, 119), 282; *ST* 1a.37.1.

32. I take this phrase from John Milbank, *The Word Made Strange* (Oxford: Blackwell, 1997), 187.

33. *ST* 1a.45.6.ad 2.

34. *ST* 1a.27.3.ad 3.

35. *ST* 1a.36.2-3.

36. Cf. discussion in Milbank, *Strange*, 172. On the commonality of the *per filium* sense of the *filioque* throughout the Christian East, see David Bentley Hart, "The Mirror of the Infinite: Gregory of Nyssa on the Vestigia Trinitatis," *Modern Theology* 18, no. 4 (October 2002): 541–61.

still from the one paternal *arche*.[37] The Son proceeds from the Father, the Spirit proceeds from the Father by the Son, ensuring the eternally distinct relations of origin of the Son and Spirit.

And yet, this divine *taxis* does not obviate the mutual inclusion of Word and Spirit, intellect and will: "The will and the intellect mutually include one another: for the intellect understands the will, and the will wills the intellect to understand."[38] Since the Spirit is what is donated to the Son in filiation, the Son's reception of the gift of the Spirit is constitutive of the Son's procession. Thus, we can say with John Milbank that the Spirit is "retroactively causal" in the generation of the Son.[39] The Spirit proceeds from the Father and Son, but the Spirit's procession is intrinsic and necessary to the prior procession of Son from Father. This is confirmed by the status of the Spirit as the love between Father and Son: the Father begets the Son in love, the Son loves the Father in return, and this love that proceeds from them is somehow coeval with their very relations.[40] There is both an irrevocable *taxis* and an ineludible paradox.

This paradox coheres profoundly with Thomas's argument for the mutual internality of will and intellect. While the intellect is, strictly speaking, prior to the will, the will is always-already present within it, functioning on both sides of the procession of an inner word. The will "follows upon intellect," as the Spirit proceeds from the Father *by the Son*.[41] But the movement of the will constitutes the intellect as such, as the Son's reception of the Spirit constitutes the Son. Thomas explains it this way: the intellect has a natural aptitude for intellection, which takes the form of desire. I come to know because I *want* to know. Once knowledge has been obtained, the intellect "rests" in its knowledge, which is also a function of the will: the intellect strives to intellection "so as to rest therein when possessed, and when not possessed to seek to possess it, both of which pertain to the will."[42] This means that the will establishes the intellect as its desire to know, while nonetheless following from its knowledge. Similarly, the divine *taxis* requires the Spirit be after the Son and yet "retroactively causal" in the generation of the Son.

Thus, for Thomas, Son and Spirit are tightly woven into an understanding of inner word and love because both are internal to the agent and irreducibly processional. To the procession of the inner word in the intellect corresponds the procession of love in the will. The Son and Spirit, like the intellect and will, mutually include one another, and while they must be distinguished, can never be separated. This entire conceptual apparatus, the symbolic inclusion of Intellect-Will in Son-Spirit, and the divine *taxis* and paradoxical mutual internality are all brought to bear on Thomas's theology of creation. God creates according to God's

37. Milbank, *Strange*, ch. 7.
38. *ST* 1a.16.4.ad 1.
39. Milbank, *Word*, 187. The concept of the Spirit deployed in this chapter derives largely from Milbank's account.
40. *ST* 1a.39.8.
41. *ST* 1a.19.1.
42. *ST* 1a.19.1.

unity in the divine processions: by the inner Word, in love. Thus, understanding both the divine *taxis* and the coinherence of the persons is "necessary for the right idea of creation."[43]

Trinity, Simplicity, and Creation

"The processions of the divine persons," Aquinas argues, "are the cause of creation."[44] Aquinas repeats this reasoning nearly twenty times throughout his career.[45] Gilles Emery concludes: "The systematic exploitation of this thesis appears as a characteristic feature of his theology."[46] Aquinas's general point is that the "procession" of creation is founded on the ontologically prior processions of the Son and Spirit. Three factors converge on this assertion: Divine simplicity, Blessed Trinity, and the external act of creation. It is the combination of the first two that guarantee the symbolic value of the latter.

God is wholly simple.[47] God is not composite, neither bodily, nor between matter and form, existence and essence, substance and accident.[48] This means that God is not included under any genus, including that of being.[49] God's words to Moses are the paradigmatic biblical ground of this understanding: "I am that I am."[50] David Burrell's translates Thomas's application of this text: "to be God is to be to-be."[51] But how can the Christian belief in the Trinity stand in the face of such a strident simplicity?

One problem with answering that question is that it tacitly assumes a complete account of simplicity to which Trinitarian theology is later added, often mapped onto philosophy and theology, respectively.[52] But as Gilles Emery notes, "[Thomas]

---

43. *ST* 1a.32.1.ad 3. The second reason knowledge of the processions is necessary for the knowledge of salvation. It is because creation is symbolic that both creation and salvation converge on trinitarian discourse.

44. *ST* 1a.45.6.ad 1. Cf. discussion in Emery, *Human Person*, 115–54.

45. Emery, *Human Person*, 122. Key instances include I *Sent.*, dist. 14, q. 1, a. 1; *de potentia*, q. 10, a. 2, arg. 19, ad 19; and *ST* 1a.45.7. ad 3.

46. Emery, *Human Person*, 123.

47. D. Stephen Long, *The Perfectly Simple Triune God* (Minneapolis, MN: Fortress Press, 2016), chs. 4–9; James Dolezal, *God without Parts: Divine Simplicity and the Metaphysics of God's Absoluteness* (Eugene, OR: Pickwick, 2011); and the recent edition dedicated to simplicity, *Modern Theology 35*, no. 3 (July 2019).

48. *ST* 1a.3.1, 2, 3, 6 respectively.

49. *ST* 1a.3.5.

50. Exodus 3:14. On simplicity as a principle of biblical interpretation in Aquinas, see D. Stephen Long, "Thomas Aquinas' Divine Simplicity as Biblical Hermeneutic," *Modern Theology* 35, no. 3 (July 2019), 496–507.

51. David Burrell, *Aquinas: God and Action* (London: Routledge, 1979), 24.

52. For instance, John Wippel argues that Thomas's philosophical content can be extracted from its theological context in *Metaphysical Themes in Thomas Aquinas* (Washington, DC: Catholic University of America Press, 1984), 28.

has no treatise 'of the one God' separated from the treatise of the Trinity."[53] Thomas is not concerned with conforming a doctrine of the Trinity to a preestablished philosophy of unified simplicity. Rather, he is concerned with what kind of simplicity is necessary to understand the Trinity.[54] Simplicity is how we speak of three divine persons who are one essence. It is a rule of Christian grammar dictated by the commitment to God as three-in-one.[55] To speak of a distinction of persons and identity of essence requires an account of simplicity, specifically trinitarian simplicity, in D. Stephen Long's words, the perfectly simple triunity of God.[56]

Consider Thomas's basic account of simplicity: God's essence and existence are the same. What God is and that God is are identical. There is not a choice, then, between a trinitarian God or a monadic God, because God's triunity is God's existence. This means there can be no temporal progression in God—we do not start with God's essence, then get the Father, then the Son, and after all this the Spirit. The language of begetting cannot imply this kind of process. All of the processions are coeval and interdependent. This commitment to the Trinity and simplicity drives Thomas's formulation of substantive relations: the Father only is in relation to the Son in the Spirit. Since there can be no progress from one person to another, there is no Father prior to the generation of the Son in the Spirit; the persons just are their relations of origin. This is nothing other than what is demanded by the grammar Christian trinitarian simplicity. But this does not imperil the *arche* of the Father, for the divine nature exists in its *taxis*. Processions are the non-temporal *taxis* of the divine nature within the paradox of coinherence.

Simplicity further demands that God's being is God's act, so that there is no shadow between what God does externally and who God is internally. Simplicity, then, is the crucial link between the doctrine of the Trinity and the doctrine of creation: God's act in creation, as God's being in eternity, is trinitarian, though the latter in no way depends on the former. Simple triunity demands that God's acts "*ad extra*" are enacting according to both the *taxis* and the unity of the divine nature. The Father who is *arche* creates; the Son who is begotten is the one *by* whom the Father creates; and the Spirit who proceeds as the love between Father and Son is the one *in* whom God creates. Creation is wholly a product of Trinitarian movement, while not identical with, or necessary to, that movement.

This is what it means to say that creation is a symbol of God. Because God acts according to God's being, God's act of creation is accomplished by the internal movement of the godhead; creation thereby bears in itself the stamp of this trinitarian pattern without being necessary to divine life. Creation is thus not a symbol in precisely the same way that the Son is the symbol of the Father.

---

53. Emery, *Trinity*, XX. Cf. Long, *Simple*, 5.

54. Long, *Simple*, 21–2.

55. Cf. Burrell, *Aquinas*, 5. The seminal text for doctrine as grammar is George Linbeck, *The Nature of Doctrine: Religion and Theology in a Postliberal Age* (Louisville, KY: Westminster John Knox Press, 1984).

56. Long, *Simple*, ch. 1.

Substantive relations demand that the Father only is inasmuch as he is symbolized in the Son by the symbolism of the Spirit. When we move to the second triad, God–creation–church, the relationship does not bear the same necessity. God does not depend on creation in order to be God, for this would violate both triunity and simplicity. If God has a necessary relationship to creation, either God will not be simple (since God would be *composed* of God's nature and a relation to creation) or God would not be triune (since creation would be a kind of fourth hypostasis). Thomas therefore describes the relation between God and creation as logical on the part of God and real on the part of creation. God is perfectly simple, and so cannot have a relation added to God's essence. Thomas therefore calls this a relation of reason. But creation *is* existentially bound to God, and hence has a real relation to him.[57] But this does not mean creation is cut off from God's life—far from it. Creation has its existence by participation in the divine life, a participation funded, as will be shown below, by the way creation arises from the trinitarian processions.

This move from Creator to creature is shaped by the twin commitments to simplicity and Trinity. Creation is symbolic because God acts according to God's essence, and the effects of God's acts therefore bear a trinitarian shape. Symbolism is first a doctrine about God and only secondarily about creation. Divine simplicity is the link between the two. The simplicity of the Trinity mandates a symbolic creation.[58]

From Intellect and Will to Creation

Divine simplicity is expressed in the trinitarian *taxis*, a "direction of travel" that applies to the act of creation as well. For Aquinas, following Augustine, God acts in creation according to God's unity, but also according to the Trinitarian order.[59] Just as "the Son receives [the one divine essence] from the Father, and the Holy Ghost from both,"[60] so the act of creation is unfolded along the same internal divine motion. Creation is enacted according to the particular "mode of operation" of each person. The Father speaks all of creation in his speaking of the Son, and loves the Son and all creation in the procession of the Spirit:

> As the Father speaks Himself and every creature by His begotten Word, inasmuch as the Word "begotten" adequately represents the Father and every creature; so He loves Himself and every creature by the Holy Ghost … Thus it is evident that relation to the creature is implied both in the Word and in the proceeding Love,

---

57. *ST* 1a.45.3.
58. So, Emery, *Human Person*, 123: "A correct and integral understanding of God's action in the world requires knowledge of the procession of the divine Persons."
59. For example, St. Augustine, *The Literal Meaning of Genesis*, I.36, trans. John Hammond Taylor, *Ancient Christian Writers* 41 (New York: Newman Press, 1982), 41.
60. *ST* 1a.45.6.ad 2.

as it were in a secondary way, inasmuch as the divine truth and goodness are a principle of understanding and loving all creatures.[61]

The *taxis* of the processions displays the order of creation. In Emery's words, "The Son *exists* in receiving eternally his being from the Father, and he *acts* in receiving eternally his act from the Father."[62] The modus operandi of each Person arises from its *modus essendi*.[63]

The Father creates by the Son in the Spirit, which, for Thomas, means by his intellect according to his will. I will take intellect and will in turn. The Father speaks the world by his speaking of the Word; he knows the world by his knowledge of himself. By understanding the eternal Word as God's knowledge, Thomas is able to say that God's knowledge of the world is the world's existence. God does not know the universe because it exists, rather, the universe exists because God knows it.[64] What Thomas means by this is that the Word is the prototype and form of the world, so that everything that is is eternally contained in the Logos. Thomas expresses this in his doctrine of divine ideas.[65] The divine ideas, the prototypes of things, are the one divine Word, and their multiplicity is nothing more than the multiple ways creatures participate in the divine essence.[66] God knows God and all things in relation to God. What is striking about this arrangement is the radical God-orientation of Thomas's doctrine of creation. Creation is known by God entirely as it participates in God's own being. And since God's knowledge of creation in accordance with his will is creation's existence, creation only is inasmuch as creation symbolizes the divine.

Doolan notes four features of a divine idea in Thomas. The first is that an idea is a form of a thing. It is the form according to which the thing is made. But this is not to imply that it is the thing's substantial form, which leads to the second feature of an idea. It is not the form intrinsic to a thing, but, so to speak, the form of the form: "A thing receives its determinate *form* from its exemplar."[67] The reason for this, as Nicholas of Cusa argues, is that if the divine idea were the substantial form

---

61. *ST* 1a.37.2.ad 3.
62. Emery, *Human Person*, 132, emphasis original.
63. *ST* 1a.89.1; Emery, *Human Person*, 134.
64. *ST* 1a.14.8.
65. The key work on this topic is Gregory Doolan, *Aquinas on the Divine Ideas as Exemplar Causes* (Washington, DC: The Catholic University of America Press, 2008). See also Gregory Doolan, "Aquinas on the Divine Ideas and the Really Real" in *Nova et Vetera* 13, no. 4 (2015), 1059–91; Norris Clark, "The Problem of Reality and Multiplicity of Divine Ideas in Christian Neoplatonism," in *Creative Retrieval of St. Thomas Aquinas* (New York: Fordham University Press, 2009), 66–88; John Wippel, *Thomas Aquinas on the Divine Ideas* (Toronto: Pontifical Institute of Medieval Studies, 1993).
66. *ST* 1a.15.2.
67. Doolan, *Exemplar*, 26. See also Mark D. Jordan, "The Intelligibility of the World and the Divine Ideas in Aquinas," *The Review of Metaphysics* 38, no. 1 (September 1984), 17–32.

of the thing, this would obliterate the integrity of the thing and reduce God to the order of nature.[68] Rather, God gives substantial form to everything as a gift from the Father of lights.[69] This gift arises from the divine ideas but only moves from the divine mind to created existence through the mediation of the divine will. This indicates the third feature of an idea: it "occurs because of an agent's *intention*."[70] A divine idea is an intentional idea, the nexus of intellect and will in the divine agent.

It might be asked at this point whether God knows the entire spectrum of possibilities God might create whether or not God in fact wills to? Yes.[71] God might know that God is capable of created spotted Zebras, but God has in fact willed to create striped ones. So the divine idea of a spotted Zebra is a possible way God's nature might be participated in. But this does not establish a Scotist realm of logically prior pure possibility (a possible world of spotted Zebras), since God always already knows spotted Zebras as that which God has not willed to create. The mutual internality of divine intellect and will, as will be made clear below, cannot be so simply sequentially parsed.

Finally, the fourth feature of an idea is that it is enacted according to an end chosen by the agent. A couple might have a child, and be the immediate givers of form to the child, but the *ends* of that form are outside the parents' control. For God, however, the form is given along with the end. The donation of form from the divine ideas is also the gift of an end, namely, the knowledge and love of the triune God. This end is wholly within the power of the giver to give, unlike the parent to the child. Thus, the divine ideas, inasmuch as they are exemplars of created things, are the intentional ideas of God, the forms of forms and the gift of an end.

Truthfulness, then, is conformity to these divine ideas. The divine ideas are the measure of all things, and anything's truthfulness is its adequation to this primordial foundation.[72] But while the divine mind is the measure of things, the human mind is, in a sense, measured by things. When the mind grasps the nature of a thing by the migration of form into the intellect, its truthfulness (i.e., the truthful perception of reality in the human mind) is measured by its adequation to the reality of the thing, which is in its turn measured by its adequation to the divine mind. Things are thus suspended between the mind of God and the human mind. Therefore, creation is known to us only inasmuch as it symbolizes God. When I recognize the form of a tree, I recognize it inasmuch as it participates in the divine idea of a tree. The tree's very intelligibility is derived from its participation

---

68. Nicholas of Cusa, *De Dato Patris Luminum*, 2.98 (Hopkins, *Complete Philosophical and Theological Treatises of Nicholas of Cusa: Volume One* [Minneapolis, MN: The Arthur J. Banning Press, 2001], 376).

69. The paradigmatic passage is James 1:17.

70. Doolan, *Exemplar*, 26.

71. See John Wippel, "The Reality of Non-Existing Possibles according to Thomas Aquinas, Henry of Ghent, and Godfrey Fontaines," *The Review of Metaphysics* 34, no. 4 (June 1981), 729–40.

72. Cf. Doolan, *Real*, 1080–1.

in the divine ideas, which are identical to God's essence.[73] All knowledge is a participation in divine knowledge, and since God knows creation as it symbolizes God, a symbolic creation, On Thomas's terms, is necessary to any knowledge whatsoever.[74]

While the divine intellect knows things according to their eternal form as various modes of participation in God, God's knowledge of creatures is not for all that merely formal. He also knows all creatures in their specificity. Thomas argues that God is not just the source of the form of things, but also of every accidental feature they might possess, every possible combination of the two, and their actual act of existence.[75] God, because he is the author and source of everything that is, at every level of existence and intelligibility, knows every minute particular of created existence. There is therefore no need for a Scotist "third-term," *haecceitas*, to account for individuation between matter and form. The noble aim of affirming the ontological uniqueness of each individual is satisfied by the universality of the divine intellect, and as we shall see, its mutual inclusion with the will. Every individual thing, inasmuch as it is, symbolizes the divine, for it is a living expression of the divine mind.

The shocking implication of all this is that "things as they are in God are the divine essence."[76] The Father knows creation in his knowledge of the Son, but his knowledge of the Son is self-knowledge, therefore creation is enfolded in God's own self-knowledge. God does not know creation as something other than himself. God knows creation in and (by participation) *as* godself.[77] In other words, God only knows creation inasmuch at it symbolizes God, for to be a symbol of God is what it means to be.

What saves Thomas from pantheism at this point is that God's knowledge of things in the divine ideas does not account for their actual existence, each thing's *esse*.[78] Creation is enacted by the intellect *according to the will*, that is, by the Son

---

73. Cf. Milbank and Pickstock, *Truth*, 12: "Since the tree only exhibits treeness—indeed, only exists at all—as imitating the divine, what we receive in truth is a participation in the divine. To put this another way, in knowing a tree, we are catching it on its way back to God." Bruce Marshall objects: "Created things exist only by their participation in their eternal exemplars, lodged in the divine Word, and we can know them only by the participation of our own intellect, through the creator Spirit's gift, in the uncreated light. But we don't have to know *about* the exemplars and the light, the Word and the Spirit, in order to have this knowledge": "Review of Truth in Aquinas," *The Thomist* 66, no. 4 (October 2002), 633. But Milbank and Pickstock are arguing for an "integral knowledge" of creation.

74. Cf. The illuminating discussion in Gilles Emery, "Trinity and Truth," in *Human Person*, ch. 3.

75. *ST* 1a.44.2.

76. *ST* 1a.18.4.ad 1.

77. Cf. *ST* 1a.105.3: "Since he is the First Being, and all other beings pre-exist in him as in their First Cause, it follows that they exist intelligibly in him after the mode of his own nature."

78. On this point, see Doolan, *Real*, 1086.

in the Spirit. So while creatures have a kind of "preexistence" in the Son, that existence is only actualized as other than God by the Spirit, the divine Will.[79] In Thomas's words: "[God's] inclination to put in act what his intellect has conceived appertains to the will."[80] Were we to stop at divine knowledge as the cause of things, God would indeed have a necessary relationship to the world. As it is, the supplement of intellect by will creates a complex concurrence of necessity and non-necessity. Creation is necessary in the divine intellect and unnecessary in the divine will. In a complex passage that deserves full quotation, the objection is raised that since God knows things necessarily, he also wills things necessarily, and since his knowledge and will are his essence, he has a necessary relation to creation. Thomas responds:

> As the divine essence is necessary of itself, so is the divine will and the divine knowledge; but the divine knowledge has a necessary relation to the thing known; not the divine will to the thing willed. The reason for this is that knowledge is of things as they exist in the knower; but the will is directed to things as they exist in themselves. Since then all other things have necessary existence inasmuch as they exist in God; but no absolute necessity so as to be necessary in themselves, in so far as they exist in themselves; it follows that God knows necessarily whatever He wills, but does not will necessarily whatever He wills.[81]

The basic distinction here is between internality and externality. The intellect knows things as they exist in the intellect (i.e., by the inner word). The mode of presence practiced by the intellect is an internal and necessary one. Thus, creation is present in the divine mind as the divine ideas. The will, by contrast is externally directed: desirous of the other *as the other*. Creation has no necessary existence in itself, being neither its own ground nor its own end. Therefore, Thomas reasons, when the divine will wills creation—being directed toward creation in itself—it wills it unnecessarily. The will wills unnecessary things unnecessarily. On this reading, the will wills God's own goodness necessarily, since God's goodness is necessary, but creation unnecessarily, because creation is contingent.

This structure has profound trinitarian resonances. We glimpse the importance of the divine *taxis* in the interplay of necessity and gratuity in creation. The necessity of creation as it is known in the Word is what secures the non-necessity of creation in the Will. Because creation is "the divine essence" as it is known in the Word, it is therefore *not its own*. If creation were a wholly separate entity to God, God would know it as something other than godself, something that has some ground

---

79. *ST* 1a.14.8: "The intelligible form does not denote a principle of action in so far as it resides in the one who understands unless there is added to it the inclination to an effect, which inclination is the through the will."
80. *ST* 1a.19.4.
81. *ST* 1a.19.3.ad 6.

outside of God. But because God knows creation necessarily as God's own essence, creation cannot be its own ground: creation is wholly and utterly dependent on God. Therefore, when God wills creation, God does so unnecessarily. Because the Son precedes the Spirit, as the intellect precedes the will, creation is first grounded in God—because necessarily known by the divine Word—and therefore willed gratuitously. In regard to creation, God necessarily knows what God freely wills, so that divine necessity is coeval with divine freedom. And this marks out the difference between creation as a symbol and the Son as a symbol. The latter is wholly necessary, the former unnecessary. But the non-necessity of creation does not posit an arbitrary relation between God and creation, rather, creation necessarily reflects the divine life (because spoken in the word), but because this life is God's life and not its own, creation is entirely contingent.

Moreover, creation is not only contingent because it has God's self-knowledge as its ground; it is also contingent because it has God's own goodness as its end. The will necessarily wills the good, and God wills the world in the willing of God's own goodness: "As he understands things apart from himself by understanding his own essence, so he wills things apart from himself by willing his own goodness."[82] Further, as Dionysius says, the good is diffusive of itself, which Thomas takes to mean that the divine will, in willing its own goodness, wills to share that goodness with others.[83] The difference is that while God's will is entirely oriented to its own goodness, creation is entirely oriented to God's goodness. Creation's end is beyond it, and so it lacks its own necessity. Creation lacks the self-sufficiency to "satiate" the divine will; creation itself therefore joins the divine will in desiring and loving God's goodness, and this telos beyond itself makes creation contingent, and therefore contingently willed. So the freedom of the divine will is guaranteed by the twin affirmations that creation is neither its own ground nor its own end.

This indicates, further, that creation is not the activation of potency in God. The divine ideas are not potencies lying latent in the mind of God until the will actualizes them. God's knowledge and love of the divine essence is fully actual, there is no potentiality in it. This is why God knows *all* the possible ways the divine nature is participable. The will, on the other hand, is fully fixed on the divine goodness and satisfied by it. Neither the intellect nor the will, neither the Son nor the Spirit, have any need for creation. Both are replete and satisfied in the divine life.[84] Creation is therefore an utterly gratuitous act. God has no need to desire and love another, for in the fullness of the Father's love for the Son, and the Son's

---

82. *ST* 1a.19.2.

83. *ST* 1a.19.2. See John Wippel, "Thomas Aquinas on the Ultimate Why Question: Why Is There Anything at All Rather than Nothing Whatsoever?," *The Review of Metaphysics* 60, no. 4 (June 2007), 731–53.

84. Cf. Simon Oliver, *Creation: A Guide for the Perplexed* (London: Bloomsbury T&T Clark, 2017), 50.

love for the Father, there is no lack. God does not create to meet some unfulfilled requirement of the divine nature. Creation in itself is entirely a gift, entirely a grace. Little wonder, then, that the Spirit is also called gift, for God's willing of creation is God's giving the gift of existence by participation in his own being.

Further, in receiving existence creation itself becomes a secondary object of divine desire. Because creation's "pre-existence" is the Logos, when creation is given gratuitous existence by the Spirit, the desire of the Father for the Son "pursues" the diffusion of the divine goodness through time, as it were. The Father loves creation in his love for the Son. This is why, Aquinas tells us, when Genesis says "and God saw that the light was good," it refers the origin of light to the Son and the light's goodness to the Spirit.[85] Creation is no sooner made (as the unfolding of the Logos) than it is pronounced upon (in the Spirit) as good, the object of divine desire. One way of stating this is to say that there is no fact/value divide in creation, for the *fact* of creation is its *value* as sharing in the divine goodness. Creation is an always-already valued fact; it *is* because it is *good* and is *good* because it *is*. God knows creation (intellect) as desirable (will), and desires creation as it is known.

But creation is not only constituted by its desirability; it is also constituted by its own desire for God. This is simply the temporal outworking of the Son's response of love to the Father. What makes creation desirable (again, paradoxically) is its original desire for God. Thomas explains this in terms of the non-necessity of the divine will. The divine will wills the divine goodness, and in creation wills others to will that same goodness. The divine will is directed toward creation *because* creation is directed toward God. Creation is the gift of desire for God. In this light, we can expand de Lubac's statement, in a letter to Maurice Blondel, to the entire created order: "How can a conscious spirit be anything other than an absolute desire for God?"[86] God desires creation as that which desires God. And as the Spirit is given to the Son in filiation and returned to the Father, so creation receives the gift of desirable existence as the gift of desirous existence. As the Spirit's *modus essendi* is the mutual play of love and desire between Father and Son, so the Spirit's modus operandi is the reciprocal acts of desire between creation and God.

The gift of existence that is God's will in creation is therefore threefold: the gift of existence, the gift of desirable existence, and the gift of desirous existence. This threefold act is a gift because it is gratuitous. But its gratuity is not funded by a separation from divine life. Rather, God's freedom in creation is secured by God's "constraint" to creation in godself. This is what it means for creation to be a symbol. It necessarily expresses the divine life as the unfolding of the Logos and is yet the

---

85. *ST* 1a.32.1.ad 3.

86. Henri de Lubac, *At the Service of the Church: Henri de Lubac Reflects on the Circumstances That Occasioned His Writings*, trans. Anne Elizabeth Englund (San Francisco, CA: Communio Books, 1993), 184.

unnecessary overflow of divine goodness. To refuse this mixture of necessity and non-necessity is to evacuate creation of symbolic value.

I have so far attempted to expound the statement that the Father creates by the Son in the Spirit. Doing so has led to a discussion of the divine intellect and will. The first correlation between them is of the divine *taxis* so that the will follows the intellect. But just as the Spirit is "retroactively causal" in the generation of the Son, so the will is "retroactively causal" in intellection: the intellect and will mutually include one another. Creation follows this dual pattern: the Spirit proceeds *ex Patre filioque*, and so creation is entirely contained in the divine intellect, and then breathed into motion by the divine will. And yet the Spirit sits on both sides of filiation, so that creation is known as it is willed, and willed as it is known. This processional paradox finally underwrites a complex coincidence of necessity and non-necessity. Creation is necessary as it is known in the divine ideas, and gratuitous as it is willed.

All of this means that creation is entirely and necessarily *theophanic* and yet gratuitously so. God is under no compulsion to create, and yet creation is truly expressive of the divine. Because God is triune simplicity, creation is a simple triune act. The Father creates by the Son in the Spirit. And this means that creation is a gift of God's own life, a gift of participation. To be a created symbol is to receive the gift of existence from the simple triune God. Throughout this section, I have not argued that the procession of an inner word in the intellect and love in the will are a literal account of generation and spiration. The language is analogical, and so is communicated with a significant amount of apophatic reserve. The Son is more truly a word, and the Spirit more truly love than anything we have access to as creatures. Meditation on these themes, then, is a way of working into the mystery of the simplicity and triunity of God. I have attempted to think with Thomas about the ways creation hums with the resonant tones of its creator.

Through the thirteenth and fourteenth centuries, a very different approach to the purpose and method of Trinitarian theology emerged, and with it material differences in Trinitarian content. Thomas's account of triune simplicity was sharply contested by the Franciscan tradition (though its proponents were not always Franciscans). It is not that the Franciscan alternative denied simplicity or triunity, but that it fundamentally rethought the links between them. Duns Scotus is the most influential of the school, and so I turn to his thought next. My argument is that to defend his Trinitarian theology, Scotus weakens the symbolic value of creation and its more meditative theological method.

Duns Scotus

A comparison like the one I am conducting between Aquinas and Scotus is common and controverted in contemporary theology. Daniel Horan pejoratively calls it "the Scotus story": "the establishment of an explicit genealogy that traces modernity, and, subsequently, the concept of nihilism as substantial *res*, back to

John Duns Scotus."[87] It is commonly associated with Radical Orthodoxy, though it neither originates with nor is limited to them.[88] Scotus, on this reading represents a definitive break in theological tradition, inaugurating a univocal ontology, and paving the way for nominalism, voluntarism, and eventually modernity and secularization. Alain de Libera summarizes the significance of Scotus: "*en quarante-trois ans de vie, Scot a inventé tout ce qui sépare conceptuellement son époque des époques antérieures.*"[89] Scotus inaugurates a univocal ontology, the story goes, where both God and the world exist under the same quasi-genus of being, flattening ontology[90]; Scotus's "formal distinction" imperils divine simplicity; a new centrality of the distinction between God's ordained and absolute power "prioritizes the possible" over the real; the individuating principle disconnects individual things from their networks of relations. All of this ultimately makes God irrelevant, since God is seen as a very big being whose work in the world becomes less obvious, and therefore of less explanatory necessity with the rise of modern science.[91] It also leads to nihilism: since the possible is given priority over actual being, nothingness is reified as a kind of thing, and a more fundamental one.[92] It

---

87. Horan, *Postmodernity*, 15. Horan's footnotes offer a significant resource to the Radical Orthodoxy literature on the subject. Unfortunately, his focus on Radical Orthodoxy obscures the far wider literature that agrees—at least in outline—with their perspective. See below for some examples.

88. Notably proponents of the genealogy include Milbank, *Theology and Social Theory*, xxv n. 41; Conor Cunningham, *Genealogy of Nihilism: Philosophies of Nothing and the Difference of Theology* (London: Routledge, 2002); Catherine Pickstock, "Duns Scotus: His Historical and Contemporary Significance," *Modern Theology* 21 (October 2005), 543–74, especially footnote 2 for a bibliography of historians of ideas that concur with the genealogy; also Brad Gregory, *The Unintended Reformation: How a Religious Revolution Secularized Society* (Cambridge, MA: Harvard University Press, 2012). This interpretation arises especially from Etienne Gilson, *Jean Duns Scot* (Paris: Vrin, 1952), but includes numerous other historians of ideas of diverse sensibility, notably Amos Funkenstein, *Theology and the Scientific Imagination*, 2nd ed. (Princeton: Princeton University Press, 1986); Alain de Libera, *La philosophie médiévale*, 3rd ed. (Paris: Presses Universitaires de France, 1998), 421–5; Olivier Boulnois, "Quand Commence L'Ontothéologie? Aristote, Thomas D'Aquin et Duns Scot," *Revue Thomiste* XCV, no. 1 (January–March 1995), 84–108; J-F Courtine, *Suarez et le Système de la Métaphysique* (Paris: PUF, 1990), and many more.

89. De Libera, *Philosophie*, 421. De Libera's list of inventions is 1) the univocal concept of being, 2) the formal distinction, 3) the intuitive knowledge of singulars, and 4) the non-static treatment of modalities. He calls Scotus the apogee of "formalist theology."

90. Cf. John Milbank, *The Suspended Middle: Henri de Lubac and the Renewed Split in Modern Catholic Theology*, 2nd edn. (Grand Rapids, MI: Eerdmans, 2005), 86.

91. Cf. Jacob Schmutz, "The Medieval Doctrine of Causality and the Theology of Pure Nature," in *Surnaturel: A Controversy at the Heart of Twentieth-Century Thomistic Thought* (Ave Maria, FL: Sapientia Press, 2009), 203–50.

92. Cf. Cunningham, *Nihilism*, chs. 1–2.

leads to nominalism, since each thing is just an individual thing, disconnected in principle from everything else: Scotus is "the unraveller."[93] According to this genealogy the specter of an atheistic, nihilistic nominalism is thus glimpsed in Scotus's work.

This has proved controversial, notably among Scotus specialists.[94] They argue that Scotus explicitly denies that God and creatures share being, and therefore the charge of a univocal ontology is fallacious.[95] Univocity is a purely semantic term for Scotus, not an ontological one.[96] The univocal *concept* of being, on this reading, entails nothing other than that "there are concepts under whose extension God and creatures fall."[97] This is not an ontological claim because Scotus is a nominalist about the transcendentals: being "is not a real feature of a thing at all, but merely a vicious abstraction, proper to nothing."[98] By definition, there can be no univocal *being* between God and creatures because there is no-thing called "being." This position is simply the logical outworking of a commitment to univocal predication combined with the classic Christian commitment to God's supremacy in all things. If the concept of being must extend equally to creatures and God, but God is not subordinated to any greater reality, then being must be *merely* conceptual, a name we use to speak our commonsense intuition that God exists.

As to Scotus's role in the development of modernity (nominalism, nihilism, atheism, etc), his defenders are simply uninterested in history.[99] If Scotus is not a nominalistic, nihilistic atheist, he cannot be blamed for their later development. I am not, however, convinced that history can be so summarily dismissed. But while I am convinced the rise of modernity is causally linked to the demise of symbolism, I do not intend to rigorously demonstrate that here. My immediate concern is the systematic theology of the symbol, so I will approach Scotus as a

---

93. Cunningham, *Nihilism*, 22; quoting Gerard Manley Hopkins, "Duns Scotus's Oxford," in Catherine Phillips (ed.), *Gerard Manley Hopkins: The Major Works* (Oxford: Oxford University Press, 2002), 142.

94. Most notably, Thomas Williams, "The Doctrine of Univocity Is True and Salutary," *Modern Theology* 21, no. 4 (October 2005), 575–85; Cross, *Duns Scotus*, 33–8; Richard Cross, "Where Angels Fear to Tread: Duns Scotus and Radical Orthodoxy," *Antonianum* Annus LXXVI Fasc. I (January–March 2001); Peter King, "Scotus on Metaphysics," in Thomas Williams (ed.), *The Cambridge Companion to Duns Scotus* (Cambridge: Cambridge University Press, 2003), 15–68.

95. For instance, I *Ordinatio* 8.1.3, no. 82: God and creatures "are, however, diverse first in reality, because they agree in no reality." All translations of *Ordinatio*, Peter L. P. Simpson, trans., https://www.aristotelophile.com/current.htm, accessed July 19, 2019. See also Joshua Benson, "Review of *The Unintended Reformation: How a Religious Revolution Secularized Society* by Brad S. Gregory," *The Catholic Historical Review* 98, no. 3 (July 2012), 508.

96. Cf. Williams, "Salutary," *passim*.

97. Richard Cross, *Duns Scotus on God* (Aldershot: Ashgate, 2005), 253.

98. Cross, *God*, 256.

99. Williams, "Salutary," 575. Indeed, few defenders of Scotus ever bother to address historical claims.

systematic theologian. Indeed, I will hew quite closely to his own texts and the interpretations of his defenders. Toward the end of my analysis I will offer a few brief thoughts on how Scotus's systematic theology contributes to the historical erosion of symbolism, as well as some of the more controverted questions of ontology. But the bulk of my argument is that Scotus's systematic theology on its own terms has no place for the symbolic, with significant consequences for theological content and method.

Powers and Persons

Compared with Aquinas, Scotus's God is "far less simple."[100] Scotus's doctrine of univocity requires the actual existence of formal distinctions in both creation and God, leading him to argue that God's one essence, God's powers and perfections, and the three persons are all formally distinct from one another. The logic is that when I say "John is a good person," I mean something distinct from "John is a wise person." These perfections may ultimately coincide in John, but they are not identical. If they were identical, we would not need two words for them. Because, then, these words are univocally ascribed to God, they must also exist in God as formally distinct, albeit without fragmentation.[101] Whereas Aquinas is happy to say that God's goodness *is* God's wisdom on the basis of divine simplicity, and are only therefore distinct for us in our temporal perspective, Scotus thinks this vitiates language too much to be intelligible. God must, therefore, have truly distinct formal properties. God's goodness is not God's wisdom. The same then holds for the divine essence and each divine person. The essence is formally distinct from each person, as well as from the divine perfections. Formal distinctions are not "real distinctions," as the distinction between John and Thomas as individuals. But neither are they purely conceptual; a formal distinction signifies a real non-identity between two terms, but not in a way, Scotus argues, that endangers divine simplicity.[102]

These formal distinctions then acquire an entirely novel, supra-trinitarian *taxis*. The divine essence alone is formally infinite, and so from the one essence "emanate all other features in an orderly fashion."[103] Emanating first from the essence "are the intrinsic essential features."[104] These are the divine intellect, will, and perfections. "Second, come the notional," that is, the three persons. Finally come "created or extrinsic things." At each stage, what is emanated receives the measure of infinity appropriate to it, in descending order. The essence is formally infinite,

---

100. Cross, "Scotus," 45.
101. Cf. John Duns Scotus, I *Ord.* 8.1.4, n. 192.
102. Cf. Scotus, I *Ord.* 8.1.4, nn. 191–2. See also, Friedman, *Trinitarian*, 109.
103. John Duns Scotus, *Quodlibetal Questions*, 5.55 in Felix Alluntis and Allan Wolter, trans., *God and Creatures: The Quodlibetal Questions* (Princeton, NJ: Princeton University Press, 1975), 127.
104. Scotus, *Quod. lib.*, 5.55.

as are the powers and perfections. The persons are not formally infinite, since the Father is not the Son.¹⁰⁵ This does not mean the persons are finite; they occupy an obscure middle ground between infinite and finite. Finally, creatures are finite because finitude "pertains to them."¹⁰⁶ That Scotus is able to narrate this scheme in a straight line, as it were, of descending levels of infinity underscores the extent of his doctrine of univocity. All things emanate from the divine essence, and the "mechanisms" of these emanations are essentially the same, as will be shown. This sequence is not merely conceptual. Each level is "produced" by the previous one. The essence produces divine intellect and will, which are then wholly possessed by the Father. The Son is then "produced [automatically] by the fecundity of the intellect."¹⁰⁷ In filiation the Son receives both the divine intellect and will. The Spirit is then produced by the divine will now shared by the Father and Son. The Son is therefore the *product* of the logically prior divine intellect in the Father, and the Spirit the *product* of the logically prior divine will in the Father and Son.¹⁰⁸

This supra-trinitarian *taxis* neutralizes any threat of mutual inclusion or paradoxical "retroactive causality." Formal distinctions police the borders of Father, Son, Spirit, perfections, powers, and essence.¹⁰⁹ The Father must be conceived as Father without the Son and Spirit, otherwise the Father's identity would not be formally prior to generation and spiration.¹¹⁰ Paternity therefore does not presuppose filiation, as this would make the Son necessary for the Father. Rather, paternity only presupposes the divine essence as a "formal reason for" generating the Son.¹¹¹ The Father is therefore constituted as such by his possession of the logically prior productive principles of intellect and will in the divine essence. The

---

105. Scotus, *Quod. lib.*, 5.57.
106. Scotus, *Quod. lib.*, 5.57.
107. Scotus, I *Ord.* 12.7.
108. Scotus, I *Ord.* 12.7: "The Father has first in origin the act of fecundity of the intellect before that of the will; in that prior stage there is communicated to the Son the same fecundity as is in the Father, because in the moment of origin—in which the Son is produced by the fecundity of the Intellect—there is communicated to him by the Father whatever is not repugnant to him, and so the fecundity of the will is communicated; therefore, in the other moment of origin, when a person is produced by the act of the second fecundity (namely of the will), that person is produced by the Father and the Son as altogether by one principle, because of the fecundity of the productive principle in them."
109. For Russell Friedman, the central aim of the Franciscan tradition was to introduce *order* into the Trinity, and so this hardened *taxis* is clearly within the scope of Franciscan theology. Friedman, *Medieval*, 39.
110. Cf. Scotus, *Quod. lib.* 4.67.
111. Scotus, *Quod. lib.* 4.67. This concept derives from Bonaventure who posited something like a "proto-Father" before generation. Freidman, *Medieval*, 27; "proto-Father" is Friedman's term for the way Bonaventure describes the readiness of the Father to produce, citing Bonaventure, I *Sent.*, d. 2, a. 1, q. 2, *solutio*. While this might seem to press Scotus toward a kind of tri-theism, it is perhaps more appropriate to call it a "logico-gnostic" myth of divine origins.

Son is then constituted by the operation of divine intellect in the Father, and since the intellect precedes the will, the Son receives both divine intellect and will in filiation. The object of the divine intellect possessed by the Father is the divine essence, so that the intellect and the essence are each a "*quasi partiale principium*" for the production of the Son.[112] What makes the Son the Son is not his relation to the Father as Father, but his production by and sharing in the divine intellect and essence. This is because, again, Paternity is in the first instance the possession of the productive principles of divine intellect and will, not the relation to the Son.

The Spirit then proceeds from the common principle of Father and Son, entirely distinct from that principle. The Spirit is *not* the love of the Father for Son and Son for Father. If Father and Son produce the Spirit as their love for one another, then the Spirit is paradoxically necessary to the Father–Son relation. This would violate the *taxis*, imperiling the logical priority of the common principle of Father and Son before spiration.[113] The Spirit is therefore the love of Father and Son for the one divine essence.[114] The precision of Scotus's formal distinctions requires developing a new *taxis* that both conditions and hardens the trinitarian *taxis* and forestalls any paradoxical mutual inclusion. Scotus has no time for "retroactive causality." Scotus does not ignore the doctrine of perichoresis, but it plays no role in his logic. For Scotus, the coinherence of Father, Son, and Spirit is only "over and above the unity they exhibit in virtue of the divine essence," so that *perichoresis* is "superfluous to the requirements" of Scotus's theology.[115] The result is that the divine relations are an afterthought—literally, thought after the divine essence.[116]

Scotus is merely reading the logic of univocity into the godhead. Because we make distinctions in temporal matters and we speak of God univocally, then the trinitarian persons must also be formally distinct. He distinguishes them by abstracting their commonality before any notion of coinherence. The result is that persons only find their divinity in a shared essence, but that essence is not defined in terms of any of the persons.[117] Persons are a postscript to essence.[118]

More precisely, persons are a postscript to divine intellect and will. As essential attributes, intellect and will are prior to the persons, and in fact are the productive

---

112. Scotus, I *Ord.* 2.2.3, n. 310.

113. Scotus, I *Ord.* 12.14; I *Ord.* 12.20.

114. Cf. Scotus, I *Ord.*12.23: "The Father does not inspirate the Holy Spirit insofar as he loves the Son first, nor the Son insofar as he loves the Father, but the Father and Son insofar as they have the divine essence present to them as the first object of their will."

115. Cross, *Scotus*, 183, n. 71. Citing Scotus, I *Ord.* 19.2, nn. 42, 54, 67.

116. In Catherine Pickstock's words, "Without recourse to substantive relation ... the attribution of intellect to the Son, and Will to the Spirit, ceases to be remote analogical naming ... and becomes the means of literal distinction." Pickstock, "Significance," 565.

117. Compare Aquinas who, as Emery argues, subsumes the one divine essence *into* the discourse on persons: Emery, *Trinity in Aquinas*, ch. 5.

118. Cross, *God*, 181: "The divine essence, as the causal power in virtue of which Son and Spirit are produced, is prior to the persons ... this essence, although not a person or suppositum, is a subsistent in itself." Citing III *Ord.* 1.2, n. 6 and I *Ord.* 28.3, n. 81.

principles of the Son and Spirit. Whereas the word from the intellect and love from the will for Aquinas and Augustine are fruitful analogies, Scotus sees them as literally the mechanisms of the processions: the production of persons "proceeds from a potency that is essential, for it is an action either of the intellect or of the will."[119] And here again formal distinctions police the boundaries of both. The divine intellect and will no longer "mutually include" one another, as for Aquinas, but are hardened into two entirely distinct operations in a series.[120]

In commenting on Aristotle's distinction between rational and non-rational potencies, Scotus argues that the intellect is "natural" in the sense that it's operations are involuntary: the intellect is "of itself determined to understand."[121] The will, by contrast, does not operate "naturally," for it is not determined to anything. The will stands equally before all logically possible alternatives and is defined—to the extent that it is free—by its equal potentiality toward its options. The intellect, then, is "not rational" because it is blindly determined by the reality it understands. Indeed, "it is rational only in the qualified sense that it is a precondition for the act of a rational potency."[122] The intellect precedes rationality as its necessary precondition, but is not itself rational. The will then "follows the intellect," but unlike the intellect "acts freely, for it has the power of self-determination."[123] The intellect recognizes and presents options to the will, which is equally disposed between them. The will then, being self-determining, chooses one. Such self-determination is possible because the will is formally distinct from the intellect. The choice of the will in turn determines the intellect to organize its powers toward the attainment of the chosen goal. The intellect then is doubly determined. In the first instance it is blindly bound to the reality it perceives, and in the second it is determined by the choice of the will. The result is that any one effect is not a product of the combination of will and intellect together, as for Aquinas, but is the direct result of the will, the only rational faculty per se.[124]

Scotists are eager to point out that this does not make Scotus a voluntarist, strictly speaking.[125] Rather, the will is a higher function for which the intellect provides

---

119. Scotus, *Quod. lib.* 1.55. Cf. Pickstock, *Scotus*, 565.

120. John Duns Scotus, *Questions on the Metaphysics* IX, q. 15, in Allan B. Wolter, trans., *Duns Scotus on the Will and Morality* (Washington, DC: The Catholic University of America Press, 1986), 141. Cf. King, "Scotus on Metaphysics," 23: "The psychological faculties of intellect and will are really identical with the soul, but formally distinct from one another since what it is to be an intellect does not include the will, and what it is to be a will does not include the intellect."

121. Scotus, *Questions* 9.15 (Wolter: 141).

122. Scotus, *Questions* 9.15 (Wolter: 142).

123. Scotus, *Questions* 9.15 (Wolter: 142).

124. Scotus, *Questions* 9.15 (Wolter: 142).

125. Cf. Hannes Möhle, "Scotus's Theory of Natural Law," in Thomas Williams (ed.), *The Cambridge Companion to Duns Scotus* (Cambridge: Cambridge University Press, 2003), 324.

a foundation. Scotus does not call into question a Scholastic intellectualism in which the will follows the intellect. Rather, he hardens the *taxis* of intellect and will by subordinating the former to the latter as a lower to a higher function. The hardening of this *taxis* guarantees the will's freedom. The will is free insofar as it is not determined to any particular possibility. It stands before the field of compossibles identified by the intellect, unconstrained by any innate directional impulse, for that would be a kind of constraint on the will. Within the realm of possibilities perceived by the intellect, the will is free insofar as it is free from reason: to put it bluntly, the will is free precisely in its ability to be unreasonable.[126] This is not to say that the will cannot be influenced by the intellect—the intellect can propose certain options as better than others on the basis of what it naturally perceives, but the *freedom* of the will is defined by its ability to ignore or embrace such recommendations. The result is both greater autonomy for the will (within the range of what the intellect acknowledges as compossible) and a greater deference to the range of givens grasped by the intellect.[127] The intellect (and nature) is more determined, the will more "free," but only because their functions have been so firmly separated. This is a long way from both Augustine and Aquinas for whom intellect operates only by right desiring, and desire only after the operations of intellect. There is no paradoxical core in Scotus's psychology—only a logically necessary and inviolable *taxis*. Moreover, because the intellect and will are the productive principles of the processions, Scotus subordinates his trinitarian theology to this psychology. Inasmuch as his psychology precludes paradox, so does his Trinity.[128] Augustine and Aquinas reconfigure intellect and will along trinitarian lines, "building in" mutual inclusion and paradoxical pre-presence[129];

---

126. Cf. Scotus, II *Ord.* I.91-92; Scotus, *Questions* 9.15 (Wolter: 142); Möhle, "Law," 324–5.

127. Because only the immanently graspable can be the object of the will, Scotus's metaphysics requires univocity to account for our desire for God.

128. It might be argued that Scotus merely shifts the location of the paradox. The "non-infinity" of the persons, the indivisibility and yet repeatability of the divine essence, or the existence of formal distinctions at all might be instances of paradox in Scotus's trinity. And yet the driving impulse of Scotus's theology *is* the resolution of any outstanding philosophical aporia, leaving the reader with the impression that if Scotus could absolve his theology of paradox, he would. See Friedman, *Medieval*, 112: "Scotus' theory ... is an attempt to explain just about *everything*." Richard Cross prefers Scotus's trinitarian theology precisely because it represents a "marked improvement over the very agnostic accounts of his predecessors"; Cross, *Scotus*, 70. For an account of why Cross cannot understand the "agnosticism" of pre-Scotist theologians, see Lewis Ayres, *Nicea and Its Legacy* (Oxford: Oxford University Press, 2004), ch. 16. Unsurprisingly, this is the one chapter that Cross takes issue with: Richard Cross, "Nicaea and Its Legacy," *Reviews in Religion and Theology* 13, no. 1 (January 2006), 16–18.

129. On Augustine, see John Milbank, "Sacred Triads: Augustine and the Indo-European Soul," *Modern Theology* 13, no. 4 (October 1997).

Scotus reconfigures trinitarian theology in terms of intellect and will, now imagined as the rigid order of operations of productive principles.

Powers and Creation

Scotus reads his psychology univocally into the divine act of creation. The divine intellect first "creates" all possible worlds.[130] These possible worlds all have a real and necessary existence in the divine intellect. These possibilities are then presented to the divine will.[131] The divine will then stands unconditioned before a vast field of options. The will then selects one. There can be no reason for this selection, not even one arising from the divine intellect, for the will is its own reason. The result is a creation inscrutably chosen by God, created by the two separate productive principles of intellect and will.

This structure makes the processions and creation two stages in a productive process, the former necessary and the latter contingent.[132] For Scotus, intellect and will are the causal principles of the processions, necessarily producing the Son and Spirit. Creation is also a production of the divine intellect and will, but a contingent one, a contingency grounded in the divine will's ability to have chosen some other creation or no creation. Because the persons are necessary, they are logically prior to the contingent production of creation.[133] Thus, the causal principles of intellect and will "pass through" the persons and are shared equally by the persons. Yet this order tends to prioritize the same productive principles of intellect and will over the persons. While the Persons thereby enact creation, they do so only by virtue of their sharing in the causal powers of intellect and will. Indeed, for Scotus, if *per impossible* there were no Trinity, "Whatever is necessary in God for causing a creature would still be possessed, for [there would be] both a perfect and complete formal principle of causing, and a *suppositum* having that formal perfect principle."[134] Because intellect and will are prior to the persons, creation is principally *of the essence*. The processions are logically prior to creation, but ultimately incidental to it. This is a perversion of the Augustinian principle that the persons act as one *ad extra*. Because Augustine and Aquinas see divine unity as the perichoresis of the persons, divine acts *ad extra* are fully trinitarian: by the Son, in the Spirit.[135] The roles of divine intellect and will are then conformed to this triune shape. Scotus, by contrast, secures divine unity by centralizing the one divine essence, rendering perichoresis superfluous. Creation is then an act

---

130. Scotus, I *Ord.* 43.16-17. Cf. analysis in Cal Ledsham, "Love, Power and Consistency: Scotus' Doctrines of God's Power, Contingent Creation, Induction and Natural Law," *Sophia* 49 (2010), 557-75.
131. Scotus, *Lect.* I.39.1-5, n. 62 (Vatican, 17:500). Cf. Cross, *Scotus*, 58.
132. See discussion in Antonie Vos, *The Theology of John Duns Scotus* (Boston, MA: Brill, 2018), 149-62.
133. Scotus, *Lect.* II 1.24.
134. Scotus, *Quod.* 14, n. 9 (Alluntis and Wolter, 323).
135. Emery, *Human Person*, 143-8.

of God's one essence, conceived as the productive principles of intellect and will. Because the intellect and will are "pre-trinitarian," creation is only symbolic of essential productive power, *not of the processional life of God*. In the first instance, it is symbolic of God's absolute power grounded in the divine intellect's knowledge of all possible worlds. Secondly, it is symbolic of God's ordained power grounded in the free choice of the divine will for *this* world. In neither instance does it refer in its deepest reality to Father, Son, and Spirit.[136]

Univocity and Symbolism

All of this is in keeping with univocity and its attendant nominalism.[137] Scotus's commitment to render theological language as intelligible as possible commits him to univocity, which requires the transcendentals be merely conceptual to avoid conflating divine and creaturely being. Once being is merely a vicious abstraction, there is nothing left to emanation other than power: creation is not the gift of a *share* in divine being, but an assertion of divine will.[138] As I will now argue, the demise of any sense of "sharing in" means that creation cannot be symbolic of God's own trinitarian reality, since symbolism requires analogy.

Funkenstein summarizes the symbolist position:

> The most natural way [for Patristic and medieval theology] to perceive God's presence in the world was symbolical. Patristic and medieval theology were inevitably led toward an interpretation of the universe as a sign, symbol, picture of God. A true symbol, to use a phrase of Durkheim, manifests a *participation mystique* with that of which it is a symbol. It is both one with, and different from, its symbol; it is much more than a linguistic metaphor. Nature reveals God's symbolic presence, and was seen as a system of symbols, of signatures of God; so also was man's soul; and so was history.[139]

It is as a late flowering of this context that Aquinas formulates his doctrine of analogy. The ontological aspects of that doctrine stipulate a hierarchy of likenesses to the divine. Because things only *are* by participation in God, then anything that *is* is an image of God, with gradations of intensity from the inert object to the fully actualized intellect.[140] To the extent that something participates in God, God is

---

136. On the influence of ordained and absolute power, see Funkenstein, *Imagination*, 124–51. Funkenstein notes, rightly, that this position at least latent in most Christian theology, the difference is that Scotus centralizes its importance.
137. I mean by this Scotus's denial of the reality of the transcendentals, not to conflate him with later nominalists.
138. While he is not a strict voluntarist, there is certainly a kind of voluntarism at work in Scotus's psychology and theology.
139. Funkenstein, *Imagination*, 49.
140. *ST* 1a.13.2; *ST* 1a.8.1.

present "in" that thing: recall, a symbol is a sign that mediates presence.[141] Thus for Thomas, God never acts at a distance from creation, for his action is always coextensive with his presence.[142] This ontological analogy requires analogical semantics since God's presence cannot mean the same thing in creatures and in God. God is "in" a creature in a very different way from the way that, for example, the Father is in the Son. But nonetheless, the difference and identity between the persons is the ground of the difference and presence of God in creation, as the analysis above showed. Indeed, unity in difference is *more* true of God than creation, but creation participates in this primordial truth.

In this context of semantic and ontological analogy Thomas deploys the psychological analogy for the Trinity. The analogy is not a "model" of the Trinity, as much as a site of analogical participation. Reflection on the human mind—the highest internal image of the Trinity—is more a meditation than a discursive argument, though it contains much discursus. It is ontologically analogical since it is the highest sharing in the *imago dei* discoverable within the human; it is semantically analogical since "word" and "love" are more true of God than of us. This enforces a significant apophatic reserve about the inner divine life. The Son is the Word, which Thomas identifies simply as something that proceeds, but we lack the intellectual, and therefore ontological, capacity to know what this means. It would be wholly inappropriate, on Thomas's terms, to suggest that the Son is literally an inner word. Human inner words, rather, are symbols of this eternal Word: they bear the ontological trace of the eternal Word, and so reflection upon them can be an encounter with the presence of the Logos. For both Thomas and Augustine, inner words and love are a symbol, reflection upon which enables the theologian to grow in the image of God.

This is not to suggest that Aquinas and Augustine treat the analogy in the same way. Thomas famously shifts from questions of the working of the mind to the ontology of the soul. But more importantly for our present purposes, Aquinas "shows less of his work" and focuses more on presenting the results of his reflection.[143] This has led to the accusation that while Augustine's analogy was a spiritual exercise, Aquinas's was a detached academic inspection.[144] But when considered within the scope of the *Summa* (a breadth far exceeding what Augustine attempts in *De trinitate*), it lacks none of the pedagogical value. The *Summa* itself is an exercise in *manuduction*, being led by the hand into a greater vision of God.[145]

If the human soul (or the working of the human mind) is a symbol, then meeting God in contemplating the symbol is symbolism, joining the symbol to

---

141. Funkenstein, *Imagination*, 54.
142. *ST* 1a.8.1.
143. Emery, *Thomistic*, 71.
144. See Emery, *Thomistic*, ch. 2.
145. Cf. Peter Candler, *Theology, Rhetoric and Manuduction* (Grand Rapids, MI: Eerdmans, 2006).

the symbolized in an act of desire and love. Thus, "symbolism" is intimately tied to Thomas's doctrine of analogy, both in its semantic and ontological aspects. What distinguishes my term "symbolism" from Thomas's *analogia* is that what I term "symbolism" attempts to articulate the Trinitarian core of the doctrine of analogy. Symbolism names the interface of the doctrine of analogy with a doctrine of the Trinity. It indicates how created symbols are themselves participants in eternal triune symbolism.[146] Their active participation in the eternal symbol by their reading of the divine signs is symbolism, a participation in the Spirit, interpreting the symbol and returning the symbol to God in praise. Symbolism thus only works with a doctrine of creation that integrates creation into the trinitarian processions. The doctrine of analogy, as a constituent part of the doctrine of creation, also has a trinitarian logic.

If analogy requires a particular trinitarian theology, the rejection of analogy requires one as well. The Franciscans did not deny the spiritual value of Trinitarian theology, nor the mystical possibilities of theological reflection. But their concerns were more firmly fixed on bringing "order" to the doctrine of the Trinity.[147] Scotus reacted, and not without reason, against late Dominican tendencies to minimize the real concourse between God and creaturely analogies. Durand of St. Pourçain went so far as to deny that the name "Word" is properly predicated of the Son, calling it a mere "metaphor."[148] This confirmed Scotus's concern: at its worst analogy is just systematic equivocation, at its best, unacknowledged univocity.[149]

For Scotus, the very discipline of theology, in both its ecclesial and evangelical aims, requires univocal semantics. There must be some concept that univocally extends to cover "John is" and "God is," otherwise we have failed to say anything meaningful at all; neither comforting for the faithful, nor compelling for the unbeliever. Scotus sees the real payout of univocity in the doctrine of the Trinity:

> Unless "being" implies one univocal intention, theology would simply perish. For theologians prove that the divine Word proceeds and is generated by way of intellect, and the Holy Spirit proceeds by way of will. But if intellect and will were found in us and in God equivocally, there would be no evidence at all that, since a word is generated in us in such and such a fashion, it is so in God—and likewise with regard to love in us—because then intellect and will in these two cases would be of a wholly different kind (ratio).[150]

Without univocity, for Scotus, Trinitarian theology suffers death by equivocation. The very proofs of God's two emanations, and thereby of the Son and Spirit, would

---

146. This is, as chapter one argued, an extension of Karl Rahner's "Theology of the Symbol" in a more complete Trinitarian direction.
147. Freidman, *Medieval*, 39.
148. Durand of Pourçain, I *Sent.* (C), d. 27, q. 3; Freidman, *Medieval*, 72.
149. Scotus, *Rep.* 1.3.1, n. 7. See Cross, *God*, 256.
150. Scotus, *Lect.* 1.3.1.1-2, n. 113, translation Richard Cross in Cross, *God*, 253.

fail to prove anything if intellect and will did not mean substantially the same thing in divinity and humanity.[151] Thus, Cross: "The very divine and human features of which the same concepts are applicable must be, at root, the same."[152] This proof, which entails the inviolable logical *taxis* examined above (from essence, through attributes, Persons and finally creation) requires univocity.[153]

And univocity requires selective nominalism. Scotus recognizes that claiming that God and creatures can be conceived as falling under a common "genus" of being is indeed idolatrous. So Scotus denies that *being* is anything other than a mental abstraction: being, and the other transcendentals simply do not exist.[154] That God falls under the same concept of being as creatures does not entail that God falls under something called being, since there is no such thing as *being*. But this is not a thoroughgoing nominalism, since Scotus wants to maintain real ascription of creaturely distinctions to God. Scotus is not a nominalist about properties, for instance. When we ascribe wisdom to God, this wisdom is real, and really convertible with the wisdom we ascribe to Socrates. In the quote above, moreover, it is clear that faculties like intellect and will are also essentially the same in divinity and humanity. When we say the divine Word emanates from the divine intellect, the emanation is real and really convertible with the emanation of our own inner words. In order to secure the stability of arguments about God (his properties and faculties), Scotus rejects "global nominalism," but so as not to subordinate God to being, Scotus adopts a nominalist view of the transcendentals.[155] Scotus has bartered real properties and faculties (for the sake of argumentative validity) for nominalist transcendentals (for the sake of orthodoxy). Wisdom is real; intellect is real; being is not.

From a Thomist perspective, this leads to an emaciated account of participation. Once being can no longer be shared, existence is still a gift from God, but only by imitation at a distance of an exemplar and efficient cause, not by an abiding inner presence. To be sure, Scotus assents to a thin account of participation, but it is accounted for solely in terms of a distant exemplar and mechanical efficient causality.[156] For since Scotus is a nominalist about the transcendentals, the goodness of any given thing is only the product of its being caused by an original good thing. It is not the ongoing presence of an original goodness in the created thing; how could it be, since goodness is merely conceptual? No instance of being, goodness, truth, or beauty indicates the presence of being, goodness, truth, or

---

151. Cf. Scotus, *Resp.* 1.3.1, n. 7 (Waddington, XI, 43^b).

152. Cross, *God*, 110.

153. Specifically, it requires semantic univocity in the case of *being*, and real univocity in the case of attributes and faculties.

154. Scotus, I *Ord.* 8.1.3, nn. 137–50. Richard Cross's most helpful treatment of this topic is "Appendix: Religious Language and Divine Ineffability," in Cross, *God*, 249–60.

155. Cross, *God*, 110.

156. Scotus, I *Ord.* 8.1.3, n. 86. Cross tends to equivocate on the extent to which this is a very different kind of participation from the previous tradition. Cross, *God*, 111.

beauty, only a mechanical dependence on a good, true, and beautiful Agent who just *is*. So what, then links this original agent with its effects? It is God's power that provides the all-important connections, but power now conceptually independent of presence. Indeed, for Scotus, God's omnipotence does not necessarily entail his omnipresence: God could exercise causal power from a distance, if, *per impossibile,* God were not essentially omnipresent.[157] Participation is then tilted toward such causality and away from presence. The reason for this is obvious: God's presence "in" something is only possible analogically and is far more difficult to isolate and secure logically. Efficient and exemplar causality (understood in terms of imitation as effect to cause, not an ontological sharing in) offers a far more robust, "scientific" basis for construing the relationship between God and creatures.[158] Participation is then not a matter of the mysterious presence of the symbolized in the symbol, but of a discursively provable correspondence between cause and effect.

To be sure, Aquinas reasons from causality, but the doctrine of analogy allows him to see divine causality as that which is most internal to a creature. While Aquinas argues for analogy on the basis of divine causality, even this term "causality" must be understood analogically, so that divine causality is not "at root the same" as creaturely causality.[159] As Jacob Schmutz notes, for Aquinas divine causality functions by *influxus* or *influentia,* so that the first cause acts "in" second causes.[160] This is an ontological affirmation: "*being* communicates itself *per influentiam* beginning with the first cause, who gives form and being."[161] God, Thomas argues, is the giver of being, that which is most intimate to everything that exists, and so God's causality acts most intimately, that is, as ontological first principle *within* the second cause.[162] God "gives being, the secondary causes only determine it."[163] By contrast, univocity forces Scotus to see divine and creaturely causation as two instances of essentially the same thing. For Scotus, divine causality thereby functions not *in,* but *with* second causes. The first cause only "concurs" with the second, making both but partial causes of one effect. Second causes, for Scotus, *add* something to the first.[164] Scotus did not initiate this evolution in the understanding of causality, but his doctrine of univocity gave it forceful expression.[165]

Thus, when *being* is nominalized, causation is homogenized. Scotus rejects Thomas's position that "*esse* is directly an effect of God," because "every composite

157. Scotus, I *Ord.* 37, n. 9. Cf. Cross, *God,* 101.
158. Cross argues that Scotus has an account of participation but fails to note the serious difference in how participation is construed.
159. Cross, *God,* 110.
160. Schmutz, "Causality," 211.
161. Schmutz, "Causality," 211.
162. *ST* 1a.105.5.
163. Schmutz, "Causality," 210.
164. Cf. Scotus, *I Ord.* 36.65; Scotus, *IV Ord.* 1.1.7.
165. It is a broader Franciscan tendency in the thirteenth century. Both Peter Olivi and Henry of Ghent doubt the viability of "*influentia.*" Schmutz, "Causality," 212.

effect can be generated by a created cause only by passing through the action of creatures themselves, who by the very fact become themselves equally 'givers of being.'"[166] Because *being* has no transcendental reality, the gift of being is nothing other than its instantiation, which can be effected by divine and creaturely causal power. In other words, creative power is reduced to productive power, a power contained preeminently in the divine essence, but possessed in essentially the same way by the Essence, the Persons, and creatures. While only God can create ex nihilo, thereafter, God and creatures become co-makers of being. This effectively removes ontological considerations from causality altogether, tilting it toward the entirely "ontic" play of productive powers, divine and creaturely, cooperating to varying degrees.

Once primary and secondary causality are conceived under a common *ratio*, it becomes necessary to delineate two distinct spheres of operation, for if creaturely and divine causality cooperate in production, this might make God culpable for human sin. Scotus uses an illustration from a medieval ball game. Divine causality is not that in which the ball moves and has its being, but "is reduced to an 'assistance or general influence' and hence designates nothing other than the 'actual conjunction of such active causes, out of which, being so conjoined and their proper activities being presupposed to the conjunction, ensues the common effect of both causes.'"[167] Now two orders of causal power concur toward a "common effect." For Scotus, this means that under the general influence of God, creaturely sin does not contaminate God, since God is only supplying the minimal requirements to ensure the effectiveness of creaturely free choice.

Ockham would then filter all of this through Scotus's distinction between God's absolute and ordained power to "eliminate the whole traditional hierarchy between first and second causes."[168] Once Scotus flattened the ontological hierarchy of causes, there was little reason for Ockham to maintain their formal order. God may as well skip secondary causes altogether, making them always potentially illusory phenomenon to which only the loose ascription of *nominales* applies. This is, for Ockham, only a possibility latent in God's absolute power; God in fact ordains the arrangement of secondary causes.[169] But this de jure situation would not last. By the sixteenth century, the possibility that God might usurp secondary causes becomes an affirmation that God programmatically does. For Luis de Molina, God's *potentia ordinata* and *potentia absoluta* map directly onto nature and grace.

---

166. Schmutz, "Causality," 213.
167. Schmutz, "Causality," 222. Quoting Scotus, II *Ord.* 3.2.1, no. 281.
168. Schmutz, "Causality," 232. Cf. Funkenstein, *Imagination*, 143: "For Thomas, 'the world' meant, first and foremost, the unity and cohesiveness of its structure. For Ockham it was derived from the brute fact that it is one aggregate. That it is well ordered he does not deny, but does not assume any order as a necessary condition for 'this world' to be one."
169. It should be noted that Aquinas would not deny God's absolute power; the point here is that the terms of the debate have so dramatically changed that Aquinas and Ockham are not having the same conversation.

God sustains the natural world by his general concurrence, but directly intervenes in that world by his absolute power to bestow grace.

In this realm of pure nature, God's action comes to be seen as "neutral" in regard to ends. God concurs with creaturely action in a way that merely follows upon the creature's free choice. Where for Scotus, the creature "adds" to divine causality, by the sixteenth century it is God who "adds" to creaturely causality: God provides the additional power necessary to accomplish an act. Quickly enough a Cistercian, Juan Caramuel Lobkowitz puts Ockham's razor to work: why retain concurrent divine causality at all?[170] If free creatures freely act and God's power secretly and imperceptibly "seals the deal," so to speak, what need is there for divine causal power at all? Would it not be simpler to inhabit a world of discreet independent causes? God may perhaps intervene occasionally, but otherwise, there is only pure nature.[171]

Pure nature has no place for symbolism. In the first instance, symbolism *requires* analogy—both ontologically and semantically (the two cannot in fact be separated). And since analogy, for Scotus and his followers, is nothing but equivocation mixed with unacknowledged univocity, symbolism must be done away with. Once *being* is no longer an analogical sharing, it becomes nothing other than an instantiation of power, thereby making the entire created order merely the expression of divine productive power. The important question then becomes not so much "what has God done?" but "what can God do?." The distinction between God's ordained and absolute power, always present in some form in tradition, takes on a novel and paramount importance. To guard the freedom of God's will, God must be capable of creating any possible world, and those possible worlds always hover in the background of this actual world. As developed by the Scotist Alexander Broadie: "since our world is one of many possible worlds that God could have created, our world is permeated by non-being."[172] Funkenstein concludes:

> The Termists could not but object to any attempt to see God symbolized in nature because the order of nature was, in their eyes, so utterly contingent upon God's will ... the nominalists had to reject the doctrine of analogy because they had already desymbolized the universe (as well as history) almost completely.[173]

In other words, the world is so exhaustively threatened by God's absolute power that nature can in no way be counted on to symbolize the divine.

---

170. Schmutz, "Causality," 248.
171. This razor cuts both ways. Calvinism and Jansenism react to the prospect of pure nature by destroying nature—there is only divine causality.
172. Alexander Broadie, "Scotist Metaphysics and Creation ex nihilo," in David Burrell, et al. (eds.), *Creation and the God of Abraham* (Cambridge: Cambridge University Press), 59.
173. Funkenstein, *Imagination*, 58.

Thus, under the weight of univocity, Scotus nominalizes *being* to avoid idolatrously subordinating God to *being*. Once Scotus reduces *being* to a vicious abstraction, there is nothing left to emanation other than power: creation is merely the result of God's ordained power, in principle always threatened by God's absolute power. Since power is *of the essence,* logically prior to the persons, creation cannot be symbolic of God's own trinitarian reality. The symbolic value of creation can only be guaranteed when creation is a *share* in the divine life of Father, Son, and Spirit; symbolism dies by univocation.[174]

Conclusion

Thomas and Scotus think very differently about the Trinity, and this alters how they think of creation. For Thomas, creation is enacted according to the persons: spoken from the Father in the Son by the Spirit. While the persons act as one in all their external acts, they act according to the trinitarian *taxis*. Creation is thus the work of Father–Son–Spirit, and carries within it the ontological trace of the triune life. While this trace must still be elevated to grace and glory, it is, nonetheless a mode of participation in the triune God. Creation is truly a symbol of God, a sign that mediates God's presence. It is this presence, moreover, that funds theology as a spiritual exercise. In "reading" the symbols of created life—in this case, the psychological analogy—the theologian encounters not just facts about God, but the vestigial *presence* of God. As Peter Struck summarizes the approach of Dionysius, symbols have "the anagogic power to lift us up" to the symbolized itself.[175] While certainly the product of a very different time and place, Thomas's theology does not depart much from the symbolism of Augustine's analogical ascent. Thomas still intends his readers to encounter God in the spiritual exercise of his reflection on the Trinity, a *manuduction* into the Trinity.[176]

For Scotus, creation "passes through" the persons, but the persons are inessential to the act of creation itself: creation, like the persons themselves, is a product of the powers of the divine essence. Creation thus symbolizes not the persons of the Trinity, but divine power. That power is formally distinct from the divine presence, so it becomes conceivable that God might act apart from God's presence. Once the distinction between God's absolute and ordained power is centralized, creation is so exhaustively threatened by God's absolute power that it cannot be counted on to symbolize the Trinity. The God who *might* have done anything from a distance, becomes a God who *does* a few things from a distance, which in turn becomes no God at all. Scotus of course is not personally responsible for every link in this

---

174. Of course, Scotus and the later nominalists did not develop these concepts in the same ways. Scotus thought univocity meant we could prove a great deal about God, later nominalists demurred.
175. Struck, *Symbol*, 262.
176. Candler, *Manuduction, passim*.

chain of events, but in prioritizing the powers of the essence over the persons in eternity, Scotus prioritizes power over presence in time, and creation ceases to be a symbol. That is, creation ceases to be a sign that mediates God's presence, only a product of divine power. And this, in turn, changes the texture of theology. No longer an exercise of spiritual ascent, theology is the discovery of or imposition of conceptual order. Scotus thought of the psychological analogy as a proof of the Trinity, in spite of Augustine's clearly different aims.[177] The purpose is no longer contemplation and ascent, but maximal discursive clarity.[178]

Thomas's account, I am arguing, better secures the symbolic quality of creation, and therefore its sacral and sacramental value. Fundamental to this theology of the symbol is the conviction that "symbolized–symbol–symbolism" is more truly said of God than creation. A systematics of the symbol, then, will turn on a doctrine of the Trinity. Only because the Father subsists as the symbolized, the Son the symbol, and the Spirit symbolism, do we have any reason to understand creation as a symbol, for created symbols participate analogically in the uncreated symbol. The Father speaks creation in the speaking of the Word, there is nothing outside this relation to ground creation—no logically prior divine essence or divine power, just the relations of the persons. And once this relation is seen in its absolute priority, we can be quite bold about the depth of connection between creation and God. Thomas will say that creation, as known in the Word, *is the divine essence*. That is a strong statement. It indicates an unspeakable intimacy between creation and God, that creation itself is revelatory, that it carries within it God's vestigial presence. And yet creation is not God. Because creation's ground and end is God, creation is not its own, it is not self-subsistent. On Thomist terms, creation *has* existence, but only God *is* existence, and thus creation is not to be identified with God. But even this "not-God" quality is itself an expression of God's life, for God's Spirit overflows in self-diffusive goodness, establishing creation as an-other that is nonetheless not at a distance. Creation's contingency is not an expression of its distance from God, but of the free and overflowing goodness of God, the willingness of God to share God's life with another.

---

177. See the argument about Augustine's pedagogical intentions in Lewis Ayres, *Augustine and the Trinity* (Cambridge: Cambridge University Press, 2010); see also Rowan Williams, *On Augustine* (London: Bloomsbury, 2016), ch. 9. Russell Freidman is thus wrong in his attempt to give Scotus the benefit of the doubt by saying that "Augustine was by no means explicit as to how he meant the psychological analogy to be taken … [both Franciscan and Dominican approaches] should be viewed as honest attempts at coming to grips with the available theological data." Friedman, *Medieval*, 61. To call the analogy "theological data" is already to misconstrue its purpose in a Franciscan direction. Of course, it was an honest attempt, but it departs significantly from Augustine.

178. The Trinity is, of course, not entirely provable, but Scotus thinks his arguments are "strongly deductive, though not demonstrative in the strict sense," since God must choose to reveal himself to us, the premises of the proof are not immediately available. Cf. Scotus, *Quod.* 14, n. 9 (Wolter, 323–4); Cross, *God*, 128.

What Thomas's analysis of creation allows us to say is that while it is indeed the work of the whole Trinity, creation's relation to the Trinity most closely approximates that of Son and Father. As the Son receives the gift of the divine essence from the Father, so creation receives participation in being from God; as the Son is the fullness of the Father expressed in another eternally and necessarily, so creation is the divine essence expressed in another temporally and contingently; and just as the Father is only known in the Son, so God can only be known within creation by created symbols. Moreover, just as the Father remains the hidden source and eternal fount of divinity, so God is the hidden source of creation who remains hidden even as revealed in created symbols.

Thus, the Son is the symbol of the Father, and creation is the symbol of God. But this does not obviate the need for redemption and elevation. Creation is indeed a symbol, but that symbol must be returned to God in a motion of symbolism. I argued above that the Spirit is necessary to the Trinity because without an "interpreter" of the Word spoken, the speaking of the Word would be a blunt self-assertion, a pulsar firing in a vacuum. Likewise it would be unfitting for the created symbol to be spoken into existence, only to remain "unread," unreturned to God in love. As the Spirit eternally "interprets" the Son and returns to the Father in praise, so creation should be read and returned to God. For this to happen, there must be a creature capable of reading the symbols. And in this creature, more than anywhere else in creation, the *paradox* of the trinitarian relations is most evidently displayed. Humanity occupies a paradoxical middle of the created order: it naturally desires the vision of God, but that desire can only be fulfilled by grace. As the Spirit follows the Son, so grace presupposes nature, but as the Spirit is paradoxically pre-present in the generation of the Word, so grace is paradoxically "pre-present" as the natural desire for the supernatural. Nature is always-already graced, a paradox grounded in the paradoxical relation of Son and Spirit. Humanity is thus suspended, always a symbol, but also always in a motion of desire toward God. As the Spirit is the paradoxical unity of Father and Son, so humanity is the paradoxical unity of all creation; the site where God and creation are destined to meet in Christ. Before turning to redemption, properly speaking, in the body of Christ, I turn to humanity, suspended in a motion of desire and love. If the human is the suspended middle of the universe, anthropology is the suspended middle of this book; it speaks of the natural inclination of all things to be rejoined to God, and yet the need for supernatural grace to achieve that union. I turn, then, to anthropology.

Chapter 3

ANTHROPOLOGY

Introduction

In the first chapter, I developed the triad symbolized–symbol–symbolism as an analogy for the Trinity. This analogy, I argued, could also be used to understand all things in relation to God, so that symbolized–symbol–symbolism analogically corresponds to God–creation–church. God is symbolized in creation, and the church is symbolism, the movement of unity between God and world. The last chapter developed an understanding of creation as a symbol of God as the temporal unfolding of the eternal Word in the Spirit. This means that our trinitarian theology is intimately connected to our doctrine of creation, as I showed in the contrast between Aquinas and Duns Scotus. The mystery and paradox of substantive relations was seen to more successfully guard the symbolic, which is to say the sacral value of creation, than Scotus's more discursively confident emanationist account of the Trinity. Creation, I argued, necessarily reflects the divine life as the unnecessary outpouring of that life; creation is a symbol not merely of divine causal power, but of the divine relations.

One potential concern with the closely linked trinitarian theology and doctrine of creation I outlined is that it seems to neglect the difference between nature and grace, between creation and elevation to grace and glory. If creation is to be *elevated* to the divine life, if nature is to be perfected by grace, then the doctrine of creation cannot be the last word. The question then arises about the relation between creation as a natural symbol, and the supernatural destiny to which it is called. I will address this issue in the present chapter in terms of anthropology. This is appropriate because, as a great deal of Christian tradition has supposed, humanity is a microcosm of the entire created order. For Thomas, for instance, in being a hylomorphic unity of body and soul, humanity joins material creation with spiritual creation, so that everything from cosmic radiation to angels is summed in humanity.[1]

---

1. Gilles Emery calls humanity the "hyphen" between material and immaterial creation. Gilles Emery, *Trinity, Church and the Human Person* (Naples, FL: Sapientia Press, 2007), 220. Citing Thomas Aquinas, *Summa Contra Gentiles* II, ch. 68 (#1453).

Human nature is created and redeemed on behalf of all nature.[2] Thus, the relation between nature and grace in the human speaks for the relation of creation to consummation in the created order as a whole. As de Lubac would say, the doctrine of creation is "symbolically included" in anthropology, so that something said of one applies to the other.

Humanity, like creation, is naturally a symbol of God. Moreover, on behalf of all creation, humanity is destined to a supernatural end. I will argue for de Lubac's view that the link between created nature and supernatural destiny is the natural desire for the supernatural. I will not be adding much by way of new argument, but I will be indicating why it is that I maintain de Lubac's position that humanity has a natural desire for the vision of God, but this desire can only be fulfilled by grace. To be a symbol is to occupy this "suspended middle."[3] This view has been expounded and controverted often. The literature is immense, and apparently intractable. In the first section, I will outline some of the issues surrounding Henri de Lubac's understanding of nature and grace, with reference to the criticisms of Lawrence Feingold, Steven A. Long and Reinhardt Hütter.[4] I will not, however, be mounting a full defense against any of them. While each has distinct and important concerns, their projects all turn on an interpretation of Thomas.[5] As important as that undertaking is, missing from any of them is the broader dogmatic context of the question. For example, one searches in vain for any reference to the Holy Spirit in Feingold or Long's work, and Hütter only glances across the surface of pneumatological thinking, a symptom of the dissolutions that de Lubac claimed could be traced back to the very doctrine of pure nature they variously defend. This chapter, then, will not attempt an exegesis of Thomas, but to ask the question within a broader frame of reference.

In particular I want to draw attention to the isomorphism identified by de Lubac between nature and grace and the Old and New Testaments. The second section of this chapter will argue that a trinitarian theology of symbols sustains an isomorphism between scripture and anthropology, so that the relation of nature to grace can be understood in light of the relation of Old to New Testament, with

---

2. This is clear, for instance, in Romans 8, where creation itself longs for its own freedom and renewal as the revelation of God's people.

3. Hans Urs von Balthasar, *The Theology of Henri de Lubac: An Overview* (San Francisco, CA: Ignatius Press, 1991), 15.

4. Lawrence Feingold, *The Natural Desire to See God According to St Thomas Aquinas and His Interpreters* (Naples, FL: Sapientia Press, 2010); Steven A. Long, *Natura Pura* (New York: Fordham University Press, 2010); Reinhard Hütter, *Dust Bound for Heaven* (Cambridge: Eerdmans, 2012).

5. Roughly, Feingold focuses on the reception history of Thomas, Long on the question of natural law and nature as a "theonomic" principle, and Hütter on the details of Thomas's text in the Summa Contra Gentiles. Of the three, Hütter's is the most sensitive to the actual questions thrown up by de Lubac's proposal and broader dogmatic concerns.

Christ standing at the middle of both. Just as Christ is only intelligible as *Israel's* messiah, as the fulfillment of Israel's founding promises, so grace presupposes and perfects but does not destroy nature. But just as there is no aspect of Israel's scripture in which the eternal Logos is not always-already present and working, so there is no pure nature not always-already marked by grace. Nonetheless, in spite of the "pre-presence" of Christ in the Old Testament and the continuity of Christ's life and work with Old Testament messianic promises, Christ comes in a manner completely beyond Israel's expectations, a fulfillment at once longed for and yet unforeseeable. So too is nature "suspended," caught up in a destiny at once constitutive of it and yet beyond it, having a natural desire for the supernatural that it is incapable of fulfilling on its own. There is thus a profound coherence or fittingness between the natural desire for the supernatural and the shape of scripture.

I will end this reflection with a reading of the opening chapter of the gospel of Luke, with particular attention to the annunciation, and Mary's *Magnificat*. Mary is shown to be a spiritual interpreter of scripture who displays in her own embodied exegesis the natural longing for God that is gratuitously fulfilled in Christ. Humanity is thus seen to be a symbol by being suspended, longing by nature for a fulfillment only possible by grace on behalf of all creation. The result is a clearer understanding of the nature of the created symbol, and its intrinsic desire for consummation in Christ. This chapter itself is a kind of "suspended middle" of this systematic theology: it articulates the relation between creation (Chapter 2) and creation's ecclesial consummation (Chapter 4). I seek to account for the hinge between symbol and symbolism, the created symbol and its gratuitous return to God. To be a symbol is to be always-already in a motion of symbolism back toward God, for nature is always-already graced.

Nature and Grace

The question of the relation of nature to grace was one of the most controverted of the last century and simmers still today.[6] While all Catholic and many Protestant theologians agree that grace perfects and does not destroy nature, the relation between nature and grace remains heavily contested. Henri de Lubac questioned the reigning neo-Scholastic synthesis in *Surnaturel*, a series of historical studies arguing that the theory of pure nature was a late aberration in Thomist theology, one that goes beyond and controverts both Thomas and the tradition Thomas

---

6. For an overview, see Serge-Thomas Bonino, ed., *Surnaturel: A Controversy at the Heart of Twentieth-Century Catholic Thomistic Thought* (Ave Maria, FL: Sapientia Press, 2009), especially chs. 1–3.

inherited.[7] De Lubac argued that humans have a natural desire for the supernatural, a desire implanted in human nature for "*l'union divine ... la participation de la Vie trinitaire dans la 'vision de Dieu'.*"[8] Such a natural desire, however, can only be fulfilled by grace. Nature is thus "suspended," driven by desire for God, but unable to fulfill that desire but for the gift of grace.[9]

For neo-Scholasticism and its heirs this violates the crucial Aristotelian axiom that desires of nature must be achievable by natural means.[10] Obviously, if the natural desire for the supernatural could be fulfilled by natural means, this would entail Pelagianism. Alternatively, if the desire is truly natural but can only be fulfilled by grace, this would seem to obligate God by justice to fulfill it. A natural desire for the supernatural would imply that human nature is only fulfilled—only fully natural—by grace, and therefore it would be ontological cruelty for God to deny nature what is natural to it. Grace would then not be gratuitous, since mandated by divine justice.[11] Moreover, if nature has this natural desire for the supernatural, it would compromise the integrity of nature, since it requires God's grace for its own fulfillment.[12] De Lubac's position, it is argued, compromises both the integrity of nature and the gratuity of grace, collapsing them together in the human spirit.

The neo-Scholastic alternative is to imagine two distinct spheres, nature and grace, two "tiers" of anthropology. Human nature constitutes a purely natural order with purely natural ends. These ends suffice for the fulfillment of nature *qua* nature, for example, building homes, agriculture, and family relations. This is the

---

7. Henri De Lubac, *Surnaturel: Etudes Historique, nouvelle edition* (Paris: Lethielleux, 2010; originally published Paris: Aubier-Montaigne, 1946); *The Mystery of the Supernatural* (New York: Herder and Herder, 1967); *Augustinianism and Modern Theology*, trans. Lancelot Shepperd (New York: Crossroad, 2000). Influential analyses of de Lubac's position include Hans Urs von Balthasar, *The Theology of Henri de Lubac*, ch. 4; John Milbank, *The Suspended Middle: Henri de Lubac and the Renewed Split in Modern Catholic Theology*, 2nd ed. (Cambridge: Eerdmans, 2005); Nicholas J. Healy Jr., "The Christian Mystery of Nature and Grace," in Jordan Hillebert (ed.), *The T&T Clark Companion to Henri de Lubac* (London: Bloomsbury T&T Clark, 2017), 181–204.

8. De Lubac, *Surnaturel*, 421.

9. Hans Urs von Balthasar borrows this term from Erich Przywara to describe de Lubac's theology. It is picked up by John Milbank. Balthasar, *Theology*, 15; Milbank, *Suspended*, 12.

10. Feingold, *Natural*, xxix: "Innate appetite is always proportionate to the nature of the creature and to his natural powers, and thus it cannot extend to something which exceeds the natural order, such as the vision of God."

11. Feingold, *Natural*, xxix: "In addition, it would put in jeopardy the possibility of a connatural end for man and thus create grave problems for the theological understanding of the gratuitousness of grace and glory."

12. Cf. Long's argument that de Lubac's position constitutes the "loss of nature as a theonomic principle" in *Natura*, especially chapter 1.

realm of common human inquiry, natural law, science, apologetics, philosophy.[13] The desire for God in this state is a desire for God as end only inasmuch as God is the one creator, in principle discoverable by unaided human reason, but not yet the trinitarian God of Christianity. Hence Steven A. Long: "yes, *God* is the natural end, but God as First Cause of these effects, not God precisely as Father, Son and Spirit."[14] Long reads a strong distinction in Thomas between a discourse on the one God and a discourse on the Trinity, corresponding to two ends, one natural and immanently attainable, the other supernatural and requiring the extrinsic addition of grace.[15] Securing a realm of pure nature therefore secures an entire range of universally available goods, including especially a basic concept of one creator God and a universally valid natural law.

Accordingly, any confusion of nature with grace destroys the integrity of those disciplines which comprise the realm of pure nature, since their internal coherence is corrupted by a natural longing for grace: natural law, science, philosophy, and apologetics lose their inherent intelligibility if human nature naturally desires the supernatural. Nature must therefore be preserved in its own order by a purely natural end, achievable by purely natural means. Grace, on the other hand, brings an entirely new order: nature is elevated, given both a new supernatural end and the supernatural gifts needed to obtain that end. Pure nature is proportionate to purely natural ends; graced nature is proportionate to supernatural ends. This is the realm of revelation, theology, sacraments, beatitude. The realm of grace is superior to that of nature, and no one who positively understands what it contains can sensibly reject it. But the realm of grace remains always subsequent to, and sharply distinguished from, the realm of nature for the sake of the former's gratuity and the latter's integrity.

---

13. Long, *Natura*, 202: "The full range of naturally knowable truth, in metaphysics, natural theology, natural philosophy, anthropology, and morality, forms a crucially central point of analogous reference for the church in her evangelical mission." One payout for Long is that pure nature secures the universal validity and availability of natural law (hence the title "theonomic"), which enables him, among other things, to uphold the American constitutional framework as a high-water mark for the political manifestation of natural teleology. See Long's chapter 4, "Why *Natura Pura* Is Not the Theological Stalking Horse for Secularist Minimalism or Pelagianism."

14. Long, *Natura*, 17. Advocates appeal to Vatican I: "If anyone says that the one, true God, our creator and Lord, cannot be known with certainty from the things that have been made, by the natural light of reason: let him be anathema," in Norman P. Tanner, (ed.), *Decrees of the Ecumenical Councils*, Vol. 2 (1990), 810. The neo-Thomist interpretation of Vatican I, however, is not necessarily original to the council; see Fergus Kerr, "Knowing God by Reason Alone: What Vatican I Never Said," *New Blackfriars* 91, no. 1033 (May 2010), 215–28.

15. Long, *Natura*, 49. He is rejecting the view of, among others, Gilles Emery, *Trinity in Aquinas* (Naples, FL: Sapientia Press, 2003), XX: "[Thomas] has no treatise 'of the one God' separated from the treatise of the Trinity."

This theory of pure nature, according to de Lubac, is too "mediocre" to risk any "rampant heterodoxy."[16] It is an over-simplification wrought by the demands of safeguarding certain aspects of truth. Those unwilling to let the paradox stand, resolve it. The problem is that every paradox has two sides and resolving it in one direction—even if satisfactory in one sense—will always be at the expense of the other. Pure nature may succeed in keeping grace from collapsing into nature, but it destroys the integral dynamism of human life toward the divine. This dynamism is lost, De Lubac argues, because of two errors: "Thinking of God in the same way as man, and thinking of man in the same way as 'natural being.'"[17] Both errors naturalize the supernatural. This needs unpacking.

Isolating the spheres of nature and grace turns on the idea that God and nature are subject to the same methodological and ontological principles. The Aristotelian principle of the proportionality of desire and ability reigns supreme. Natural desires must be obtainable by natural means, so God, on pain of being unjust, cannot give a creature a natural desire without also giving those creatures the natural means to attain that desire. For example, it would be ontological cruelty for God to create humans who hunger for food in a world with nothing edible. For grace to be gratuitous, then, the desire for God must be purely "elicited," arising entirely from wonder at creation and terminating in an entirely *natural* knowledge of God. The natural desire for God thus begins and ends as any other desire in a neo-Thomist anthropology: consequent upon knowledge and naturally attainable. Knowledge provokes wonder and desire to know, just as knowledge of Texas barbeque provokes hunger and desire to eat. The latter knowledge provokes a sense appetite; the former knowledge provokes an intellectual appetite. Because an intellectual appetite is more profound than a sense appetite, the natural desire for God is more important than any desire for smoked brisket, but the structure of desiring is identical. The fact that the terminus of the desire is God makes no difference to the process of desiring. Here is no ontological *elán*, no natural dynamism, just wills desiring objects wholly known within the ambit of nature, and whose significance remains wholly immanent. God is thus objectified, reduced to the realm of the naturally knowable and therefore naturally desirable.

The reason for this strict proportionality, according to Long, is that everything is defined by its proportionate end. So a natural desire for the supernatural would transgress the boundaries of what makes humanity an intelligible species. Such a desire would make humans indistinguishable from angels, since angels also have the vision of God as their supernatural end.[18] But even more strikingly, Long argues that if human nature were to have an intrinsic desire for the beatific vision, this would erase the very difference between God and creation:

---

16. De Lubac, *Mystery*, 166.
17. De Lubac, *Mystery*, 163.
18. Long, *Natura*, 91.

> How would God Himself distinguish nature and supernature were it not the case that between the divine nature and the nature of the created person there are naturally diverse ends? A natural end is that toward which a being naturally tends as to the perfection proportionate to it and from which its species is distinguished ... only the divine nature is defined by intrinsically supernatural and deific felicity.[19]

Long's point is that definitions matter. God and creatures are defined differently (and therefore are really different) because they have diverse ends. A natural desire can only correspond to a natural end, and so a natural desire for the supernatural, in spite of unsavory appeals to paradox, makes glory the de facto natural end of humanity. But only God can have God as a naturally proportionate end. But what is striking about this passage is the univocity with which he treats Divine and creaturely nature and knowledge. Just like creatures, God's nature is defined by a proportionate end and is subject to the epistemological constraints of the law of proportionality. Hence, for Long, if humanity has a supernatural destiny inscribed on its nature, it would, as the serpent in the garden put it, be like God. So inviolable is the law of proportionality that even God would be confused about where God's nature ends and human nature begins if humanity were to have a natural desire for a supernatural end. But this is to treat the divine nature as one nature among others, and the divine mind as one mind among others. If we remember that we live and move and have our being *in* God, then it is clear that the divine nature is not a nature like any other, and God's knowledge is subject to *none* of the epistemological constraints of creaturely knowledge. Why should we assume that a creature endowed with a natural desire for the supernatural would be confusing for God, whose nature is fully known only to God and whose knowledge is the very existence of what is known? Long has risked naturalizing God, now so readily definable in wholly natural terms and so firmly subject to the epistemological methods and constraints of creatures.

The naturalization of God is risked in Long's argument, but it is not his point. His point, rather, is that a natural desire for the supernatural is simply incoherent, and God can no more be expected to recognize such a creature than to create a rock too big for God to lift. The law of proportionality is simply, for Long, the law of non-contradiction applied to the question of desire. A creature is only capable of desiring that which it is capable of attaining, at least formally: a fish cannot desire a tenure-track position at a research university. A natural desire for the supernatural is simply a logical contradiction, and like a tenured fish, an absurdity that no epistemology, no matter how mystical, can overcome. This insistence that de Lubac's understanding of the natural desire is a contradiction requires a flat-out denial or complete ignoring of paradox. Reinhard Hütter, for example, makes "avoiding the paradox" the payoff of his own proposal.[20] Faced with an apparent

---

19. Long, *Natura*, 29.
20. Hütter, *Dust*, 178. Also Long, *Natura*, 234n. 33. This is one of the few places Long mentions paradox, and he marks it off with scare quotes to signal his distaste.

contradiction, or at least ambiguity, in Thomas's texts on the natural desire for the vision of God, neo-Thomism resolves it by further definition, specification and delineation. Those taking their bearings from de Lubac are more likely to argue that the tension in Thomas serves to clarify a central Christian paradox, namely, the paradox of a nature destined beyond itself.[21] For John Milbank, who presses the Lubacian paradox as far as it can go (certainly further than de Lubac himself does), the natural desire for the supernatural is something wholly nature and wholly grace, unmixed and undivided, at the core of human reality, a kind of Chalcedonian moment that frames the entirety of human existence from and to God.[22]

The paradox of a natural desire for the supernatural is only a contradiction if the divine nature is a nature like any other and therefore desired like any other good. But because God is not a nature among others, God is not desired as one good among others. Since all our knowing and willing occurs *in* God, the desire of nature for the vision of God necessarily takes the form of an ontological élan. If we truly live and move and have our being in God, then our desire for God cannot precisely mirror our desire for finite objects. It must be more aboriginal, more intrinsic, coded in the very structure of desire itself. Indeed, the very shape of finite desire takes its motion from this original desire for and movement toward God. My desire for God is not merely the intellectual version of my desire for barbeque. Rather, my material desires arise only within the horizon of this original desire; the natural desire for God is not *a* desire, it is the condition for the possibility of any desire whatsoever, since it marks out my motion in time from and to God.[23] If God were one nature among natures, then the disproportion between God and creatures would indeed make such a natural desire for the supernatural a contradiction. But because God's nature is the exclusive context of created existence, transcendence rather than proportionality becomes the operative principle. A third way is thereby opened up between contradiction and resolution, namely, the paradox of a desire constitutive of nature that can nonetheless only be fulfilled by a supernatural gift of grace.[24]

---

21. On the centrality of paradox to de Lubac's theology, see Rowan Williams, "Forward: A Paradoxical Humanism" in Hillebert, *Companion*, xiv-xix.

22. Milbank's is overtly a radicalization of de Lubac's paradox. It is not the only interpretive option for understanding de Lubac's paradox of nature and grace. For a contrasting position, see Jordan Hillebert, "Introduction to Henri de Lubac" in Hillebert, *Companion*, 22. Hillebert's forthcoming book will fill out this alternative interpretation.

23. The language of "horizon" is Rahner's, borrowed from Heidegger. Karl Rahner, *Foundations of Christian Faith*, trans. Williams Dych (London: Crossroad, 1978), 63.

24. Hence, Rahner: "Preaching is the express awakening of what is already present in the depths of man's being, not by nature, but by grace. But it is a grace which always surrounds man, even the sinner and the unbeliever, as the inescapable setting of his existence." *Theological Investigations*, Vol. 4, trans. Cornelius Ernst, (New York: Helicon, 1966), 181.

This paradoxical desire is an echo of humanity's trinitarian origin. Thomas follows Augustine in arguing that while the Father speaks creation in the speaking of the Logos, the Spirit is the life of creation, drawing it back to God.[25] The *movement* of creation, its drive toward God is its participation in the Spirit. This aspect of movement toward another is precisely why the will is taken as an analogy for the Spirit in Thomas's trinitarian theology.[26] The will is an outward motion toward another. While the intellect sustains an interior mode of presence by the inner word, the will creates a form of "external" presence by desiring and loving things in themselves. Because the Spirit is the union of Father and Son, their mutual movement toward one another, the Spirit is correlated to the divine will, since by the Spirit the Father and Son desire and love each other *as the other*. And just as, paradoxically, there is no Son not already loved and desired by the Father in the Spirit, so there is no creation not already desirous of God in the Spirit. The *modus essendi* of each Person is its modus operandi; in creation the Spirit works to draw nature beyond itself toward God. The Spirit does this not by some extrinsic intervention in an otherwise pre-constituted world, but by establishing the very life of creation as a sharing in the life that is the Spirit. The desire for God is a finite participation in the Spirit; to desire God is to be an intellectual creature in motion by the Spirit, that is, a created spirit.[27]

This is important when it comes to questions of gratuity, since Thomas secures the gratuity of the created order by the operation of the divine will. Recall that creation is a contingent act of God's will *not* because God made a choice between two options—God could have refrained from creating, but this bare fact is not how Thomas ensures the contingency of creation. Rather, creation is contingent and therefore gratuitous because the will is directed toward things in themselves, and since creation is neither its own ground nor end, when God's will is directed toward creation in itself, it is directed to something contingent, and therefore

---

25. Thomas Aquinas, *Summa Theologiae* Ia.45.6.ad. 2: "by his sway [the Holy Spirit] governs and quickens what is created by the Father through the Son," in Laurence Shapcote, O.P., trans., *Latin/English Edition of the Works of St. Thomas Aquinas* (Lander, WY: The Aquinas Institute for the Study of Sacred Doctrine, 2012), 469. Hereafter *ST*.

26. Cf. Simon Oliver, *Philosophy, God and Motion* (London: Routledge, 2005), 115: "God's knowledge becomes the cause of creation and the ground of the continual subsistence of the cosmos, while the Holy Spirit, which proceeds from the Father and Son by way of love, is properly described as the principle of the motion of nature."

27. See de Lubac's articulation of this position outlined below. See also Rahner, *TI* 4, 179: "We must say that for Scripture, the communication of the Spirit (the divine *pneuma*) is not just a trans-conscious entitative 'elevation' of the conscious moral acts of man, which remain existentially the same and are only changed extrinsically by the *fides ex auditu*. It is 'life', 'unction', 'light', the inexpressible co-intercession of the Spirit, *pneuma* which is more than *nous*, an inward attraction, testimony given by the Spirit."

wills it contingently.[28] The divine will is fully satisfied by the divine essence, and so does not require the willing of creation for its own fulfillment. So when God wills creation, it is willed as something both unnecessary to the divine nature and wholly ordered toward it. In fact, creation is wholly unnecessary to the divine nature precisely because it is wholly ordered toward it. Were creation its own ground or end, it would be a legitimate "end" for the divine will, an end that would compete with the divine goodness for the divine will's attention. But creation's end is the *divine* goodness, so that when God wills this creation, it is wholly within the replete movement of God toward God; creation is the gift of sharing in God as end and is therefore entirely contingent. And since within the godhead this movement of unity from God to God, Father to Son, is the person of the Spirit, creation's contingency is an expression of its temporal sharing in the life of the eternal Spirit.

This way of securing the gratuity of creation has the significant benefit of making creation's ongoing actual existence entirely gratuitous. Gratuity is ensured not by appeal to some alternate universe rejected by a divine decision made "prior" to time, but by the very structure of divine willing in this creation right now. The very structure of created existence ensures that it is a free gift of God. This concept of gratuity is a long way from Scotus's gratuity of exhaustive alternatives. This is important because the bare fact that God may have done otherwise gives rise to the question of God's freedom once the initial decision to create has been made. Is God then constrained by this decision? Scotus resolves this by maintaining the ongoing reality of compossibles—the creations not chosen lurk in the background of all that is.[29] Aquinas, alternatively, secures the ongoing gratuity of *this* creation by appeal to its being entirely directed toward God as source and end. Creation's directedness toward God secured by its position in the trinitarian act of creation means that anytime God wills anything in regard to creation, this willing is entirely gratuitous.[30]

---

28. ST 1a.19.3.ad 6: "As the divine essence is necessary of itself, so is the divine will and the divine knowledge; but the divine knowledge has a necessary relation to the thing known; not the divine will to the thing willed. The reason for this is that knowledge is of things as they exist in the knower; but the will is directed to things as they exist in themselves. Since then all other things have necessary existence inasmuch as they exist in God; but no absolute necessity so as to be necessary in themselves, in so far as they exist in themselves; it follows that God knows necessarily whatever He wills, but does not will necessarily whatever He wills." See the discussion in John Wippel, "Thomas Aquinas on the Ultimate Why Question: Why Is There Anything at all Rather than Nothing Whatsoever?," *The Review of Metaphysics* 60, no. 4 (June 2007), esp. 745–6.

29. See Alexander Broadie, "Scotist Metaphysics and Creation ex Nihilo," in David Burrell, et al. (eds.), *Creation and the God of Abraham* (Cambridge: Cambridge University Press, 2010), 59.

30. This is why Feingold's sidelining of the "platonic" scheme in Thomas is a fatal error, for it is precisely the platonic framework of emanation and return that makes creation an ongoing act of gratuity, irrespective of questions about divine justice. Feingold, *Natural*, 31.

But this indicates a surprising inversion. In a particularly experimental mode, we might say that if the gratuity of creation is founded on creation's orientation toward God as source and end, and if this is not some generic one-God, but is the trinitarian God of Christianity, then the gratuity of creation is in fact inextricably bound to the gratuity of grace and glory. Creation is gratuitous because its end is God, and that end is accomplished through the humanity and divinity of Jesus Christ, so the grace of creation by the Logos cannot be separated from the grace of redemption and beatification in the Logos incarnate. And this re-centers the conversation on the subject from which it never should have strayed: the concrete center of the person and work of God incarnate. Precisely *because* the incarnation makes *reditus* possible, the gratuity of creation is inseparable from the grace offered in incarnation.[31] Where a doctrine of pure nature requires that nature be thought without Christ, the logic of gratuity requires that all creation be understood as creation in and for Christ, as Colossians 1 makes abundantly clear.[32] Here we must part company with Thomas; not only is the incarnation the point of creation, on Thomas's own terms the incarnation is inseparable from the gratuity of creation.

Rahner is particularly helpful in this regard. "Grace is God himself," Rahner rightly says, "the communication in which he gives himself to man as the divinizing favour which he is himself."[33] Rahner continues: "Such grace, from the very start, cannot be thought of independently of the personal love of God and its answer in man."[34] Christ is this personal love and human answer—Logos and humanity, Symbolized and symbol. Christ is not, therefore, the merely de facto agent of grace since the *felix culpa* of the fall. Rather, Christ is "the person who by his free Incarnation creates the order of grace and nature as his own presupposition (nature) and his milieu (the grace of the other spiritual creatures)."[35] Creation, as I argued in the previous chapter, is the unfolding of the Logos in time, and thus the nature necessarily presupposed in the incarnation of the same Logos. The incarnation then is the joining of created reality to its eternal source. This is nothing other than to specify how God is the beginning and end of creatures. The Logos is the source and archetype of creation; it is in the Logos incarnate that creation returns to God.[36] Or again, creation is an ecstatic outpouring of love from the Logos, the same Logos whose *kenosis* in Christ is an ecstatic outpouring of love

---

31. De Lubac by no means denies the order of creation, or a natural end for human nature. The two form "a real and ordered duality" which can never be separated. De Lubac, *Augustinianism and Modern Theology*, 130-1. See discussion in Healy, "Christian Mystery," 194–5.

32. Cf. Healy, "Christian Mystery," 181; Aaron Riches, "Christology and *duplex hominis beatitudo*: Re-sketching the Supernatural Again," *International Journal of Systematic Theology* 14, no. 1 (January 2012), 44–69.

33. Rahner, *TI* 4, 177.

34. Ranner, *TI* 4, 177.

35. Rahner, *TI* 4, 176.

36. Of course, both creation and incarnation are accomplished in the Spirit. See below.

for creation's deification.³⁷ Creation and incarnation are thus two expressions of the same Logos. And because creation and incarnation are of the same love, there is no reason to think the incarnation was God's plan B. Rather, the love of God in creation is the love of God in deification, and the former was made for the latter.

But if the incarnation is inseparable from the gratuity of creation, since it secures creation's *reditus* to the Father, does this not make grace necessary to creation, and therefore no longer gratuitous? It is in this context that de Lubac's appeal to the logic of gift is important. God, in creating ex nihilo, gives gifts that entirely constitute the recipient. That God creates a creature with a natural desire and a destiny beyond its nature establishes no obligation on God, for there is no prior substance toward which God could be obligated.³⁸ God's determination to create such a creature is coextensive with God's determination to offer that creature beatitude, for there is but one divine act. In de Lubac's terms:

> As soon as I say "I," I exist and I have being; and once I exist and have being, I have a finality. It is impossible to dissociate in reality these three elements by spreading them out over three instants in time with gaps between them.³⁹

This does not mean that the offer of grace is the same as creation. Grace is indeed a second gift, but like the Spirit to the Son, it is "retroactively causal" in the first.⁴⁰ Nature precedes grace, but nature is given for grace and in grace, as the Son is generated by his reception of the gift of the Spirit. This is because if nature is a symbol of God, then grace is the gift of unity between symbol and symbolized, and thus mirrors the role of the Spirit. Nature and grace therefore follow the *taxis* of Son and Spirit, but this *taxis* does not obviate the paradox. That paradox is the utter transcendent unity of God, in whom the twofold act of creation and salvation are finally one. God is beyond any law of proportionality: God cannot be desired as one good among others, even as the largest good among others. God is goodness itself, and the desire for this end is inscribed on my very nature. The transcendent unity of God sustains creatures in a paradoxical desire for a supernatural end.

And this leads to the second error de Lubac identifies: thinking of human nature as "natural being." De Lubac points out that Thomas follows the entirety of Christian tradition in arguing that humans are unique among created things: "There is something in man, a certain capacity for the infinite, which makes it impossible to consider him one of those beings whose whole nature and destiny

---

37. See Simon Oliver, "Trinity, Motion and Creation *ex Nihilo*," in David Burrell, et al. (eds.), *Creation and the God of Abraham* (Cambridge: Cambridge University Press, 2010), 133–51.

38. See Milbank, *Suspended*, 48–50.

39. De Lubac, *Mystery*, 79. Nor does *humani generis* conflict with this account. God *could* have created a rational creature and withheld beatitude from it, but de Lubac is right that this would not be the same humanity.

40. De Lubac, *Mystery*, 76–9.

are inscribed within the cosmos."⁴¹ The theory of pure nature tends to conflate human nature with the natural, a conflation which ignores humanity's supernatural vocation. Rahner makes the point forcefully:

> It might be asked whether the scholastic concept of "nature" as applied to the "nature" of man does not still owe too much to the model of what is less than human .... What is signified by the "definition," and hence the circumscription, of man's "nature," if he is the essence of transcendence, and hence the surpassing of limitation?⁴²

Analyses of human nature in terms of other natures in the world can only be carried on analogically. The human calling is a calling to transcendence, and hence to break the strictures of Aristotelian definition and natural proportion.⁴³ It turns out that neither God nor humanity can be circumscribed within the law of proportionality. But once human nature is elevated, and this is the heart of the mystery of the Logos incarnate, *all creation* is elevated with it. The entire natural order is elevated to the life of God in the transcendent nature of humanity by the redeeming work of the Logos. This again re-centers the question of nature and grace on the concrete center of Jesus Christ, and that means we must return to scripture, the word that witnesses to the Word. It is, de Lubac suggests, patristic exegesis, with its reading so radically centered on the work of Christ, that places in sharp relief the anthropology of nature and grace.

Anthropology and Fourfold Exegesis

Reinhardt Hütter describes two general approaches to anthropology. One, typified by Augustine's restless heart and advocated by de Lubac, sees nature as driven toward grace by an inner dynamism.⁴⁴ The other, Hütter argues, takes its starting

---

41. De Lubac, *Mystery*, 110.

42. Karl Rahner, *Theological Investigations Vol. I* (London: Longmann, Dartmon and Todd, 1963), 317. De Lubac cites this and other passages from Rahner to show their essential agreement. De Lubac's complaint against Rahner is that the language of "supernatural existential" does not really answer the question, it just displaces it behind additional, and therefore superfluous, terminology. Cf. De Lubac, *Mystery*, 101–2, n. 2.

43. This is, I take it, the heart of Rahner's "transcendental anthropology." To probe the question of humanity's transcendent source and end is not so much a Kantian *a priori* to police the boundaries of the finite, as a grappling with the mystery of creatureliness, a mystery rooted in nothing other than the inexhaustible mystery of God. See the essay presented at a symposium alongside de Lubac and other *ressourcement* figures, "Theology and Anthropology," in T. Patrick Burke (ed.), *The Word in History* (London: Collins, 1968), 1–24.

44. Hütter, *Dust*, 129. Of the theologians of pure nature engaged in the chapter, Hütter's is the most sensitive. My engagement with him here is critical but appreciative.

point in the Psalm, "what is man that thou art mindful of him and the son of man that thou dost care for him?" (Ps 8:4, RSV).[45] This approach sees humanity as fragile and sinful, for which sinfulness alone the eternal Son became incarnate, "not primarily to perfect creation by inchoately ushering in its transcendent end."[46] This vision understands the natural desire to see God,

> like Abraham having not the slightest inkling about his eventual calling and surely no desire for it ... like Israel being created out of the "nothingness" of Egyptian slavery and being called to something (Lev 19:2) for which it had no antecedent desire ... so also "the many" (Mk 10:45) from Israel and the nations are called to a supernatural destiny categorically transcending the range of human imagination and desire. This destiny grants its own supernatural desire with the call to it.[47]

Hütter goes on to advocate the neo-Thomist view of the natural desire for the vision of God (proportionality, specific obediential potency, etc.). Now this brief interpolation from Scripture is not the core of Hütter's argument. He does not need Abraham, Israel and "the many" to be suddenly commandeered by grace as if by lightning on a clear day to sustain his argument. His argument centers on Thomas and his commentators. But since he has claimed at least broad and programmatic support from Scripture for his position, it is worth asking whether this neo-Thomist anthropology actually coheres with the story of Abraham, Israel, and the many. How does Hütter know that Abraham "surely" (!) had no desire for his calling, especially since the natural desire for the supernatural is an *ontological* élan? Abraham need not have been sitting in Ur expressly wishing that God would call him to be the patriarch of a Messianic people to naturally desire God. Again, on what grounds does Hütter know that Israel had no desire for deliverance into freedom, even while they were calling out for this very thing from the nothing of slavery? This is especially problematic since Israel was not first created and later awarded a destiny. Israel was born in the promise to Abraham, always-already destined to the promised land and to be a blessing to every nation on the earth. While enslaved in Egypt it would only have been natural to desire that God fulfill this founding promise. How could a desire that God fulfill the promise for which Israel was created be some kind of pelagian presumptuousness? As for "the many" in Mark for whom the Son of Man came to give his life as a ransom, the immediate context is of desirous expectation for the Kingdom of God. When James and John ask in the preceding verses to sit at Jesus right and left hand it is in expectation of his coming exaltation as Israel's Messiah, in fulfillment of the founding promises of Israel made by God to Abraham. The disciples were undoubtedly wrong about the shape of that Messianic calling, which is the point of Jesus's reproof, but the passage

---

45. Hütter, *Dust*, 131.
46. Hütter, *Dust*, 131.
47. Hütter, *Dust*, 132.

quite clearly indicates that they desired the Kingdom without either knowing its exact shape or being capable of attaining it on their own. We will return to false expectations of the Kingdom presently, but none of these passages support a neo-Thomist anthropology.

It is important to note once again that this brief appeal to scriptural motifs of calling is not the heart of Hütter's account. Indeed, it is not at all clear that an appeal to Scripture can be anything other than a post-hoc gloss on Hütter's argument. For Hütter,

> Thomas is not concerned [in the texts on the natural desire to see God] with the concrete givens of the one obtaining order of providence … Any attempt to read particular statements or conclusions from Thomas's precisely delimited metaphysical argumentation here as *prima facie* theological claims about the obtaining order of providence as it coincides with the economy of salvation can only obfuscate the status of the conclusions reached.[48]

While Hütter is attempting to pinpoint just what exactly Thomas is and is not saying, the implication of his strategy is that—lest we disturb the metaphysical purity of Thomas's conclusions—it is unwise to bring Abraham, Israel, and the many into the argument at any of its formative stages. Only after Thomas and his commentators have done the metaphysical heavy-lifting without recourse to scripture or theology should we read scripture and do theology—at least in regard to the natural desire for the vision of God. With this methodology in place it is now clear how Hütter is so sure that Abraham did not desire his calling from God. Abraham did not desire his calling because Thomistic metaphysical inquiry has ruled out such a desire beforehand. But of course, Christian theology has traditionally been characterized as a reflection arising from scripture and its context in Christian worship, not to scripture and worship from *a priori* natural metaphysics.[49] Hütter recognizes the historical novelty of this procedure, and concedes that it is not strictly speaking how Thomas proceeds, even in the *Summa contra Gentiles*.[50] Nonetheless, Hütter maintains that this method is present enough in the structure of the *Summa contra Gentiles* to warrant using it as a programmatic hermeneutic, in spite of Thomas's occasional (mis?)uses of theology and scripture.

---

48. Hütter, *Dust*, 188.
49. See Lewis Ayres, *Nicea and Its Legacy* (Oxford: Oxford University Press, 2004), ch. 16. It is true that, as Hütter points out, Pope Benedict advocated metaphysical inquiry as its own proper science, but he never advocates subjecting scripture to this kind of *a priori* metaphysical analysis.
50. Hence, the "older discursive tradition" of commentarial Thomism "is not *the* oldest way of doing theology," Hutter, *Dust*, 140. As to Thomas's untidy deployment of theology and scripture in "philosophical" writings, see page 189: "A strict and clean separation between these two parts [i.e. theology and philosophy] is not possible. Elements of the one are clearly present in the other."

The historical novelty of this foundational metaphysics can be seen in light of de Lubac's recovery of patristic exegesis.[51] For de Lubac, it is the ancient practice of spiritual interpretation that contains and displays the entire vista of ancient faith. The spiritual interpretation of scripture is a "theory that even in its very form, owes everything to this Christian faith, and that, in its content, seeks to give it full expression"[52]; it contains "a whole mental universe"[53]; it is "a complete act."[54] The principles of spiritual exegesis lie, as de Lubac quotes Louis Bouyer, "at the heart of the Christian faith itself."[55] It is not that the Bible provided important data for theologians, and the Fathers were privileged interpreters of that data, but that exegesis was the very form of their religion, and the fourfold form of their exegesis contains and displays their entire theological paradigm. Christian theology was not founded on an *a priori* metaphysics, but on the sustained engagement of the church with Christ in Scripture. This is not to say that Christians have ever had access to the Bible unmediated by metaphysical assumptions and uninfluenced by philosophy. Far from it. But never has theological inquiry been so exclusively founded on natural metaphysics, and certainly not a metaphysic which exerts its right to proceed free from theology and scripture without returning the favor.[56]

De Lubac describes the shift to this protocol as the rise of "dialectical theology," which slowly displaced the older "symbolism" that had conceived and sustained spiritual interpretation.[57] *Medieval Exegesis* traces this decline of spiritual interpretation from Paul and Origin, through the Middle Ages into early modernity. Christian theologians had always attended to the *disputatio* of questions thrown up by history. By the twelfth century, such *disputatio* became a more clearly defined genre; "'questions' began to proliferate at an unprecedented rate."[58] The flowering of learning in the twelfth century renaissance sustained a new approach to knowledge, one that began to look more "scientific" and less mystical. By the thirteenth century, "the break has taken place; 'dialectic' and its 'questions' have won the day."[59] Fourfold exegesis remained "even after the advent of the Questions, even after the victory of the Summas," but it "was no longer

---

51. See Susan K. Wood, *Spiritual Exegesis and the Church in the Theology of Henri de Lubac* (Grand Rapids, MI: Eerdmans, 1998).
52. De Lubac, *ME* 1, 235.
53. De Lubac, *ME* 1, XIV.
54. De Lubac, *ME* 1, XIX.
55. De Lubac, *ME* 1, XX. Citing Louis Bouyer, *La vie de la liturgie* (Paris: Editions du Cerf, 1957), 261–2.
56. No doubt Hütter would object to this reading, but it seems to be the de facto status of a metaphysics that is in no way dependent on theology. See Chapter 5 in this volume for a discussion of the relation between theology and metaphysics.
57. See my account of this in the introductory chapter of this book. De Lubac gives this account in different forms throughout his work, but its core can be found in *Corpus Mysticum*, trans. Gemma Simmonds CJ (London: SCM Press, 2006), ch. 10.
58. *ME* 1, 60.
59. *ME* 1, 73.

the place where these vital elements [of exegesis, theology and spirituality] met, or rather, the place where they achieved union."[60] The spiritual interpretation of Scripture, always affirmed, "became a lifeless shell."[61] Under the dialectical impulse, scripture, while not necessarily eclipsed, was displaced from the center of theological inquiry.[62]

De Lubac unfolds the fourfold sense as given by a thirteenth-century distich which takes its cue from Thomas: the literal, the allegorical (we might call it christological/ecclesial), the tropological (moral), and the anagogical (eschatological). For Aquinas, "the literal sense is that which the author intends," and the author of scripture is God.[63] Because creation is divine speech, God communicates through events and things, not just words. Thus, the events and things portrayed in scripture are the bearers of meanings beyond themselves, meanings written into them by their author, God. The literal sense thus opens onto the spiritual contained within and beyond it.

The spiritual sense of scripture is always Jesus Christ and by extension the church. The four senses of scripture finally converge upon Jesus, the exegete par excellence, whose life is the very meaning of the text. Because of this, de Lubac only permits a christological and ecclesiological allegory. This is, for de Lubac, what sets Christian allegorical interpretation apart from its pagan uses. The meaning of all scripture is Christ, and by the unity he establishes with his body, the church. The remaining two spiritual senses follow from this. The moral sense is how we are to live as members of Christ's body. The eschatological sense is the hope toward which we live as his Body. But it is Christ who remains the definitive meaning of every text.

This call to return to the multiple senses of scripture has been enormously successful, with "theological," "spiritual," or "figural" interpretation of scripture becoming more common in biblical studies, alongside continuing theological reflection on the theme.[64] But in an important essay, Lewis Ayres points out that

---

60. *ME* 1, 74.

61. *ME* 1, 74.

62. Since de Lubac wrote this, a great deal has been published on Thomas as an exegete, and even on the centrality of exegesis to Thomas's task. See Thomas Prügl, "Thomas Aquinas as Interpreter of Scripture," in Rik Van Nieuwenhove and Joseph Wawrykow (eds.), *The Theology of Thomas Aquinas* (Notre Dame, IN: University of Notre Dame Press, 2005), 386–415.

63. *ST* I.1.9.

64. Examples in biblical studies include Richard Hays, *Reading Backward: Figural Christology and the Fourfold Gospel Witness* (London: SPCK, 2015); Walter Moberley, *Old Testament Theology: Reading the Hebrew Bible as Christian Scriptures* (Grand Rapids, MI: Baker Academic, 2013); Francis Watson, *Text and Truth: Redefining Biblical Theology* (Edinburgh: T&T Clark, 1997). Examples from theology include: Andrew Louth, *Discerning the Mystery* (Oxford: Clarendon Press, 1983); Ephraim Radner, *Time and the Word* (Grand Rapids, MI: Eerdmans, 2016); and many more.

biblical studies, even as it has embraced multivalent readings of scripture, has still failed to reckon with the anthropology required to sustain such readings.[65] The spiritual interpretation of scripture demands a robust notion of the soul, one which recognizes the central place of the soul in becoming an integral reader of scripture. Of the twofold division of scripture into literal and spiritual (letter and spirit), the three subdivisions of the spiritual sense are the realm of the soul. The soul learns to see Christ in the literal sense of scripture as it learns to read in the church (allegorically), is conformed to the image of Christ in faithful obedience (tropologically), and moves toward the fulfilment of its blessed calling in the eschaton (anagogically). These "levels" of interpretation are not extrinsically related to one another; they cohere in a single reality. In Ayres's words:

> Tropology discloses not simply the moral implications of Christian belief, but the shape of the life of one who lives within Christ, within the *ecclesia*. This disclosure is only possible when one has discovered the doctrinal matrix disclosed by allegorical reading. The two reading practices are thus part of one whole: the deeper one penetrates the mystery of God's action in Christ the more one comes to see how the action of Christ as and on the church is an action which shapes each Christian.[66]

The doctrine of multiple senses requires a robust account of the soul because it is the soul that the senses are meant to in-form. In spiritual reading, the action of God in Christ glimpsed in scripture becomes the action of Christ in the reader, forming a whole person into the image of God.

It is for this reason that exegesis, for de Lubac, is not primarily about "reading"; exegesis is primarily a mode of action, a way of being in the world. If learning to read scripture is a process of the development of the soul, then it will ultimately converge on action, a union of body and soul. This is why Christ is the exegete par excellence. While Christ is the meaning of scripture, since "the spirit of the letter is Christ,"[67] Christ is also its exegete: "Christ's exegesis, insofar as it is essential and decisive, does not consist of words first and foremost. It is actual. It is Action."[68] Before Christ explains scripture to the disciples on the Emmaus road, he fulfills scripture on the cross. Thus, the spiritual interpretation of scripture is a participation in Christ's exegetical action—it is to learn to live in time as Christ, truly becoming his body.

Such a christological reading is possible because the Old Testament is the history of the eternal Word unfolded through time.[69] Christ is not foreign to the

---

65. Lewis Ayres, "The Soul and the Reading of Scripture," *Scottish Journal of Theology* 61, no. 2 (2008), 173–90.
66. Ayres, "Soul," 175.
67. De Lubac, *ME* 1, 237.
68. De Lubac, *ME* 1, 238.
69. De Lubac, *ME* 1, 142.

Old Testament, not a "second layer" added onto a complete first layer, for the Old Testament is always-already the eternal Word spread through time. To interpret scripture spiritually, therefore, is to find Christ hidden both within and beyond the letter, and to learn to live according to Christ's own exegetical action. The Old Testament, then, is the symbol of Christ. It is a vast sign in which the ontological trace of Christ is hidden: Christ is the treasure hidden in the field of the literal sense. And here an entire trinitarian texture becomes clear, for to read Christ in the letter, to join symbolized to symbol, is to read *spiritually*. To read in the Spirit is to join in the Spirit's work of unity, discovering Christ hidden within and beyond his symbol, the Old Testament. This "reading," like the Spirit to the eternal Word, is not the impersonal recognition of meaning, but a wholly personal response in love. As the Spirit is the wholly personal agent of unity and love between Father and Son, so the spiritual exegete is the wholly personal agent in whom the meaning of the text is revealed and returned to God in an act of loving devotion.[70] To read the Word spoken in scripture by the Father is to join in the Spirit's work of uniting symbol and symbolized.

Buried not far beneath the surface of this analysis is an understanding of nature and grace.[71] The reason for this proximity is the unity of the divine Word. Creation is spoken in the same eternal Word who is hidden in the scriptural word. The book of nature and the book and scripture have the same eternal source, and both bear the same symbolic structure. Where Christ is hidden within and yet gratuitously beyond the letter of the Old Testament, so the incarnation reveals Christ to be hidden within and yet gratuitously beyond the "literal sense" of nature. The revelation of Christ in the New Testament presupposes, perfects, and does not destroy the Old Testament, but Christ is not wholly external or superadded to the Old Testament after the fact, for that would leave the unity of God's purposes divided.[72] In the same way, grace presupposes, perfects, and does not destroy nature, and this grace is not a wholly extrinsic addition to an otherwise natural perfection. Because there is only one Word, creation and redemption must be held together, even while being differentiated. It will not do to divide them into a sphere of pure nature, to which is later added an additional layer of perfection.[73] For that

---

70. This is not to deny the integrity of the Hebrew scriptures, for the spiritual sense presupposes the literal, and while the literal sense has its own historical integrity, the presence of Christ may be discerned within it *in faith*.

71. This isomorphism is noted by Susan Wood, *Exegesis*, 119, n. 148.

72. In de Lubac's words, "The second arises from the first and does not repudiate it. The second does not destroy the first. In fulfilling it, it gives it new life and renews it. It transfigures it." This is about scripture, but the isomorphism with nature/grace is abundantly clear. *ME* I, 228.

73. This is Feingold's understanding of pure nature: that there is a replete natural order, perfect in its own sphere, proportionate to its own ends, to which is superadded grace. That grace is accompanied by a new and second end, along with the resources to meet that end. Feingold, *Natural*, 336.

would divide Christ in whom all things were created and by whom all things are redeemed.

Human nature is thus suspended in the same way as the Old Testament. De Lubac highlights Jerome's articulation of the paradox: "such, according to Saint Jerome in his translation of Origen, is the double significance of the Greek word used by Saint Luke at the beginning of his Gospel, a word that can only be translated by the conjoined words 'fulfilled' and 'manifested'."[74] To fulfill implies a perfection not previously present; to manifest is to show a reality already present. As the New Testament both fulfills the Old and reveals what was always true of it, so grace both fulfills nature and reveals the dynamism always at work within it.

De Lubac understands this natural dynamism as the natural desire for the supernatural. De Lubac further identifies this desire with the nature of humanity as a created spirit. Here too, then, the trinitarian dimension is key, for to desire God by nature is to be a spirit—a finite participation in the eternal work of the Spirit as desire and love between Father and Son. In an unfinished draft of an essay on mysticism, de Lubac advocates this view in reference to a tripartite anthropology. He argues that Paul's usage in 1 Thess 5:23—"may your spirit and soul and body be kept sound and blameless"—is not just a haphazard borrowing from Platonic philosophy.[75] It is not actually platonic, for Paul substitutes *pneuma* for *nous* as the highest of the three. This difference is crucial, for de Lubac, since it recalls the Spirit/breath of God breathed into the first man in Gen 2:7. The difference is thus a biblical one, one that instantiates a link between God and humanity, a sharing in divine life. But this sharing is not some little portion of God that constitutes the human. The human *pneuma* is not the Holy Spirit. De Lubac points to Paul's usage in 1 Cor 2:11 ("who ... knows the secrets of a man if not the spirit of the man which is in him") to pinpoint the paradox. This is clearly not the Holy Spirit, for God's Spirit is compared to the human spirit in the next verse. Rather, this spirit is something in humanity that is nonetheless not of humanity:

> Thus, what par excellence makes a man, what constitutes man in his worth among the beings of the world, much more, what makes him a being superior to the world, would be an element that, rather than being "of man", would be "in man."[76]

De Lubac traces the ambiguity of *pneuma* through the patristic era: from Irenaeus who "spoke particularly of the Spirit of God, even when that Spirit, shared,

---

74. De Lubac, *ME* 1, 238; citing *In Luc.*, h. 1, Jerome's translation. See Joseph Fitzmyer, *The Gospel According to Luke (I–IX)* (New Haven, CT: Yale University Press, 2009), 292–3; Fitzmyer concludes that it means fulfill, picking up on the promise-fulfillment motif in Luke.

75. De Lubac, "Tripartite Anthropology," in *Theology in History*, trans. Anne Englund Nash (San Francisco, CA: Ignatius, 1996), 117.

76. De Lubac, "Tripartite," 129.

[becomes], by consent of the soul, the spirit of man,"[77] to Origen who spoke "more explicitly about the spirit of man, insofar as an opening to the Spirit of God."[78] This analysis continues through Augustine and Thomas. De Lubac summarizes:

> The *pneuma* that is "in man," in every man, assures a certain hidden transcendence of the man over himself, a certain opening, a certain received continuity between man and God. Not that there is the least identity of essence between the one and the other ... but it is, at the heart of man, the privileged place, always intact, of their encounter.[79]

The summary is of Origen, but the view is de Lubac's. The human spirit is the soul in self-transcendence, that is, in concourse with God. One way of stating this, but that de Lubac warns is open to misrepresentation, is that the spirit is the graced soul.[80] The danger is that this might falsely be taken to imply that there is some other part of the soul that could be described as "reason without grace," separable from the spirit.[81] Such a misconstrual only shows, de Lubac argues, that "the Pauline concept of *pneuma* is a concept 'of which our modern anthropologies can absolutely not take account.'"[82] Lewis Ayres summarizes de Lubac's position:

> At its "highest" or "deepest" the soul is *constituted* by a gift which is nevertheless its own and which enables contemplation of the Spirit and Christ whose life wells up within and through this gift: this gift is not truly "of" us but is "in" us.[83]

This anthropological truth is mirrored in the relation of the Testaments: at its deepest level the history of God's interaction with Israel is constituted by Christ who is nonetheless a gratuitous gift beyond Israel's expectations, a reading I will argue below from the first chapter of Luke. Moreover, this "suspension" of the Old Testament is an expression of the Spirit's work: Christ is present in the Old Testament by the Spirit; Christ is the spirit of the letter.[84] In spiritual exegesis, the spirit of the letter calls out to the human spirit, deep unto deep, that the whole human, body, soul, and spirit might be formed more fully into the image of God.[85]

---

77. De Lubac, "Tripartite," 136.
78. De Lubac, "Tripartite," 136.
79. De Lubac, "Tripartite," 141.
80. De Lubac, "Tripartite," 126.
81. De Lubac, "Tripartite," 126.
82. De Lubac, "Tripartite," 129; quoting Max-Alain Chevallier, *Esprit de Dieu* (Paris: Delachaux and Niestle, 1966).
83. Ayres, "Soul," 181.
84. De Lubac, *ME* I, 261.
85. De Lubac should not be understood as arguing that human nature is *essentially* spirit to the exclusion of soul and body, for the human spirit is only finally formed by exegetical *action*, which is embodied action in time. Hütter mistakenly ascribes this view to him. Hütter, *Dust*, 213.

This isomorphism is of course not an identification. The Thomist reading of nature and grace is a metaphysical analysis, whereas the relation of Old to New Testament is theological and historical. The Old Testament is the record of God's dealings with Israel, and so presupposes the work of grace. So I am not suggesting that the Old Testament just is nature and the New Testament just is grace, certainly not that the Old Testament is a purely natural reality and the New a supernatural one. I am, however, attempting to think the metaphysics of nature and grace in dialogue with the history of God's action in the world, the nature of God's triune life, and the Christian discipline of spiritual exegesis. And herein is the key difference between de Lubac and neo-Thomists both new and old. De Lubac's anthropology, because rooted in the interpretation of scripture, remains tethered to history. According to the theology assumed by patristic exegesis, history is exhaustively defined by its relation to the death and resurrection of God incarnate and the sending of the Spirit.[86] Spiritual interpretation of scripture is "an entire theology of history."[87] It organizes the whole scope of human history and meaning "around a concrete center, which is fixed in time and space by the Cross of Jesus Christ."[88] Nothing remains untouched by God's action in the world:

> Time and space, heaven and earth, angels and men, the Old Testament and the New, the physical universe and the moral universe, *nature and grace*: everything is encompassed, bound together, formed, "structured," and unified by this Cross, even as everything is dominated by it.[89]

While Hütter celebrates Feingold's complete disregard for history, which is, let us be clear, the sidelining of the entire scriptural witness to God's action in the world, de Lubac aims to reclaim a theology inseparable from exegesis, inseparable from the *history* of God in the world. For it is only in the telling of this history that my own history might finally be meaningfully illuminated.[90]

There are trinitarian reasons for thinking that any analysis of human nature will need to center on the history of God in Scripture and not be the sole purview of *a priori* and ahistorical metaphysics. Recall that for Thomas, creation is spoken in the Father's speaking of the Word. He conceptualizes this as creation being contained in the divine ideas. But the life of creation, its movement through time back toward God, is the life of the Spirit. And, crucially, the Son is never without

---

86. On the Spirit, see De Lubac, "The Sense Given by the Spirit" in *ME* I, 261–7.
87. De Lubac, *ME* I, XIX.
88. De Lubac, *ME* I, XIX.
89. De Lubac, *ME* 1, 111, emphasis mine. See also *ME* I, 239: "By this sacrament of the Cross, he unites the two Testaments into a single body of doctrine, intermingling the ancient precepts with the grace of the Gospel."
90. Hütter, *Dust*, 138. On de Lubac's understanding of history and scripture, see the excellent article by William M. Wright, "Patristic Exegetical Theory and Practice in de Lubac and Congar," *New Blackfriars* 96, no. 1061 (January 2015), 61–73.

the Spirit. If one is to think of humanity, one must attend to the ways human beings are *living* beings, caught up in histories not entirely their own. And this requires thinking of them as always-already in movement through time, always-already called in grace. In the language I have been developing, humanity is symbol—as a temporal unfolding of the eternal Word—and the symbol cannot be understood in isolation from *symbolism*, from the movement of desire and love back toward the symbolized that constitutes the symbol as a symbol. The account of that motion is given in scripture, and the actualization of that motion comes from the spiritual reading of scripture, from embodied exegesis of its spiritual senses. There is no Son without Spirit, no symbol without symbolism: human nature cannot be understood apart from its fundamental relation to the Trinity, created with a natural desire for a supernatural destiny. As Thomas would say, "There are two reasons why the knowledge of the divine persons was necessary for us. It was necessary for the right idea of creation ... In another way, and chiefly, that we may think rightly concerning the salvation of the human race."[91] The road between creation and redemption is trinitarian, and neither can be understood without this Logos and Spirit, this logic and life.

Thus, while I am not arguing discursively from spiritual exegesis to the natural desire, I am arguing that the isomorphism between the spiritual interpretation of scripture and nature–grace commends de Lubac's understanding of the natural desire as a dynamic fitting of the history of God's dealings with his people. To think of natures in motion in this way presses us into the realm of narrative, in particular, the narrative of God's engagement with creation through his people. Narratives do not operate on the rules of logical necessity, but have an aesthetic logic all their own, what the medievals called *convenientia*, or fittingness. Denys Turner has described *convenientia* as "narrative necessity," an aesthetic fittingness to what went before and what comes after, like a Mozart melody that does not have to end the way it does but only seems right the way Mozart ended it.[92] Thomas appeals to fittingness to account for the propriety of divine action in history. The category of *convenientia* enables Thomas to articulate why it is appropriate for God to be revealed through the material history of the literal sense of scripture and above all in the incarnation.[93] The incarnation, and the revelation of God in scripture, for Thomas, are not strictly necessary given God's omnipotence, but the most fitting ways to accomplish the divine plan.[94] There is a narrative necessity to God's revelation in scripture and the incarnation. This is the most fitting action

---

91. *ST* 1a.32.1.ad 3.

92. See Denys Turner, *Faith, Reason and the Existence of God* (Cambridge: Cambridge University Press, 2004), 243–5; he puts this idea to work in *Julian of Norwich Theologian* (New Haven, CT: Yale University Press, 2011), 44–5.

93. Scripture: *ST* 1a.1.9-10; Incarnation: *ST* 3a.1.

94. Cf. John Milbank and Catherine Pickstock, *Truth in Aquinas* (New York: Routledge, 2001), ch. 3.

God could have taken, a beautiful harmony of God's character as self-diffusive goodness and the multivalent effectiveness of the incarnation.

This coordination of God's character and the shape of the narrative relies on an "aesthetic" judgment that what God has done is appropriate for God. And this turns on an account of beauty. As Thomas Sammon has argued, for Thomas beauty is "the *ratio* of being that orients the good to the cognitive faculties."[95] Beauty is what makes the good intelligible, that which draws the intellect into "being's intensive depths." The reason for this is that beauty is founded on the relation between the Son and the Father: as the Son draws us into the Father, so beauty draws us into being. The *integritas, proportio,* and *claritas,* of the Son's representation of the Father are the archetype of every beautiful thing, each of which re-present the beauty of the filial relation by re-presenting beauty itself.[96] Because creation is spoken in the eternal Word, every individual component of creation exhibits beauty to the extent that it participates in the eternal utterance of the Father.[97] Fittingness is the extent to which divine action in time conforms to the eternal reality of the Word, which is why the incarnation is the supreme moment of fittingness, for by it the Word takes on a human nature, perfectly—and paradoxically!—fitting created life to divine life. While this was not strictly necessary in a logical sense, and was not in any way owed to nature, it was a narrative necessity founded on the character of God as self-diffusive goodness, and the nature of creation as the unfolding of the eternal Word. We recognize the events and things of scripture and the incarnation as divine revelation because of the integrity, proportion and clarity with which they express the divine life. It is the beautiful relation of the symbols of scripture to Christ, and the beautiful relation of the symbol of Christ's humanity to his divinity that allows us to recognize God in him. The spiritual interpretation of scripture is thus the search for these harmonious resonances, it is an "aesthetic" exercise in finding God in the beautiful correlations between creaturely life and divine life.

We could never recognize God's self-diffusive goodness if it were not beautiful, for we would have no inherent attraction to it, no reason to want to know it. Just as we only know the Father in the Son, so we only know goodness in its beauty, which is why Feingold and Hütter's appeal to *convenientia* as a construal of nature and grace does not really resolve the issue.[98] They argue that grace is fitting to nature, not by any necessity latent in nature as such (and so not logically necessary), but

---

95. Thomas Brendan Sammon, *The God Who Is Beauty: Beauty as a Divine Name in Thomas Aquinas and Dionysius the Areopagite* (Cambridge: James Clarke Company, 2014), 341. The theologian most well known for work in aesthetics is undoubtedly Hans Urs von Balthasar, *The Glory of the Lord: A Theological Aesthetics*, 7 vols (San Francisco, CA: Ignatius Press, 1984–90); also influential is Gilbert Narcisse, *Les Raisons de Dieu* (Fribourg: Éditions Universitaires Fribourg Suisse, 1997).

96. ST I.39.8.

97. Sammon, Beauty, 349: "What makes the participant beauty-filled, one might say, is a procession from beauty itself as a creaturely recapitulation of the Son's procession."

98. Feingold, *Natural*, 425. Hütter, *Dust*, 179.

in the way that we can recognize God's action after the fact as something befitting of God. Grace fits nature as an aesthetic rightness. This, for Feingold, preserves the possibility or "non-absurdity" of God creating an intellectual creature in pure nature. But this merely defers and does not answer the question. For to rely on the category of fittingness is to rely on an aesthetic construal of nature and grace, which is an appeal to beauty. Grace is thus the elevation of nature that is supremely beautiful. But how can a human recognize the call of grace as a fitting or beautiful and so a desirable elevation of its nature, if humans do not have a natural inclination toward beauty itself? It would seem that the category of fittingness only works if humans have a natural desire for ultimate beauty, a desire for the vision of God only available in the Son.

This *desire* for beauty is itself a finite participation in the Spirit, who forever joins symbol to symbolized. If beauty is the proportion between symbol and symbolized, the Spirit is the desire for this proportion and the love of it once found. Again we see that even in the register of the aesthetic, the human spirit is an absolute desire for the vision of God. In terms of scripture, what connects the literal sense to the spiritual senses is this same Spirit. Only the Spirit can unlock the presence of Christ hidden within and beyond the literal sense. It is, for this reason, spiritual exegesis: a reading in the Spirit. Our own transcendence is expressed by this same word, we are spirit because we long to transcend the confines of our nature, to be joined to that which we symbolize. We are symbols, and this means we long for union with the symbolized. Thus even after our neo-Thomist metaphysicians punt the ball into the realm of aesthetics, it remains a question of God the Trinity and the natural human desire for this ultimate source and end.

This appeal to *convenientia*, then, is an appeal to a beautiful narrative, a story of a life in time demarcated by fitting symbols. This life is *beautiful* to the extent that it participates in the Son's representation of the Father, and it is *life* to the extent that it participates in the dynamic movement of the Spirit between Father and Son. What the patristic practice of exegesis points to is the hidden transcendence embedded within the literal sense of our natures, which can nonetheless only be fulfilled by grace. It is, moreover, only in the living exegesis of this scripture in prayer, liturgy, and love of others that such a desire can be satisfied. The spiritual interpretation of scripture indeed contains "a whole mental universe";[99] it is indeed "a complete act."[100] Both turn on a trinitarian logic of symbols. Symbols long for union with the symbolized, a longing called symbolism. One cannot think of the human as a symbol of God without thinking of the movement of desire and love at once "in" nature but not "of" nature, for the Son is never without the Spirit. The understanding of the Trinity is thus necessary for the right idea of creation and salvation, nature, and grace. We come to know the Trinity and conform to the life of the Trinity in the spiritual reading of scripture. And to sever our analysis

---

99. De Lubac, *ME* 1, XIV.
100. De Lubac, *ME* 1, XIX.

of human nature from the trinitarian witness of scripture is indeed supremely unfitting.

Lest this analysis remain entirely abstract, I turn now to an exegesis of scripture. When the natural desire is brought to fulfilment in living exegesis, the result is an incarnation: the body of Christ is born in the spiritual exegesis of scripture. This is nowhere more evident than in Mary's exegesis of Israel's scriptures. There she discovers a destiny at once intrinsic to Israel's and her own history, and yet in gratuitous excess of Israel's and her own greatest desires and expectations. Her reading of the symbols in her very own life brings God into the world.

Mary the Exegete

Luke is concerned to narrate the story of Jesus as "the continuation of the story of Israel,"[101] and goes so far as to imitate septugintal Greek to "begin [his] Christian Gospel as though it were a part of Israel's Scriptures."[102] In typical Lukan fashion, the arrival of Gabriel to the Virgin Mary recalls without quoting Daniel's encounter with the same angel. In Daniel, Gabriel arrives with the declaration that Daniel is "greatly beloved" and prophesies the forgiveness of sin, atonement, and an anointed one abandoned to death. This whole context is invoked in Gabriel's appearance to Mary, both foreshadowing the ministry of Christ and placing Mary in the context of Israel's scriptures. Luke thus depicts Mary as between the Old Testament and the New, the promise and its fulfillment, suspended between a destiny greatly desired but as yet unknown.

With Luke, Old Testament imagery comes thick and fast. Having invoked Daniel 8 and 9, with its apocalyptic and messianic overtones, Gabriel then paraphrases the Davidic promises of 2 Samuel 7 and Psalm 89: Jesus's greatness, sonship, eternal reign and eternal kingdom are all direct citations of God's promises to David.[103] This places this moment at the very center of God's work in the world: "Luke places the fulfillment of the promise to David at the heart of his promise-fulfillment scheme—not in isolation, but as the epitome and summation of the promises, oaths, and covenants which God made to his people."[104] On this annunciation rests all the promises of God's history with his people, and through them the entire created order. This is the fulfillment long promised and long desired. Founded in

---

101. Michael Wolter, *The Gospel According to Luke*, trans. Wayne Coppins and Christopher Heilig (Waco, TX: Baylor University Press, 2016), 25.

102. David Ravens, *Luke and the Restoration of Israel*, Journal for Study of the New Testament Supplement Series 119 (Sheffield: Sheffield Academic Press, 1995), 29.

103. Combining imagery from Daniel and David is common in first-century messianic texts, especially Enoch and 4 Ezra, see Mark Strauss, *The Davidic Messiah in Luke-Acts* (Edinburgh: T&T Clark, 1995), 46–7; for a discussion of parallels between Gabriel's annunciation and Davidic promises, see pages 88–9.

104. Strauss, *Davidic*, 97.

the Abrahamic promise, deepened in the Davidic, tested and refined in exile, this is the moment Israel has desired, a desire now concentrated in Mary.

But this does not mean that Mary's desire comprehends its object. Gabriel's promise of fulfillment from Israel's messianic calling is met by a question from nature: "How can this be, since I have no husband?" Such a response is part of the literary form of angelic birth announcements. The recipient is expected to respond with a question, but in Mary's case the question takes on a new potency. The bare physical fact is urgent enough. The promise will require a profound physical miracle. But the question from Israelite history is equally urgent: God has often delivered his people by miraculous birth, but this has never been accomplished by a *virgin* birth. An elderly Sarah, a barren Hannah, the barren mother of Samson, these are among the Israelite women who would miraculously conceive by otherwise-normal sexual means. But this cannot be the case with Mary. Mary's response is thus more profound than Zechariah's, whose question regarding the conception of John could just as well be found on the lips of Abraham, Elkanah, or Manoah. John's birth is a miracle wholly in keeping with Old Testament precedent.[105] But Mary's question has no precedent; no one could have anticipated this kind of fulfillment.

An unfortunate feature of popular theology and well-intentioned apologetics is to assume the evangelists considered scripture a catalogue of prophecies to be checked off a list. *None* of the gospel writers treat scripture this way.[106] Rather, under the impact of Christ's work and the power of the Spirit, Christians learned to "read backward," seeing Christ everywhere in places not previously expected.[107] Luke sees Jesus as integral to the Old Testament—truly its content and purpose—but nonetheless a surpassing perfection of it. Thus, while the virgin birth is only intelligible as the fulfillment of the promises at the heart of Israel's identity, it arrives as something completely new and unanticipatable.[108]

Gabriel's answer is stunning. We should not allow familiarity to obscure its strangeness: "The Holy Spirit will come upon you, and the power of the Most High will overshadow you; therefore the child to be born will be called holy, the Son of God."[109]

While David, the king and Israel itself are said to be the "son of God," this is always in the context of *adoption* for a particular purpose. The Spirit is likewise shown to give life to creation, individuals, and the dead, but this is never linked

---

105. John is thereby placed in the lineage of prophets, and according to Jesus in Luke 7:26, more than a prophet.

106. See Richard Hays, *Echoes of Scripture in the Gospels* (Waco, TX: Baylor University Press, 2016), 192.

107. This is Richard Hays's phrase. Hays, *Echoes*, 5.

108. See Strauss, *Davidic*, 29: "One of Luke's central purposes is to show that Jewish expectations concerning the messiah were inadequate and incomplete."

109. Lk 1:35.

with sonship.¹¹⁰ Nowhere is the Spirit's *creative* power associated with the identity of a Son of God.¹¹¹ While David is adopted as a son in order to be king of God's people, Jesus is both Son and King from his conception. His sonship and kingship are not functions of his calling; rather, his sonship and kingship are his identity.

The surpassing quality of this miracle can only be seen if we read diachronically. Richard Hays advocates "reading backward," learning to read the Old Testament in light of Christ. This, he argues, is the strategy of the New Testament authors, and he is undoubtedly correct. But "reading backward" should be qualified: only *after* reading forward is reading backward possible.¹¹² The symbols of the Old Testament are fundamental to recognizing the symbolized, that is, Christ. Only in *this* symbolic world in which Davidic kings are sons of God, is Christ recognized as the King-Son par excellence. Only in the symbolic world of Sarah, the mother of Samson and especially Hannah is Mary's miraculous conception seen to be a deliverance beyond all others. The danger of reading backward is that it can abstract the story from history as a process through time. As Rowan Williams points out, a reading that claims to perceive the whole from the end implies a total spatialization of the text, which, like a painting can be glimpsed all at once.¹¹³ But a story, in contrast to a painting, must be traced, followed in its ambiguities and undulations through time. It is only in attending to the time of the text that a reader may engage its literal sense. This is simply the logic of symbolism, for we only have access to the symbolized in its symbols. We only come to know God through the material conditions of life in time—there is no access to God unmediated by material history. This is, moreover, why spiritual exegesis is ecclesial exegesis, for to read across time requires a material community that has learned to speak the language of the symbols, that has come to inhabit the symbolic world given by the literal sense of the text. This is one significance of Luke's use of septuagintal Greek. It places Luke in a concrete interpretive community (Second Temple, Greek-speaking Judaism), and it is Luke's inclusion in this community that enables him to "read backward" from Christ. There can therefore be no sharp distinction between the time of Israel and the time of Christ, as has been influentially argued by Hans Conzelmann, for such a sharp distinction

---

110. Gen. 1:2; Ps. 33:6; Job 33:4; Ps. 104:30 and others. See the references at Strauss, *Davidic*, 91.

111. Strauss concludes that this is Luke's "original application of the creative role of the Spirit," *Davidic*, 91.

112. This is advocated by Hans Frei's reading of Calvin's exegetical practice. Hans Frei, *The Eclipse of the Biblical Narrative: A Study of Eighteenth and Nineteenth Century Hermeneutics* (New Haven, CT: Yale University Press, 1974), 36; cited in Hays, *Echoes*, 370 n. 15.

113. Rowan Williams, "The Literal Sense of Scripture," *Modern Theology* 7, no. 2 (January 1991), 121–34.

would destroy Luke's entire reading strategy.[114] It is the continuity of a community reading forward that enables Luke to read backward.

Reading forward allows us to see the stunning newness of Christ. Between John the Prophet and Jesus the Messiah there is a fundamental qualitative difference.[115] Mary's question from nature, which is also a question from history and a question from scripture is a question of how this difference can be bridged: "How can this be, since I have no husband"? Gabriel's answer is the Holy Spirit. What connects these scriptural promises, motifs, and metaphors with this fulfillment in the body of this woman? The Spirit, the original "symbolic inclusion" between Father and Son, continuing its work of unity, drawing these scriptural symbols into unity with the Symbolized in the body of the Virgin. It is this act of symbolism in Mary's history that brings about the incarnation.

Even in Mary's acceptance of this divine calling, Luke is pointing us to the Old Testament. Joel 2:29 prophecies that God's Spirit will be poured out on female servants. Mary's response, "I am the handmaiden of the Lord," contains an exact verbal correlate to the translation of Joel 2:29 in the Septuagint.[116] It is, moreover, this passage from Joel that frames Peter's Pentecost sermon. The birth narratives thus have a strikingly pentecostal quality, and Pentecost an annunciatory quality. Nearly every participant in the first two chapters is filled with the Spirit, and that Spirit-filling is what enables them to recognize Christ as Israel's Messiah. When Mary who has conceived by the Holy Spirit comes to Elizabeth, Elizabeth is filled with the Spirit and proclaims, "Why is this granted me, that the mother of *my Lord* should come to me?"[117] Gabriel announced that John would be filled with the Spirit from the womb. When this Spirit-filled gestational John recognizes the presence of Jesus, he leaps for joy. Those filled with the Spirit recognize Christ *as the fulfillment of Israel's scripture*, at once at home in those scriptures and yet beyond them. As Joseph Fitzmyer argues, the "assurance" that Luke promises Theophilus is not the product of Luke's faithful recording of the finer points of the apostolic *kerygma* but is the gift of the Holy Spirit.[118] Elizabeth recognizes Christ, John rejoices because of him, Mary carries him, and we are led by Luke to join these characters in worship *by the Spirit*. Luke thereby foreshadows the descent of the Spirit at Pentecost where a community of Christ-followers is formed by the

---

114. Conzelmann proposes a threefold theology of history in Luke: the time of Israel, the time of Jesus, and the time of the church. Scholars are divided on its validity. To sustain his reading, Conzelmann dismisses the birth narratives as inauthentic, a move that has been nearly universally critiqued. Hans Conzelmann, *The Theology of Saint Luke*, trans. G. Buswell (London: Faber and Faber, 1961).

115. Strauss, *Davidic*, 23: "Jesus is presented as the messianic king promised to Israel. Yet he fulfills the Old Testament promises in a new and surprising way."

116. Ravens, *Restoration*, 27.

117. Luke 1:43. Fitzmyer, *Luke*, 363: "Elizabeth is filled with the Spirit and inspired to interpret the sign thus given to her."

118. Fitzmyer, *Luke*, 13.

filling of the Spirit. Here in Luke's opening scenes, we the readers are invited to join two women and two babies for the first Christian church service, which is nothing other than a recognition of Christ as the gratuitous fulfillment of scripture.[119]

Mary's receptivity in her *fiat* should not be overplayed. Her acceptance of the divine calling is an act of boldness and freedom. In his book defending the Christian humanism of Pico della Mirandola, De Lubac describes human dignity: "*la dignité suprême de l'homme réside avant tout, essentiellement, disons même uniquement dans la liberté.*"[120] That liberty is not humanity's ability to choose between options, but is rather the freedom of spirit, the freedom to transcend the boundaries of nature by participation in the life of the Holy Spirit.[121] Mary's *fiat* is thus a supreme act of freedom in which Mary transcends all the natural expectation of her cultural history to achieve a union with God unimaginable in any prior epoch and unequalled since. This freedom in transcendence is a constitutive part of Mary's identity as the highly favored one and is expressed in her radical reinterpretation of Scripture. In the Magnificat Mary interprets scripture *spiritually*, that is, in the freedom of transcendence that allows her to move both with and beyond the literal sense. She rearranges scripture, especially the song of Hannah, around her own life and calling as an expression of her own supreme transcendent freedom.

Mary reinterprets scripture in the Magnificat, and in freedom she provides new meanings to old songs, re-centering them on herself and her son. In her hands, the song of Hannah, as well as in a secondary way those of Miriam, Deborah, and Judith, and a great many other Psalms and prophecies, are recast in light of the outpouring of the Spirit. This is funded, in the first instance, by an understanding of the literal sense of Hannah's song. Hannah was a barren woman who prayed for son. She then dedicated that son to the Lord's service, becoming the prophet Samuel who was to anoint David. God's miraculous provision for her was also God's provision for the whole of Israel. It is the literal sense of this story that funds any connection to Mary's. And so Mary takes up the story precisely because of its literal continuity with her own.

But Mary does not stop there, for the literal story of Hannah opens onto the story of what God is doing in history now, that is, it opens onto God's provision for his people in Christ. As the story looks forward to the birth of Christ, the entire song of Mary takes on christic meanings: God shows his strength, casts down the proud and exalts the lowly, remembers his mercy and helps his servant Israel *in Christ*. And God's action in Christ is the culmination of his mercy "from generation to generation."[122] With all its pentecostal overtones, the Magnificat thus

---

119. This motif continues: both Zechariah and Simeon are filled with the Spirit; Anna, though the Spirit is not mentioned, her proximity to the story of Simeon and her role as temple prophetess would all imply the role of the Spirit.

120. Henri De Lubac, *Pico Della Mirandole* (Paris: Aubier Montaigne, 1974), 64.

121. De Lubac, *Pic*, 66.

122. Lk 1:50.

looks forward to the church as the community of the Spirit continuing Mary's work of reinterpreting scripture.[123] The history of Hannah, the literal sense of scripture, thus opens onto the allegorical sense of Christ and his church in Mary's song.

The Magnificat is, moreover, a kind of moral response from Mary. Exalting the Lord and rejoicing in God are not spontaneous and uncontrollable spasms of excitement. Mary has *decided* to accept God's calling, she has "believed that there would be a fulfillment," she has taken the decision to visit Elizabeth, and has wrapped her self-understanding of all these decisions in the clothing of Hannah's song. Scripture has opened for Mary onto a tropological plane: she must now act, and inasmuch as that action is an exegesis of scripture, it is also an enormous risk. She is risking the violence of history. Here is no prescinding from the real. In taking God into her body, she risks everything, as Simeon will make clear to her in chapter 2. Yet she embraces this calling not because loss and diminishment are key to human existence. Mary risks because in a fallen world scripture requires moral actions that the world cannot recognize or understand. The sword that pierces Mary's heart is not good in itself, but Mary shares in Christ's tasting of the evil of the world so that, as Paul will say, she might share in his glory.

And if Mary's exegesis is her action risked in time, then it also looks forward to the end of time. All generations will call Mary blessed, God is merciful toward those who fear him from generation to generation, and finally, tying it all together, God's promises to "our fathers" are given "to Abraham and to his posterity forever." The fulfillment of these promises is nothing other than God himself, who is faithful to all generations who fear him, now and forever. Mary's song is in fact a delicate balance of past, present, and future. Luke has her consistently use the *aorist* tense, giving most of the song the appearance of an orientation toward the past. This would perhaps be the shape of the song sung in a worship setting recalling God's past provision for Israel. But the immediate context implies God's present action. This serves to rhetorically underline the rootedness of God's present action in Israel's history,[124] a way of saying that what is happening now is the fullness of what happened then. The allusions to the eschatological day of the Lord then ensure that this song covers all time: Hannah's deliverance, God's present action in the world (and Mary's action in response), and God's future and final action. The Magnificat thus plays between the literal, analogical, tropological, and anagogical senses.

This reading is only possible by the Holy Spirit. In the opening chapters of Luke, only those filled with the Spirit recognize Christ as the Messiah, foreshadowing Pentecost. Symbolism is an apt description of what is happening in these passages. Jesus is symbolized in the diverse symbols of Old Testament messianic expectations, but the only way to join them together is by the Spirit, the unity between symbolized and symbol that is symbolism. This finds ultimate expression in Mary; the symbols of Old Testament expectations and the Symbolized, Christ,

---

123. Luke clearly has Pentecost in mind as he writes his infancy narratives. See Ravens, *Restoration*, 27.

124. See Ravens, *Restoration*, 36.

are literally joined together by the Spirit in Mary's own body. Mary thereby becomes the paradigm of spiritual exegesis as her understanding of Christ in scripture becomes her own embodied action in the world.

This mode of exegesis is not unique to Mary's high calling. Rather, she has embodied precisely the kind of exegesis that every person is invited into. She has read the symbols, including the symbol she has been called to be, an interpretive endeavor that involves her whole life: body, soul, and spirit. In ascending through the senses of scripture, Mary discovers that stories she has known her entire life contain a hidden transcendence, an inner dynamism at once constitutive of them and yet from beyond them. She makes those stories her own when by the power of the Spirit she transcends all cultural and historical nature to become the mother of God. The result is incarnation. The Word has taken on flesh, the Symbol has arrived in time, unlocking all symbols and revealing their ultimate referent. Thereafter, all of life becomes a kind of spiritual exegesis, and all exegesis becomes a kind of incarnation. What is born into the world is Christ and christological, the one who bears Christ is Christian and mariological.

Mary thus embodies both the desire and the gratuitous surprise of the relation between the testaments. That relation, I am arguing, shares a profound isomorphism with the relation of nature and grace. Like the hidden transcendence that Mary discovers in the song of Hannah, so nature has a natural desire for the supernatural, a calling at once its own and yet wholly beyond it. To receive Christ as the fulfillment of that desire is to learn to read in the Spirit, to discover Christ hidden within and beyond the literal sense of human nature, as Mary discovers Christ hidden within and beyond the literal sense of the Old Testament. Thus, a trinitarian logic of symbols sustains both a theology of scripture and an anthropology as symbols that must be read together in the symbolism of the Spirit. Christ is born into the world wherever his people learn to read themselves as symbols in a story written by God, little words and little spirits, symbols and symbolism in motion back to the Father. It is to this motion toward God that I now turn. The church, I will argue, is symbolism, the unity of desire and love between God and creation.

Chapter 4

ECCLESIOLOGY

Introduction

As outlined in the introduction, de Lubac first uses the term "symbolism" in *Corpus Mysticum*, a groundbreaking work that tracks changes in ecclesiology and attempts to account for them in terms of the demise of "symbolism."[1] Symbolism was a mode of doing theology that enabled theologians from the patristic era to the high Middle Ages to hold together diverse topics and diverse disciplines in one vibrant whole—Ecclesiology and Christology, prayer and theology, reason and mysticism, etc. The church was "symbolically included" in the eucharist, and both church and eucharist were symbolically included in the mystery of Christ. So close were their relationships that to say something about one was to say something about the other, a kind of exchange of idioms between the symbolized and the symbol. And the cast of mind that allowed theologians to read these symbols and thereby unite symbols with the symbolized, de Lubac calls symbolism. There is thus a threefold pattern to the structure of de Lubac's thought: symbolized–symbol–symbolism. I have developed this in trinitarian terms as the Father, the Son/Word, and the Spirit who unites Son to Father and Father to Son. Creation, in turn, is a symbol of God, as the unfolding of the Logos through time, animated by the symbolism of the Spirit. Humanity is the summit of this unfolding, the little word and little spirit desirous by nature for its source and end in the triune life of God. This natural desire can only be fulfilled by grace, the utterly free gift of God's very self. Creation, in humanity, participates in the original symbolic movement of God, and the structures of this movement frame the structures of life in time.

The triad symbolized–symbol–symbolism is not a reified ontic thing; it is, rather, a structure of relations. The structure of relations does not fix things in ontic space; it rather attempts to narrate theological themes and topics in terms of the relations by which they subsist. This structure of relations allows me to examine diverse topics within a logic governed by trinitarian theology—without thereby lapsing into a crude personalism or social trinitarianism: "There can

---

1. Henri De Lubac, *Corpus Mysticum*, trans. Gemma Simmonds CJ (London: SCM, 2006), 221–47.

be no question, we must repeat, of merely transposing into the natural order what faith teaches us about the supernatural world: that would be to transform the divine reality, which must be believed and lived in mystery—*mysterium unitatis*—into a dangerous kind of secularization."[2] The triad, then, is a contemplative tool, a way of exploring all things in relation to God. While this method certainly has its limits, it allows me to examine diverse topics under a trinitarian unifying theme.

As I turn to ecclesiology, I will deploy the triad in two ways. The first is an examination of the threefold body of Christ. I will argue that prior to the late Middle Ages, the threefold body was understood with Christ–church–eucharist corresponding to symbolized–symbol–symbolism. The church was the symbol of Christ, his true presence in the world, while the eucharist was the dynamic union of church with Christ, symbol with symbolized. This configuration slowly evolved until the last two terms were switched: the eucharist came to be seen as the symbol of Christ, his real presence, while the church came to be seen as symbolism, the external structure that guaranteed the unity of the eucharist with Christ. This is a "rescription" of the story de Lubac tells in *Corpus Mysticum*. My aim is to illuminate the inner-relations of the threefold body as the One Body of Christ, the *totus Christus* in motion through time toward God.

The second inquiry considers the One Body—the eucharistic church in union with its head—in relation to creation and God. The resulting speculation is that the One Body can be appropriated to symbolism, the dynamic unity of creation the symbol with God the symbolized. The church in its life and especially its sacraments returns creation to God in praise, not as a contrast to creation, but as the revelation of its deepest life. In this way we can understand de Lubac's assertion that the church is a sacrament. It unites creation to God, symbol to symbolized.

To say the church is a sacrament is to say it is causes what it signifies. But this creates two concerns. In an engagement with two contrasting texts from John Webster, I will show that this "sacramental causality" is not Pelagian. Then, in an engagement with Louis-Marie Chauvet, I will show that this is not ontotheological. My own language of symbols—distinct from, though closely related to Chauvet's—has the benefit of uniting a sacramental ecclesiology to trinitarian theology, making reflection on the church itself a site of meditation on the being of God, an ascent through the chain of symbols to the eternal and transcendent "play" of symbolized–symbol–symbolism, Father–Son–Spirit.

Symbolism and Ecclesiology

In *Corpus Mysticum*, de Lubac traces shifts in the meanings and uses of its two eponymous words. The words *Corpus Mysticum* originally applied to the eucharist

---

2. Henri De Lubac, *Catholicism*, trans. Lancelot Sheppard and SrElizabeth Englund, OCD (San Francisco, CA: Ignatius, 1988), 364.

as the body of Christ in its sacramental state; "mystery" and its related words had always been used in relation to sacraments. It denoted a liturgical act, something done or celebrated. What was accomplished in that act issued in the unity of the church, the ecclesial body of Christ. Hence, the eucharist makes the church. De Lubac traces the slow severing of this link between the eucharist and the church, as the words *corpus mysticum* evolved to signify the ecclesial body, eventually taken in isolation from its eucharistic center. The driving factor in this evolution was the conflict with Barengar, for whom the traditional phrase "mystical body," when applied to the eucharist, meant less-than-real. The word "mystical," under the impulse of dialectical rationalism, had come to be opposed to real. Traditional terminology thus shifted to account for this new meaning. Challenging Barengar's conclusion, but not his rationalism, theology eventually—if grudgingly—ceded the ground and adjusted its terminology accordingly. The eucharist became the true body of Christ, real presence winning the day over any references to "mystical" presence, now in danger of non-realist interpretation. This had the effect of sidelining the eucharistic center of the church, since the key issue was not how the eucharist made the church a unified body, but how the eucharist was the true body of Christ. The ecclesial and social implications of the eucharist were diminished in favor of real presence. I think this story can be helpfully illuminated with the triad I have developed—which terms are assigned to which realities is enormously consequential.

Christ–Church

Initially, according to de Lubac, there was no need to distinguish between the three bodies of Christ. When Almarius of Metz coined the term "threefold body of Christ," Florus of Lyon reproached him as "the greatest enemy of the unity of the church."[3] To make distinctions in the one Body was to imperil its fundamental unity. Of specific concern was the unity of the church with Christ its head:

> The body *par excellence*, the one that always comes first to mind, the one that needs no other designation is the Church ... The mysterious continuity linking the incarnation to the church was strongly felt by all ... Is the church not the continuation of Christ?[4]

De Lubac's point is not that these ninth-century writers cared more for the church than the eucharist, but that even when they began to elaborate on three distinctions

---

3. De Lubac, *Corpus*, 23–6. Citing Almarius of Metz, *Elogae de officio missae* (PL105, 1328 C); Florus of Lyon, *Adversus Amalarium* 1, n. 7 (PL 119, 76–7) and II, n. 7 (PL 119, 85–7).
4. De Lubac, *Corpus*, 23–4.

in the body, the church required no qualification as did the historical body and the mystical or sacramental body. The church was the body of Christ *simpliciter*.[5]

The church was therefore, in my language, the symbol of Christ, that in which Christ is seen and known in the world. Hence de Lubac's famous phrase, "If Christ is the sacrament of God, the Church is for us the sacrament of Christ; she represents him, in the full and ancient meaning of the term; she really makes him present."[6] For de Lubac to call the church a sacrament is to say that the church effects what it signifies, that is, that it both images Christ and mediates his presence and work. The church images Christ by displaying in its sacraments, liturgy, and life the shape and pattern of Christ's own life. The mediation of the church follows from this: it mediates Christ's presence and work by extending in its sacraments and liturgy the salvation secured once for all by Christ on the cross. De Lubac quotes Gregory of Nyssa, "He who beholds the church really beholds Christ."[7]

My language of the symbolized–symbol relation helps to indicate the extent to which this is founded on a trinitarian logic. The Son is the symbol of the Father, the replete self-representation of the Father. In an analogical way, the church is the symbol of Christ, Christ's ongoing self-expression in the world. As the Son proceeds from the Father, so analogically the church proceeds from Christ, sharing in his humanity and by his humanity with divinity. Christ thus retains priority *over* the church as the symbolized. But this priority is one of service, for the traditional imagery sees the church born from Christ's side as it is pierced.[8] Christ is "over" the church because he is raised over it on the cross. Christ exercises his authority over the church as one who serves, as in the washing of the disciples' feet or the husband washing with the water of the word.[9] Thus, ecclesiologically, Christ is the symbolized, the church the symbol, and the founding principle of this relation is the Son's procession from the Father.

There is a paradox in this relation. As the Father only is as he is symbolized in the Son, so Christ has elected to only be present in the world in relation to his body, the *totus Christus*. Paul McPartlan is right that de Lubac underplays this paradox. This is, in fact, McPartlan's principle critique: de Lubac consistently distinguishes Christ from the church, so that, as McPartlan interprets him, the church is a "second phase" of the divine economy.[10] In contrast, McPartlan prefers Zizioulas's undifferentiated identification of Christ with the church in the eschatological mystery of the eucharist. On this reading, the "future" is made contemporary each time the eucharist is celebrated. Because the church truly *is* this eschatological reality, then it is always united to Christ and Christ cannot be thought without it.[11]

---

5. De Lubac, *Corpus*, 79.
6. De Lubac, *Catholicism*, 76.
7. De Lubac, *Catholicism*, 73.
8. Jn 19:34.
9. Jn 13:1-7; Eph 5:25.
10. Paul McPartlan, *The Eucharist Makes the Church* (Edinburgh: T&T Clark, 1993), 23, 65, and elsewhere.

Zizioulas sought "the de-individualization of Christ," so that Christ is constituted as a *corporate person*; the church *just is* Christ.[12]

It is true that de Lubac is eager to distinguish the church from Christ, but McPartlan has curiously missed the logic of this distinction. The union of the church with Christ is a sacramental union, which is to say that it turns on a logic of symbols. The church is the sacrament of Christ, and so is the re-presentation of Christ in which he is truly present. McPartlan seems at times to deploy an either/or logic, missing the centrality of paradox to de Lubac's thinking. To give just one example, "The personification of the church as spouse uttering her 'I' of response to Christ conflicts with de Lubac's conviction that the 'I' of the church is Christ."[13] Either the church is the bride of Christ, or the church is Christ. But of course, *Paul* invokes bridal language to indicate precisely a unity that transcends either/or. The bride and bridegroom become one body, so that their *distinction* as bride and bridegroom enables their profound identification: "He who loves his wife loves himself."[14] Within Paul's bridal framework, the church is certainly constitutive of Christ, but only on the basis of its sacramental *relationship* to Christ, that is, the relation of symbol to symbolized. The bridegroom is only the bridegroom in relation to the bride—otherwise he is just a bachelor; the Messiah is only the Messiah in relation to the people he is anointed to redeem; Christ is only Christ— that is, specifically, the one anointed to save—in relation to the church. Because all of these are relational terms, this is nearly tautological. De Lubac need not abolish the distinction of Christ and church to secure their unity. Indeed, the distinction makes the unity.[15]

But the differences run deeper. For de Lubac, the church we encounter and know in its institutional or everyday form is not coextensive with Christ's work in the world: "The church, insofar as it is visible, is not the Kingdom."[16] If the visible church is indeed the sacrament of Christ, it is so in its movement toward the kingdom, its characterization *as* the way. De Lubac is keenly attentive to the historical movement of the church, its current state being fragile and incomplete. McPartlan, while agreeing with the current fragility of the church, seeks to overcome this by appeal to Zizioulas's all-determinative eschatology. In the eucharist, the future becomes present, the *totus Christus* in its eschatological fullness is truly made present and "identical" with the gathered assembly.[17] Eschatology, however,

---

11. McPartlan, *Eucharist*, 89.
12. McPartlan, *Eucharist*, 23; quoting John D. Zizioulas, "The Mystery of the Church in Orthodox Tradition," *One in Christ* 24 (1988), 299.
13. McPartlan, *Eucharist*, 94. There is a whole nest of issues in this book that I do not have space to address, chiefly, the ecumenical question of the *filioque*.
14. Eph 5:28, RSV.
15. This is not to suggest that Paul's nuptial mystery is *only* about the structure of the relationship.
16. De Lubac, *Catholicism*, 67.
17. McPartlan, *Eucharist*, 187–211.

is doing too much work here, not least because we are left with the awkward situation in which the future arrives at every eucharist, and then disappears again until the next.[18] For Zizioulas, this eschatological shot-in-the-arm strengthens believers for the in-between time, but it cannot account for the ways Christ is his church in the troubled and faltering ways it makes its way through history; indeed, it risks turning the eucharist into an escape *from* history.

A better, but still not perfect, approach is John Milbank's essay "The Name of Jesus," in which Christ is truly constituted by the church, but only inasmuch as Christ's life is to be re-presented by Christian practice in time. Milbank notes that Christ's "personality" is noticeably absent from the New Testament. Rather, the New Testament speaks of Christ already from an ecclesial perspective. Jesus is indeed a "minimal" historical personality, but he is primarily depicted as "the event of a transformation which is to be non-identically repeated, and therefore still made to happen."[19] Scripture presents Christ as always-already received by the church, so that the key question is not the personality of the historical Jesus, but rather, how Jesus's life and teachings establish a *way*; the name of Jesus is the name of the form of existence we call the church. That this perfect form of human existence coincides with a single person nurtures reflection on Jesus's divine identity, so that dogmatic theology is itself contained in the historical unfolding of this way. Milbank's essay does indeed risk evacuating Christ—and therefore the church—of historical constitution: it verges dangerously close to sheer idealism. But I take his central point to be that there is no uninterpreted "life of Christ" beneath the text that operates independently of the church that bears his name. When the church, therefore, looks back to Christ, it does so as to the one who makes its own life intelligible and possible.

Thus, for example, it is well known that the gospel of John substitutes the washing of the disciples' feet for the eucharistic narrative, with the implication being that Christ is present in his body within and as the servant practices of the community. In substituting the foot-washing for the eucharist, the gospel writer is not playing off ethics and institution. John 6 is abundantly clear about the priority of the eucharist. Rather, John is indicating the extent to which Christian life mediates the life of Christ. After having their feet washed—and in view of the Passion—the disciples act as Christ, and anyone who receives them receives Christ.[20] It is in washing feet that the disciples act *in persona Christi* and instantiate his presence in the world; the church participates in Christ's life of service, and in so doing constitutes his presence in the world. Christ's body must still be his body at 10:00 a.m. on a Tuesday. Again, this is not at the expense of the eucharist, but it does serve to illuminate de Lubac's statement in a letter to McPartlan that "[*la*] *question du rapport entre l'Eucharistie et l'Eglise ne préjuge en rien l'idée qu'l'on peut*

---

18. McPartlan, *Eucharist*, 169.

19. John Milbank, "The Name of Jesus," in *The Word Made Strange* (Oxford: Blackwell, 1997), 153.

20. Jn 13:20.

se faire de la structure visible de l'Eglise."[21] The washing of feet is always a contingent and local affair, one reflected in the practical structures of the church established to meet such local needs.[22] It is more a process of discernment and prophetic action than a prescriptive blueprint on the basis of eucharistic theology.[23] In this way, Christ is constituted in the world by his church, not at the expense of the eucharist, or indeed at the expense of his historical personality, but by the historical church acting in history in the name of Christ.

McPartlan does note that de Lubac's account is more attentive than Zizioulas's to the evangelical requirements of *proclaiming* the gospel.[24] The church's structures serve the proclamation of the gospel, and because this proclamation is always local, the structures themselves cannot be exclusively prescribed by eucharistic theology. But even here we could press further. The church's core structures—especially the episcopacy and baptism—themselves proclaim the gospel. In one of the twentieth century's most remarkable ecclesiological works, *The Gospel and the Catholic Church*, Michael Ramsey argues that the church catholic is also the church evangelical.[25] The church's catholic structures, especially the episcopacy and sacraments, actively proclaim the gospel. The episcopacy, as the visible symbol of church unity across time (by apostolic succession) and geography (by the structural communion between bishops) proclaims the gospel invitation to join the family of God. This is an invitation to rebirth to, as de Lubac might say, a new mother in the church and a new Father in God. And rebirth requires a death of an old self. For Ramsey, this signals the fundamental importance of baptism. In baptism, all die with Christ. This is not merely an "entrance fee" into the rest of the sacraments; it is a continuing reality. "One died for all, therefore all died" means that "the fact of Christ includes the fact of the church."[26] The death and resurrection of Christ is both the shape of the gospel and the heart of the church. Practically, this means that the Christian life is always a dying and a rising.

---

21. Henri de Lubac, *Letter to Paul McPartlan*, July 4, 1986; quoted in McPartlan, *Eucharist*, 98.

22. I am not claiming that church structures are *all* transient, only that many forms are culture-specific. Another aspect—which McPartlan is attentive to—is the importance of the proclamation of the gospel served by the structures of the church. I would only add to this that the enduring structures of the church themselves proclaim the gospel. See Michael Ramsey, *The Gospel and the Catholic Church* (London: SPCK, 1990).

23. Nicholas M. Healy has sought to centralize this prophetic aspect in a way that systematically refuses to "prejudge" its content in *Church, World and the Christian Life: Practical-Prophetic Ecclesiology* (Cambridge: Cambridge University Press, 2000). The term "blueprint ecclesiology" is his.

24. McPartlan, *Eucharist*, 289–91. Though McPartlan attributes this to an excessive anthropomorphism in de Lubac, and a mere lack of detail in Zizioulas.

25. Ramsey, *The Gospel and the Catholic Church*.

26. 2 Cor. 5:15. Ramsey, *Gospel*, 34.

Of course, baptism is *intrinsically* linked to the eucharist, which "proclaims the Lord's death until he comes."[27] There is no need to play one off against the other. But in its enthusiasm for sociality and unity, communion ecclesiologies such as those that follow Zizioulas and de Lubac have often failed to recognize how the eucharist requires a death, a conversion, a prophetic renunciation of sin enacted in baptism. Rowan Williams notes that when communion ecclesiology meets political theology, it has served to undermine the church's prophetic witness as that which *cannot* be in unity with current social structures.[28] What is lost is the church as irritant, as prophetic witness against the very unity with which society proclaims false gospels. And because the church is always a part of the societies from which it is drawn, this prophetic witness must always take the form of self-criticism. Baptism enacts this self-criticism in a visible and structural way. As Romans 6 makes clear, baptism is death to sin, but a death which must be constantly recalled, constantly instantiated in practice. It is a prophetic criticism of society and of our corporate and individual selves. That criticism takes the form of a calling to come and die and be raised again. Thus, as Michael Ramsey indicates, baptism helps explicate a eucharistic ecclesiology in gospel terms.[29]

With McPartlan, then, we should say that the church is constitutive of Christ. But where this has been conceived in exclusively eucharistic terms, it has tended to minimize the church's calling as the redemption of history itself, limiting its gospel witness both to the church itself and its culture. Rather than an absolute eschatological presence, it is better to think of the eucharist as a movement, a dynamic exchange between symbol and symbolized. As the Holy Spirit is the movement and life of creation, so the eucharist is the movement of the church toward Christ, and of Christ toward church, in a mystery of consummation that is at the same time a proclamation of death and new life. I turn now to this pneumatological account of the eucharist.

Christ–Church–Eucharist

De Lubac was not blind to the pneumatological function of the eucharist:

> Over and above the institutional unity ... faith recognized within it an internal unity. It assigned to it a mysterious source of life: the very Spirit of Christ ... Now, the eucharist is the mystical principle, permanently at work at the heart of Christian society, which gives concrete form to this miracle. It is the universal bond, the ever-springing source of life.[30]

---

27. I Cor. 11:26, RSV.
28. Rowan Williams, "Incarnation and the Renewal of Community," in *On Christian Theology* (Oxford: Blackwell, 2000), 225–38.
29. Gary Badcock, *The House Where God Lives* (Cambridge: Eerdmans, 2009), 99.
30. De Lubac, *Corpus*, 88.

To the "mysterious source of life" that is the Spirit corresponds the "mystical principle" of the church, the eucharist. It is the concrete form of the church's union with Christ. Just as the church is the symbol of Christ, participating in the Son's relation to the Father, so the eucharist is symbolism, uniting church to Christ by participation in the work of the Spirit. The eucharist is a pneumatological mystery not just because of the reintroduction of the epiclesis into contemporary liturgies, but because the work of unity it accomplishes is the unity of the Holy Spirit. The eucharist makes the church because the Spirit makes the church.

Like the Spirit, the eucharist is a movement between symbol and symbolized; it is a finite participation in eternal symbolism.[31] It marks the church's motion toward Christ as its fullness and head. It is an action, a mystery accomplished, not a static thing or a reified space: the church in motion toward God.[32] The everyday motions of the church, as well as all the other sacraments, are gathered together in the eucharist. As Johann Adam Mohler points out, the other sacraments are positioned at key points in life so that the very course of life in time is sustained by a sacramental process: baptism at birth, confirmation at emerging adulthood, either marriage or holy orders in the time of family life, confession and penance for the ongoing struggle with sin, and anointing of the sick, in Mohler's time, at the point of death.[33] Every stage of life is marked by a sacrament, so that in its administration of the sacraments, the church redeems life across time. What ties all of these time-markers together is the eucharist, when the whole church joins together in communion with God and one another. There is indeed an eschatological reality to the eucharist in which the church joins with all creation in worship and communion. But it does this not by interjecting eternity into time in an enclosed moment, rather, it is the redemption of time itself, all our history offered to God in thanksgiving and praise. The eucharist is thus not so much a reified thing, as the ever-flowing "source and summit" of life itself.[34] It is symbolism, the movement of the symbol toward the symbolized.

But every sacramental action is not just the movement of the church toward Christ. It is also the movement of Christ toward the church. The significance of

---

31. Nor was Scholasticism blind to the ecclesial implications of the eucharist. The presence of Christ in the sacrament was the *res et sacramentum* "between" the *sacramentum tantum* of the ritual and elements and the *res tantum* of the church. Eucharistic presence was conceived as *toward the church*. See Brett Salkeld, *Transubstantiation* (Grand Rapids, MI: Baker Academic, 2019), 130; Emery, "The Ecclesial Fruit of the Eucharist in St. Thomas Aquinas" in *Trinity, Church and the Human Person* (Naples, FL: Sapientia Press, 2007), 155–72.

32. Cf. Henri de Lubac, *Corpus*, 49–50.

33. Johann Adam Mohler, *Symbolism*, trans. James Burton Robertson (New York: Crossroad Publishing, 1997), 212.

34. *Dogmatic Constitution on the Church: Lumen Gentium*, 11. Available at https://www.vatican.va/archive/hist_councils/ii_vatican_council/documents/vat-ii_const_19641121_lumen-gentium_en.html

this should not be missed. The Spirit is the movement of Father toward Son and Son toward Father as desire and love, and so symbolism is a two-way street. In the eucharist, Christ comes to meet his people; he offers himself in the offering of the people and he is returned to the people in communion.[35] This is not a "meeting-in-the-middle" of two terms, for that would require two independent, preexistent, and self-possessed entities, a kind of eternal compromise between distinct agents. Rather, the church only is as it receives itself from Christ. It is ever in the position of the symbol, entirely dependent on the gift of donation from the symbolized. There is no meeting in the middle because there is no church that is not always-already the body of Christ who is its head. This is the significance of the eucharist as a divine act. It is an act of God that creates the church, which flows from Christ's side, on analogy to the emanation of creation from the Trinity. The church is born in the eucharist, an act of God that unites symbol to the symbolized. Without this union, this union and love of the Spirit, the church would not be the body of Christ, and therefore would not be the church. The eucharist makes the church because Christ makes the church, and the eucharist is the self-offering of Christ to the church and to God, uniting both in his person.[36]

This indicates that the church is never a *subject* standing over and against an object. One cannot conceive of the relation of church to Christ, or church to eucharist, or even church to world, in terms of a separation between subject and object. Just as the church is always a part of its worldly milieu and can never step outside its place in history (for to do so would be to refuse its salvific function *toward* history), so the church is always a part of its divine milieu, ever a society whose founding and sustenance is God. There is not first a church that then needs to be connected to Christ for which the eucharist might provide the necessary technology. Rather, the church is established precisely in this relation to Christ: it finds itself to be his body, often enough to its own surprise.[37] "In theology as in philosophy, subjects can truly 'grasp' nothing without at the same time recognizing themselves to be already grasped by it";[38] this is why, traditionally, to understand

---

35. The mutli-directional nature of this gift is explored in Catherine Pickstock, *After Writing* (Oxford: Blackwell, 1998), 240–7.

36. This points toward Thomas's conception of instrumental causality, where, in this case, the eucharist is the instrumental cause in the constitution of the church, which remains ever a divine act. Thomas Aquinas, *Summa Theologiae* 3a.62.1. All quotations from the Summa from Laurence Shapcote, O.P., trans., *Latin/English Edition of the Works of St. Thomas Aquinas* (Lander, WY: The Aquinas Institute for the Study of Sacred Doctrine, 2012). Hereafter, *ST*.

37. See Pickstock, *Writing*, 238–48.

38. Louis Marie Chauvet, *Symbol and Sacrament*, trans. Patrick Madigan and Madeleine Beaumont (Collegeville, MN: Pueblo, 1995), 43. He continues: "In showing why we must renounce, as much as this can be done, the scheme of 'explicative' causality and embrace rather the symbolic scheme of language, of culture, and of desire, we set up *a discourse from which the believing subject is inseparable*—just as language is inseparable from being or *Dasein* from *Sein*."

Christianity requires an understanding of the lives of the saints and an attempt to live such a life.[39] Ecclesiology is, in the first instance, a reflection on the church's gift of itself from Christ.[40]

In this way we can speak of the church as the symbol of Christ and the eucharist as symbolism, the union of body with head. Just as in trinitarian theology, there is a network of paradoxes nested in these relations. The classic *taxis* of Father–Son–Spirit prescribes that the Spirit proceed from the Father *per filium*. On my terms, this means that symbolism (Spirit) proceeds from symbolized by way of the symbol. So the eucharist proceeds from God by way of the Church which is the context assumed for its performance. It is the priest who consecrates the elements under the authority of the bishop whose authority descends through the ages from Christ; the eucharist proceeds from the charism given to the Church by its head. But as the Son is constituted by his reception of the Spirit from the Father, so the Church is constituted by its reception of the eucharist from Christ, even as the eucharist proceeds from the church. The eucharist is, like Spirit to Son, retroactively causal in the generation of the church. Moreover, while Christ is the head from whom the church invariably proceeds, nonetheless Christ is constituted across time in and as the eucharistic Church. Christ is only present by his symbol, and so in life in time there is a kind of subsistent relationality between Christ and his church. The head is only where the body is, and the church is the ineludible context of Christ's presence in the world. There is no Christ, as God incarnate, not in relation to his body, the church. While de Lubac never formulates the mystery of the church in precisely these terms, my account coheres profoundly with his presentation of patristic ecclesiology. The church is the symbol of Christ, the society of his real presence, the sacrament of Christ in the world. The eucharist is symbolism, the dynamic union of the ecclesial body with the historical body. All three taken together are the *totus Christus*, the One Body of Christ. As de Lubac narrates, such an ecclesiology would not last.

Christ–Eucharist–Church

De Lubac's account of the *demise* of a eucharistic and communion ecclesiology can also be re-narrated in terms of the triad I have developed. The crisis initiated by Barengar's non-realist reading of Augustine caused the terms to be switched to better emphasize the real presence of Christ in the eucharist. To symbolized–symbol–symbolism was now joined Christ–*eucharist*–church. The eucharist came to be seen as the symbol of Christ, his real presence, and the church came to be seen as symbolism, the guarantor of the union of Symbolized (Christ) with

---

39. For example, Athanasius, *On the Incarnation*, 57 in *Nicene and Post-Nicene Fathers*, Second Series, Vol. 4. Available at http://www.newadvent.org/fathers/2802.htm

40. Moreover, the church is also an eternal reality, and so its instantiation in time is always a donation from eternity. The church is not exclusively, or even primarily, the church militant.

symbol (eucharist). This risked devolution into an understanding of the church as the external authority that secured the internal miracle of transubstantiation. By making the church the guaranteed location of the Christ–eucharist relation, the dynamic sociality of the church was diminished, degenerating into an individualistic piety internally and a juridical structure externally. No longer the corporate body living by a unifying miracle, the church became the objective space of divine action guarding the object miraculously produced.

Historians and theologians have vigorously debated the accuracy of de Lubac's account, a debate that has become heated in the wake of the Second Vatican Council's liturgical reforms.[41] Eamon Duffy has argued the vitality of pre-reformation and counter-reformation Catholicism, which was by no means wholly individualistic and clerical.[42] Some have extolled the late Medieval liturgy as a premier example of "affective piety" which could point the way toward a new evangelization.[43] Others have pointed out that while the laity of the late Middle Ages and early Modernity lacked "full conscious participation" in the liturgy, they nonetheless played a significant role in the liturgical drama, and that conscious participation is itself only an ideal of the enlightenment.[44] Generally speaking, the early modern church was precisely that—early modern—and exhibited all the complexity of its era. How a scholar perceives modernity, whether as something to be overcome, embraced or as merely "there" without any need for normative evaluation, will influence how she evaluates the changes that led to its development. Nonetheless, a number of things seem clear. By the early modern era one can see a strong centralization of liturgical protocol with local rites and customs pressured into conformity. This accompanied a decline in liturgical participation by the Laity which was by no means uniform but is certainly detectable. Together with the rise of the *devotio moderna* with its emphasis on individual piety, this tended to emphasize the "spiritual" and individual over the corporate gathering. Finally, a growing divide between theology as an Aristotelian science, spirituality as a personal Neoplatonic exercise, and liturgy as principally the concern of canon

---

41. The debate surrounding liturgical reform is complex. For an overview and bibliography, see Alciun Reid, *The Organic Development of the Liturgy*, 2nd ed. (San Francisco, CA: Ignatius Press, 2005). For a variety of perspectives, see Alciun Reid, ed., *The T&T Clark Companion to Liturgy* (London: Bloomsbury T&T Clark, 2016). This volume plays out as an extended debate over a range of related issues, and is immensely valuable.

42. Eamon Duffy, *The Stripping of the Altars* (New Haven, CT: Yale University Press, 1992). See a similar argument in Virginia Reinburg, "Liturgy and the Laity in Late Medieval and Reformation France," *The Sixteenth Century Journal* 23 (1992), 526–47.

43. James Monti, "Late Medieval Liturgy: A Celebration of Emmanuel—'God with Us,'" in Alcuin Reid (ed.), *The T&T Clark Companion to Liturgy* (London: T&T Clark, 2016), 93–107.

44. Alcuin Reid, "In Pursuit of Participation—Liturgy and Liturgists in Early Modern and Post-Enlightenment Catholicism," in *T&T Clark Companion to Liturgy* (London: Bloomsbury T&T Clark, 2016), 133–53.

law ensured that even while the ecclesial fruit of the eucharist was maintained in much scholastic theology, it failed to substantially influence piety and liturgical reflection.[45]

These factors tended to objectify the eucharist, with a juridical concern to ensure a canonically valid sacrament that "worked." There is a discernable *technologization* of the eucharist in this era, even while it remained the center of a certain kind of social vitality.[46] This dynamic can be seen in the dramatic increase of votive and requiem masses. John Bossy points out that the rise of masses said for dead individuals expressed a kind of sociality—a social network encompassing both the living and their dead relatives and friends—and that this sociality required the living to do their part in securing the beatitude of dead relations.[47] But this is to turn the mass into a technology for procuring improved relations with God for friends in purgatory, an exchange mirrored in its more infamous cousin, the selling of indulgences. While religious life remained intimately tethered to the social, it began to be tainted by the logic of trade, with the eucharist becoming an object for the procurement of an outcome.[48] Hence, while Bossy is eager to defend the Mass and eucharist as social institutions, he describes it as having "secured or reenacted the 'paying' of God, the appeasement of his anger, the restoration of diplomatic or social relations between God and man, the return of the universe to a condition of peace."[49] While these motifs are common throughout Christian history, they take on a new primacy in the transition from the Middle Ages to Modernity.

It is this objectification of the eucharist that de Lubac protests. My argument is that this story can be told as the move from seeing the eucharist as the pneumatological core of church life to seeing it as the objective presence of Christ. The church is then the indefectible guardian of the miraculous object, an indefectibility guaranteed by the Spirit. Indeed, as Congar rightly argues, the Spirit was often blatantly replaced by this indefectibility.[50] This identification with the Spirit is a way of seeing the church as symbolism, as the term of union, but its overly juridical tone focused on the church as a static reality, a structure sustained by the Spirit to house and guard the christic symbol. Symbolized–symbol–symbolism was appropriated to Christ–eucharist–church.

---

45. These are well-documented. See Gerard Rouwhorst, "The Mystical Body Falling Apart?," *Religion and Theology* 23 (2016), 35–56. The debate tends to be over their evaluation and cause.

46. John Bossy, "The Mass as a Social Institution 1200-1700," *Past and Present* 100 (1983), 29–61.

47. Bossy, *Mass*, 37–42.

48. This is related to the rise of nominalism and univocity. For the ways this influenced Luther's rejection of Catholic sacramental theology, see Salkeld, *Transubstantiation*. See my review in *Modern Theology* (forthcoming) for a critical evaluation of some aspects of Salkeld's argument.

49. Bossy, *Mass*, 33–4.

50. Congar, *I Believe in the Holy Spirit*, trans. David Smith (New York: Crossroad, 1997), 162–3. The Pope, in this passage, is the figure of the church's indefectibility.

In an otherwise-flawed book (see below), Louis Marie Chauvet presents an alternative to this mechanized view of the eucharist.[51] Chauvet objects to any sense in which sacraments *produce* grace, for grace can never be a product of technology, however "spiritual" that technology might be. Grace is more like the *mannah* that fed the Israelites in the wilderness: "It's very name is a question: *Man-hu?* Its name is 'what is this?'" It seems to be a thing, and yet it melts in the sun; it has no measure, for those who collect little have enough, and those who collect much cannot use the excess. Grace thus refuses any element necessary to sustain a logic of exchange: "grace as a question, grace as a non-thing, grace as a non-value."[52] As Peter remonstrates Simon the Sorcerer, the gift of God transcends the transactional. The eucharist is not principally a means of negotiating good relations with God, a gross devolution of the mystery to which the reformers rightly reacted (which is not to say that they reacted rightly).[53] The point here is that, like *mannah*, the church is governed by the logic of the gift: the gift of Christ to the Father on the cross, the gift of the Spirit to the church at Pentecost, the gift of itself received at the altar. Like *mannah*, the church is more of a question, a non-thing, a non-value, for it is precisely the grace of God at work in the world, a work that can neither be quantified nor exchanged.

This is not to deny the institutional structure of the church. But this structure itself is founded on a question: Peter receives his commission to feed Christ's sheep only after Christ's question, "do you love me?"[54] This question is not a one-time query; it is the question that continues to stand at the fountainhead of the priesthood whose founding principle is not authority, but love. The institutions of the church are a perpetual response to an abiding question. The first response of the world to this society founded on gift and love as it observed Pentecost is also a question: "What does this mean?"[55] *Man-hu?* When Ananias and Sapphira try to bargain their way to status in the community, the results are disastrous.[56] Simon the Sorcerer cannot buy the Spirit.[57] Neither status nor Spirit operates on the logic of exchange. Both are, in fact, the same thing, as Peter discovers at Cornelius's house, when to his surprise the Spirit falls on gentiles, indicating that they are now full siblings in the house of God.[58] A question: do you love me?; a non-value: the gift of Christian community; a non-thing: the gift of the Spirit.

The question, "what is this?" cannot be definitively answered on earth. For one thing, the church is an eschatological reality, and until all have become saints, the

---

51. Chauvet, *Symbol*, 44.
52. Chauvet, *Symbol*, 44.
53. This, alas, in spite of my own Protestantism. Cf. Liam Walsh, "Sacraments," in Rik Van Nieuwenhove and Joseph Wawrykow (eds.), *The Theology of Thomas Aquinas* (Notre Dame, IN: University of Notre Dame Press, 2005), 328.
54. Jn 21:15-19.
55. Acts 2:12.
56. Acts 5:1-11.
57. Acts 8:9-24.
58. Acts 10-11.

church remains incomplete, a pilgrim city. The final identity of the church will only be known when all have been gathered together. But more fundamentally, the question cannot cease to be asked, for to ask the question is to name the church precisely as an inexhaustible gift, one which is suited to the "needs of the day," but which nonetheless can never be possessed by anyone. To "go on asking the question," as Rowan Williams might put it, is to learn to be the church. The church takes the form of innumerable acts of discernment played out at every level, from the most intimately local to the public and universal. It is a patient and humble self-questioning: what is the church in this situation?[59] The church abides by the law of love, whose definitive shape is given by Christ on the cross, but whose particular enacting is only possible by the Spirit of Christ at work in his Body. To go on asking the question is to live the life of the church in time, to refuse to prescind from the realities of history and to work always within the relational logic of gift, the law of love.

While it is not possible to merely replace a modern ecclesiology with a premodern one, it is possible to search for modes of reflection that help us re-learn the distant past. This will not be merely to repeat the past, for while one can attempt to re-learn pre-Modernity, one cannot un-learn Modernity. The triad I have developed is a kind of pedagogy. It seeks to illuminate without capturing the mystery. In its light, we can say the church is the symbol of Christ, Christ's real presence in the world; the eucharist is symbolism, the dynamic movement of unity of church and Christ. The result is *One Body* in motion through time, the *totus Christus*. I have not described three separate things to which relations are later added. Rather, the threefold Body is One Body composed of these relations. This One Body, in turn, stands in fundamental relation to God and the world. I now turn, then, from the dynamics of the threefold body to the relation of this One Body to God and the world. Here the terms are aligned differently. I take the church to be the *totus Christus*, itself composed in the threefold way outlined above. But taken as a unity, the threefold body takes on its own position in relation to God and creation, which I will now explicate.

God, Creation, and the One Body

In this systematic theology I have argued that creation is a symbol of God, truly the unfolding of the Logos in time. We are now in a position to finish the triad that structures this account: God is the symbolized, creation is the symbol, and the

---

59. Pope Francis, *Amoris Laetitia*, especially §300, where the Pope explicitly refutes the possibility of a transactional logic in discernment and accompaniment. The pastoral responses imagined by the encyclical are relational, examining all relations involved: the couple, their children, their parish, the engaged and newly married around them, etc. Available at: https://w2.vatican.va/content/dam/francesco/pdf/apost_exhortations/documents/papa-francesco_esortazione-ap_20160319_amoris-laetitia_en.pdf

One Body of Christ is symbolism, the unity of love and desire between creation and God. The One Body of Christ, that is, the eucharistic church in union with its head, is the world in motion toward its creator. The *totus Christus*, to borrow Augustine's famous phrase, is the unity of creation with God, or, in that other famous Augustinian phrase, the world reconciled.[60]

Just as the Spirit is the love of the Father for the Son, so the One Body is God's love toward his creation, his desire for its fulfillment and his action for its redemption. It is thus *God's* society, a divine gift for the sake of all. We must resist, then, any attempt to conceive of the One Body in purely functional and managerial terms: the Body is not an assembly line, and ministers are not "line managers," "production managers," or even "leaders."[61] Such titles are broadly used, and are conceived entirely along the lines of trade: governance structures of the modern American corporation have become the governance structures of many portions of the church. While the One Body is always embedded in and expressive of its particular culture, it is not clear that any of these terms have actually been *redeemed*; the logic of trade suffuses their practice. Rather, the Body is the gift of God's sacramental presence, the visible community through which God redeems the world. Its priests, whatever their organizational duties, are first and foremost the sacramental presence of Christ and the sacramental figures of their communities. Their calling refuses all logic of exchange and governance structures designed to maximize their "output."

But if the model is the Spirit as the unity of Father and Son, then symbolism must be mutually internal to both symbolized and symbol. The One Body, then, is also the movement of creation toward God. It is the love and thanksgiving—the *eucharisteo*—offered to God. This is not in exchange for salvation and presence but is the logic of a gift received and returned. The One Body, while entirely of God (symbolized), is entirely of the world (symbol). It is thus never able to excuse itself from the affairs of daily cultural life; it is in no way a flight from the material contingencies of life in time into the security of a future kept in promise elsewhere. It is entirely *in* the world for which it is called. That is to say that the One Body only ever exists as the redemption of the societies in which it is found, and thus bears their life, their culture, history, pain and victories in itself, as itself. This is not a neo-colonialist "claim" on the goods of non-Christian cultures, though it risks becoming this. Rather, it is the claim of all cultures on the body of Christ. The Body can never be owned by any particular culture, but the truth of every society

---

60. Augustine, "Homilies on 1 John," Homily 1, §2, *The Nicene and Post Nicene Fathers*, ed. Philip Schaff (New York: The Christian Literature Company, 1888), 461; Sermon 48, §8, NPNF, 410.

61. Such titles are used throughout non-denominational churches, low churches, and even the Church of England. Even in places where the titles are lacking, the mentality is often present. The mega-industry of "leadership development" resources testifies to this.

has a legitimate claim on the attention and affection of the Body.[62] The One Body receives itself as it patiently discerns and nurtures the truth, beauty and goodness of every culture: servant of all, possession of none.

The same paradox we have encountered again and again in this systematic theology holds true here as well. As the Spirit is "retroactively causal" in the generation of the Son, so the One Body is retroactively causal in the creation of the world. It is the "first of God's creatures" in the sense that the body of Christ is the life for which creation is set in motion.[63] The eucharistic church in unity with Christ is not, therefore, in an inversely proportional relation with the world, so that one must *conquer* and subjugate the other. It is clear from the life of Christ that the world will often have this attitude toward the Body, but the Body can never have this attitude toward the world. The One Body is precisely the refusal of conquest, for it is the power at work *in* the world, the leaven in the bread. De Lubac describes the church as "the only reality which involves by its existence no opposition. It is therefore the very opposite of a closed society."[64] What he means is that the body of Christ is not competing for space in the world—it is not struggling to carve out a niche for itself in an agonistic climate. Rather, it finds itself fundamentally on the side of any and every culture precisely in its goodness and strength, and opposed only to that which is evil, i.e., the privation of this good. Indeed, the One Body just is this goodness and reality summoned together sacramentally in eucharistic motion.[65]

This arrangement guards against the temptation to abstract the church from its place in history. If the One Body is the world in motion toward God, then those still pilgrims in the world can never flee temporal concerns. Indeed, the church precisely is this redemption of time.[66] It must be attentive, then, to its own time, even while living always in reference to the time of scripture, and the eschatological future. The body of Christ is a product of its age, always influenced by its surroundings and shaped to greater or lesser degrees by its culture. This is why we must "go on asking the question" of the church, for only thus can we live in time reflectively, not to master and so leap from our place in history, but to faithfully live in the time given us by God. This process of discernment cannot be resolved by any *a priori* evaluations. Asking the question requires the patience and discipline to learn to see our own contexts rightly, even though this is a never-ending task. But we can go on asking the question of the church in *this* culture at *this* time because we have faith

---

62. De Lubac addresses these issues in *Catholicism*, 282–302. De Lubac's most direct engagement with other cultures is through his work on Buddhism. His most well-known work is *Aspects of Buddhism* (London: Sheed and Ward, 1954). For an overview, see David Grumett, "De Lubac, Christ and the Buddha," *New Blackfriars* 89, no. 1020 (March 2008), 217–30.

63. Shepherd of Hermas 2.4, *The Fathers of the Church: The Apostolic Fathers*, trans. Francis X. Glimm, et al. (New York: Christian Heritage, 1947), 241–2.

64. De Lubac, *Catholicism*, 298.

65. Of course this means the institutional church is not coextensive with the One Body.

66. Cf. John Milbank, "Enclaves, or Where Is the Church?" *New Blackfriars* 73, no. 861 (June 1992), 341–52.

that inasmuch as we are never outside our own culture, so also we are never outside the gracious movement of God. Our very existence is as a word spoken by God, the unfolding of the eternal Word by the Spirit, and there is never a moment in our history not always-already embedded within this trinitarian movement. All of history is circumscribed by Trinity. And this sustains our discernment, to look to the symbols of creation, history, and culture in hopeful expectation that by the Spirit, the Logos will shine through, revealing the Father.

The reason the One Body can maintain this posture of "openness toward" creation is because the One Body is *not* the symbol of God, creation is. The point is not that there is this thing called the world out of which the church is revealed. Rather, the One Body is the world in its most revelatory form: the Body is the revelation of the world. And this implies that the Body can never adopt a "colonial" attitude to any aspect of creation. The Body just is creation at its fullest, and so is nothing more than each culture, each time's, reception of itself as a gift from God in Christ, the giver of every good and perfect gift.

For these reasons it is entirely appropriate to call the church a sacrament, in the specific sense that the eucharistic church in unity with its head is a sacrament. Only the threefold body is the sacrament of God and creation. The external structures of the church in themselves are not rightly considered a sacrament of God and creation, nor is the eucharist in abstraction from its ecclesial context. Nor—and this is controversial—is Christ a sacrament except in his ongoing unity with the visible church in the eucharist. The logic of the last statement is simply that Christ is not known in the world without his material instantiation in the church, and that instantiation is secured by the eucharist. Once the unity of the threefold body is established, the relation of this One Body to creation and God becomes clear. The One Body effects what it signifies; it signifies God's redemption of the world and is the instrument by which that redemption is wrought. Thus, to symbolized–symbol–symbolism corresponds God–creation–church.

A Few Critiques

This arrangement is not without possible criticisms. Two, in particular, will be addressed below. The first is a Barthian critique about the priority of God in all things. If even Christ is not a sacrament without the eucharistic church, how does this not infringe on divine perfection? Is it not better to conceive of the church not in sacramental terms, but in the gospel terms of *hearing* and *responding*? If the Barthian critique worries about the dangers of semi-pelagianism in ecclesiology, a Heideggerian critique worries about ontotheology.[67] To call the One Body a

---

67. The term is most influentially developed by Martin Heidegger. In contemporary theology, it has come to indicate an inappropriate forgetting of the radical difference between God and creatures. See Judith Wolfe, *Heidegger and Theology* (New York: Bloomsbury T&T Clark, 2014).

sacrament is to say that it causes what it signifies. Louis-Marie Chauvet rejects the notion of causality as implementing a productionist scheme of grace. To think that the sacraments in some way *cause* grace is to reduce God to an ontic force, to forget the utter transcendence of God. Better, then, to conceive of the sacraments along the lines of human symbolic meaning to respect both the transcendence of God and the irreducibility of human language. I will argue that *contra* Barthians this is not semi-Pelagian; *contra* Chauvet this is not ontotheological. There are, of course, numerous other objections one might imagine: a Marxist objection that I have neglected the dynamics of power; a Thomist objection that I have merely obscured what was made clear in the scholastic framework of *res et sacramentum*; a postcolonial objection that I have underplayed the church's enmeshment in social sin; a Zwinglian objection that sacraments lack the power of presence; etc. Unfortunately, rather than answer every conceivable objection, what follows will have to merely indicate the *kind of thinking* I would pursue in answering such questions. First, the Barthian concern.

John Webster on Divine Perfection

John Webster underwent an astonishing development in his understanding of divine perfection: from a Barthian concern to protect a sphere of pure divine causality, to a Thomist understanding of perfection as the sharing of causal power. Outlining this development helps me address the Barthian concern that a sacramental ecclesiology infringes on divine perfection. In "On Evangelical Ecclesiology," John Webster calls Henri de Lubac's *Catholicism* one of the "magisterial ecclesiological texts of the last century."[68] But Webster's point is not so much to praise the text, as to discover the conditions under which it might avoid falling into a kind of sacramental semi-pelagianism. Webster worries that behind talk about the Church as a sacrament, behind a strong identification of the church with Christ in the eucharist, lies a disorder of dogmatic protocol: a failure to think Christ and gospel first, and church second; a conflation of the work of God and the work of creatures. To embrace this magisterial text, Webster argues, it must be shorn of its tendency to identify the church with Christ and Christ's gospel.

Standing behind Webster's concern is Eberhard Jüngel, and Barth before him. Jüngel expresses deep reservation about the sacramental ecclesiology championed by de Lubac, Rahner and others. For Jüngel, "the 'sacrament of unity' is not the church but Christ himself."[69] For Karl Barth, the trouble with the Catholic doctrine of the church is simply the trouble with the doctrine of Mary:

---

68. John Webster, "On Evangelical Ecclesiology," in *Essays on Christian Dogmatics II* (London: Bloomsbury, 2016), 172. Originally published in *Ecclesiology* 1, no. 1 (2004), 9–35.

69. Eberhardt Jüngel, "The Church as Sacrament?" in *Theological Essays*, trans. John Webster (Edinburgh: T&T Clark, 1989), 191.

In the doctrine and worship of Mary there is disclosed the one heresy of the Roman Catholic Church which explains all the rest. The "Mother of God" of Roman Catholic Marian dogma is quite simply the principle, type and essence of the human creature co-operating servantlike (*ministerialiter*) in its own redemption on the basis of prevenient grace, and to that extent the principle, type and essence of the church.[70]

The concern for each of these theologians is that the church has transgressed the territory that belongs exclusively to Christ, as God's redemptive action in the World, and thereby exchanged divine supremacy for a semi-Pelagian notion of cooperation. The church is the people defined by their hearing of the gospel, the recipient of divine action, and like Mary, perpetually a virgin, i.e. perpetually under the repudiation of human capability. Webster's essay is profound summary of this central Protestant critique.

Webster outlines the relation between the church and the gospel, that is, the relation of the church as a visible human community and the divine work that creates and sustains it.[71] Webster is explicitly trying to avoid an ecclesiology in which the gospel is only extrinsically related to the visible life of the church. He is therefore sympathetic to the concerns of "communion ecclesiologies" that seek to make the action of Christ internal to the action of the corporate body of the church.[72] But such ecclesiologies, Webster argues, go too far. They collapse Christ into the church, voiding an all-important dogmatic protocol: "The gospel proceeds and the church follows."[73] To show this, Webster begins with divine perfections, on the principle that an ecclesiology is only as good as the theology, properly speaking, that underlies it: "As the perfect one, God is utterly realized, lacks nothing, and is devoid of no element of his own blessedness. From all eternity he is wholly and unceasingly fulfilled."[74] God's "internal" perfection implies the perfection of God's "external" acts. There is "no point at which God must call upon the assistance of other agents to bring his work to its completion."[75] Of course, God graciously and freely chooses to include other agents, but this is election for a particular service; in election, God "does not bestow an enduring capacity on the creature so much as consecrate it for a specific appointment."[76] The perfection of God's life entails the

---

70. Karl Barth, *Church Dogmatics* Vol. 1, 2 (Edinburgh: T&T Clark, 1956), 143.
71. Webster, "Ecclesiology," 153–4.
72. Communion ecclesiologies are a family of ecclesiological thought tracing back to de Lubac's *Corpus Mysticum* and *Catholicism* that emphasis the sociality of the church, conceived as the unity of people among themselves and participation in the unity of God and centered on the eucharist. For an overview, see Dennis M. Doyle, *Communion Ecclesiology* (Maryknoll: Orbis Books, 2000).
73. Webster, "Ecclesiology," 154.
74. Webster, "Ecclesiology," 157.
75. Webster, "Ecclesiology," 157.
76. Webster, "Ecclesiology," 171.

perfection of God's acts, which only include creatures to the extent they are elected for a specific purpose within it.

But at no point do creatures participate in either the divine work or the divine life. Webster frames this in terms of a strict dichotomy: is God's perfection "inclusive" or "exclusive?"[77] If inclusive, then God needs creation for his perfection. If exclusive, then creation cannot participate in God:

> God's relations to that which is other than himself are real; but they are expressions of divine freedom, not of lack, and in those relations creatures *do not participate in God*, but are elected for fellowship and therefore summoned into God's presence.[78]

This is borne out christologically, where the incarnation is "an absolute beginning, the introduction into creation of an absolute *novum*, unconditioned and unexpected."[79] The work of Christ, as the work of God, is therefore unparticipable, unrepeatable, and even "non-representable."[80] And all of this finally issues in a firm "distance or difference" between Christ and his church, even while remaining united by election.[81] The death, resurrection, and ascension of Christ enact "his over-againstness to the church."[82] "The perfection of Christ," as the perfection of God, "is not integrative or inclusive, but complete in itself."[83] To be complete, God's perfection must be exclusive.

Two features of this argument are troubling. First, its nominalism. This is most obvious in Webster's account of the incarnation. In order for the incarnation to be an "absolute *novum*," the humanity of Christ must be an absolute creation ex nihilo, which calls into question any *real* human nature common to all humans and Christ. For Webster, there can be no "pre-existing creaturely coordinate" for the incarnation's occurrence.[84] He interprets such a situation as requiring a kind of adoptionist pelagianism: "The humanity of Jesus is thus not a creaturely quantity which is annexed or commandeered by God, for then it would precede the incarnation as its creaturely condition."[85] There can be no real common human nature because that would condition God's act in the incarnation, diminishing God's perfection by imposing a creaturely precondition. Moreover, a common human nature would mean that humans are united to Christ by *participation* in that common nature, illicitly insinuating humanity into this divine act. This pays

---

77. Webster, "Ecclesiology," 158.
78. Webster, "Ecclesiology," 158.
79. Webster, "Ecclesiology," 163.
80. Webster, "Ecclesiology," 172.
81. Webster, "Ecclesiology," 170.
82. Webster, "Ecclesiology," 173.
83. Webster, "Ecclesiology," 174.
84. Webster, "Ecclesiology," 172.
85. Webster, "Ecclesiology," 172.

out immediately in soteriology: "In Christ, God unites himself to us, but he does so only in this one person, and this one person is not the symbol of some more general communion or identity."[86] Christ's life and work are not salvific on the basis of the nature common to him and us, but only inasmuch as Christ substitutes his own solitary individuality for ours: "His humanity only gathers all others into itself as substitute; it includes all in itself only as it also excludes them."[87]

But we should ask, what does it mean for God to become a creature if not to subject the Word to a "creaturely condition"? Webster secures divine perfection at the cost of real natures, for a nature common to human creatures would indeed be a precondition for incarnation. This necessitates nominalism because were humans to share a common nature, but Christ be some peculiar instance of creation ex nihilo, his humanity could not meaningfully be our own. To avoid creaturely preconditions and still affirm the full humanity of Christ, *every* human would have to be an isolated instance of creation ex nihilo, bound together not by common nature, but pure divine decree. Christ is therefore a unique, unrepeatable, unparticipable, "insistent singularity" from which all other humans are excluded.[88] That exclusion, ensured by nominalism, is then bridged by God's free and spontaneous choice in election to have this insistently singular individual stand-alone before God's judgment as a substitute for every (singular) other.

To this christological nominalism corresponds an ecclesial one. Even though the proclamation of this exclusively divine act generates a community, the material practices of that community can only be said to be the "phenomenal form of the church."[89] Webster makes the perfectly valid argument that the Spirit is what makes the phenomenal practices of the church *the church*. And yet, the phenomena of church life cannot be said to be the work of God, for in its phenomenal acts, "the church simply points."[90] That is, the church testifies to what God has done *elsewhere*, i.e., to the insistent singularity of Christ's action in which the church cannot participate. The church is "strictly subordinate to that which it is appointed and empowered to indicate [signify], raised up not to participate in, extend, or realize a reality that lies quite outside itself."[91] Here a nominalism of signs lurks. The sign does not participate in the signified; the church is no symbol. The church is a pointer that those filled with the Spirit can recognize, but only a pointer. The symbolized has done all the work, and there remains nothing for the symbol to do but to evacuate itself in unreserved witness.

This indicates the second troubling feature of the text. The nominalism of Webster's account, in both its christological and ecclesiological instantiations, coincides with a competitive relation between God's perfection and creaturely participation. Here, the doctrine of creation ex nihilo serves to sever any

---

86. Webster, "Ecclesiology," 173.
87. Webster, "Ecclesiology," 173.
88. Webster, "Ecclesiology," 172.
89. Webster, "Ecclesiology," 181.
90. Webster, "Ecclesiology," 185.
91. Webster, "Ecclesiology," 185.

concordance between divine and human action: "It is a basic entailment of the doctrine of creation *ex nihilo* that God and creatures are in a certain sense inversely proportional."[92] That "certain sense" is the absolute priority of divine perfection in act, such that at every decisive moment—Webster lists the incarnation, the ascension and Pentecost—"God acts alone."[93] The reason for this, as we have seen, is that a perfect act can require no "other agents."[94] Were there some human correlate to these divine acts, it would imperil their perfection. The result is that divine acts must not only be divine, but exclusively so. Therefore, Webster argues, a concept of the eucharist as a participation in Christ's self-offering "undermines the *alien* character of Christ's person and work, and so compromises their perfection and grace."[95] This last statement summarizes the logic of the essay: if Christ is not *alien* to the world, and the world alien to Christ, God's perfection is compromised. His worry about "other agents" is telling, for it indicates that creaturely participation is really, in spite of protests to the contrary, competitively arrayed against divine agency. Here, nominalism and a univocal ontology lurk hand-in-hand.

And yet, nine years and a great deal of Thomas Aquinas later, Webster argues this:

> Perfect power does not absorb, exclude or overwhelm and dispossess other dependent powers and agents, but precisely the opposite: omnipotent power creates and perfects creaturely causal capacity and movement. Exclusive power is less than perfect and falls short of divinity.[96]

Here the question is again divine perfection, and the founding premise is the same—creation from nothing entails the absolute priority of divine action—but this time the doctrine serves rather to undermine attempts to play God and creatures off from one another. He identifies a pressing theological–historical task as discovering "how there has arisen a condition in which the axiom *aut Gloria Dei aut Gloria homini* has gathered such cultural authority, one in which God and creatures are natural antagonists, 'two units in a symmetrical or asymmetrical relationship, each poised in such contradiction that one must sink if the other is to rise.'"[97] Efforts at undertaking that task have traced the condition to:

> a narrowing of divine causality to efficient causality; decline of appeal to final causality in the explanation of nature, or the reorientation of final causality to human, not divine, purposes; a sense that natural motion is self-contained,

---

92. Webster, "Ecclesiology," 171.
93. Webster, "Ecclesiology," 171.
94. Webster, "Ecclesiology," 157.
95. Webster, "Ecclesiology," 173.
96. John Webster, "*Creatio Ex Nihilo* and Creaturely Goodness," *Modern Theology* 29, no. 2 (April 2013), 170.
97. Webster, "*Creatio*," 168; quoting Michael J. Buckley, *Denying and Disclosing God: the Ambiguous Progress of Modern Atheism* (New Haven, CT: Yale University Press, 2004), 94.

not requiring talk of God's creative and providential operations to render it intelligible; in short, the retraction of the concept of a divine *source* for natural and human movement.[98]

With the collapse of formal and final causality into efficient causality, it has become increasingly difficult to see how God might be a first cause operative *within* creatures. As Jacob Schmutz has argued, this reduces God to acting alongside or upon creatures.[99] In this scheme, divine action could only be conceived as somehow achieved at the expense of human action: "The idea whose spell must be broken is that God is a supremely forceful agent in the same order of being as creatures, acting upon them and so depriving them of movement."[100]

The trouble with this spellbinding idea, as Aquinas points out, is that perfect power cannot be in competition with anything. It is far more perfect to bestow both being and causal power than to withhold causal power out of anxiety about losing a causal monopoly.[101] Webster appeals to *creatio ex nihilo* precisely to avoid a situation in which creatures and creator compete in ontic space, allowing creaturely action to be authentically creaturely and yet never in fact separated from divine action. And this, at the very least, opens the possibility that God need not "act alone" to maintain the priority of providence and the ultimacy of divine glory.

This does not entail a repudiation of Webster's previous concerns. The priority is still divine action, but the mode of this action is now recast according to a clearer truth of perfection: divine perfection is displayed precisely in its *sharing* of causal power, its bestowal of agency, its generosity. Everything, then, is founded upon creation, a divine act in which "God acts alone." But that act creates and sustains other actors, so that from Gen 1:1 on, God never acts alone, at least not in the sense of competitively replacing second causes. This is not merely the result of the divine will in election—though it is indeed that—it is also an indication of God's very nature as goodness itself, which seeks to share itself, and in so doing freely

---

98. Webster, "*Creatio*," 167. For an account of these shifts, see Simon Oliver, *Philosophy, God and Motion* (London: Routledge, 2005).

99. Jacob Schmutz, "The Medieval Doctrine of Causality and the Theology of Pure Nature," in Serge-Thomas Bonino (ed.), *Surnaturel: A Controversy at the Heart of Twentieth-Century Thomistic Thought* (Ave Maria, FL: Sapientia Press, 2009), 203–50.

100. Webster, "*Creatio*," 170.

101. Thomas Aquinas, *Summa Contra Gentiles* (Notre Dame, IN: University of Notre Dame press, 1975), III.69.15: "The perfection of the effect demonstrates the perfection of the cause ... So, to detract from the perfection of the creature is to detract from the perfection of divine power. But, if no creature has any active role in the production of any effect, much is detracted from the perfection of the creature. Indeed, it is part of the fullness of perfection to be able to communicate to another being the perfection one possesses. Therefore this position detracts from the divine power."

creates creatures whose existence is their sharing in that original goodness. Gone, therefore, is Webster's allergy to the language of participation: "Participation is theologically to be understood in terms of the operation of creative benevolence, and so in terms of the *differentiated* sharing of creator and creature in the good of being, each in their proper order and mode."[102] The creature exists by participation in being, according its proper mode as a creature. This does not detract from God's perfection but is funded precisely by God's perfection which is perfect enough to share itself. This sharing takes the form of the most intimate form of causality. God is *first* cause because God works at the deepest level of creaturely life, both giving and sustaining being, and giving and sustaining agency. It is creation ex nihilo that ensures this most intimate involvement: "Even after it has come into being, the creature is not a reality to which God is 'other,' some correlate in a common order."[103] In other words, God cannot be "alien" to the creature, for the creature only ever *is* in God.

While he likely would still have maintained that communion ecclesiologies go too far in uniting church to Christ—and not entirely without reason[104]—his later outlook lacks the anxiety to protect a sphere of exclusively divine causality. If we follow Webster's turn to Thomas, where does that leave the church? If creaturely causality need not infringe on divine perfection, we need not be as worried about the church participating in Christ's work. But I think Webster would want to know—with great specificity!—just what kind of causality we are talking about when we speak of the church in relation to the divine economy. Clearly the work of the church is not run-of-the-mill human action. Nor are we speaking of a moment where God unequivocally "acts alone," since this formula assumes a competitive contrast between divine and human agency. I have claimed that the church stands between God and the world as symbolism, which is to say, as a sacrament, then something like *sacramental causality* will need to be examined. But before that, I must answer an objection from an entirely different direction: a Heideggerian objection to any language about causes whatsoever.

Sacraments, Causes, and Symbolism

What might it mean for the church to occupy the place of symbolism, a sacrament of world and God? If the church in some way participates in God's work of redemption, what kind of causality is at work here? To understand this, we need to look at sacramental causes. To explain such causality, it might help to start with a misunderstanding, specifically, Louis Marie Chauvet's misconstrual of sacramental causality as a kind of technologization of mystery. For Chauvet, "The communication of grace is to be understood, not according to the 'metaphysical' scheme of cause and effect, but according to the symbolic scheme of communication

---

102. Webster, "*Creatio*," 164.
103. Webster, "*Creatio*," 171.
104. See discussion above on Zizioulas.

through language."[105] Chauvet argues this as both an affirmation and a critique of Thomas's view of the sacraments. He applauds Aquinas's late attempt in the *Summa* to "subordinate the notion of causality to that of sign."[106] While the rest of Middle Ages saw it necessary to add the notion of causality to Augustine's "definition" of sacraments as signs, Thomas adds only that it is "a sign of a sacred thing inasmuch as it sanctifies human beings."[107] Here, Thomas studiously avoids conflating signs with causality, prioritizing the sign-value of sacraments, and so the priority of the symbolic over the technological.

But this prioritization would not last. When Thomas turns to examine the operations of the sacraments, he immediately switches to a discourse about causes. This, according to Chauvet, removes the discussion from the realm of the symbol and into the realm of the mechanical. Moreover, once the symbolic has been abandoned, Thomas must bracket out the church from the functioning of the sacraments. Even though he has maintained the ecclesial connection with the eucharist, when Thomas turns to its mode of functioning, the language of causes forces him to focus exclusively on the efficient causality of God and the instrumental causality of the sacrament, occluding the church until after the "how" of the sacraments has been examined. The all-important vision of the mutual constitution of the *totus Christus* in the threefold body of Christ is lost to the language of causes. Grace is then something that the sacraments *produce*, with subsequent centuries taking the ontotheological bait and technologizing the sacramental life of the body of Christ.

In order to unlearn the logic of causes, Chauvet turns to Heidegger and the logic of symbols. All of reality is mediated through language and culture, so that it is impossible to get behind our symbolic understandings of the world to a pure, unmediated moment. The world is always-already mediated through language, through rites and rituals, through society, whether the casual society of pop culture, the formal structures of the Royal Society, or the heavenly society of the church. The sacraments, then, are to be understood as mediating rituals, rites that both institute and are instituted by the community. They are formative rituals that bind together past with present and future, uniting the community together and to God. They *function* to the extent that they signify, that is, to the extent that they mediate reality through a particular ritual and linguistic culture. Because the real is unavailable except through the mediation of language and ritual, the sacraments witness to the presence of the absence of God; God is certainly "here," but because the real is always mediated, God is not available for inspection, and is certainly not subject to possession or manipulation. The sacraments institute and are instituted

---

105. Chauvet, *Symbol*, 139. For an accessible introduction to Chauvet's thought, see Lieven Boeve, "Theology in a Postmodern Context and the Hermeneutical Project of Louis-Marie Chauvet," in Philippe Bordeyne and Bruce Morill, SJ (eds.), *Sacraments: Revelation of the Humanity of God* (Collegeville, MN: Pueblo, 2008), 5–24.

106. Chauvet, *Symbol*, 12.

107. Chauvet, *Symbol*, 15; Citing his translation of *ST* 3a.60.2.

as an exhaustive *hermeneutic*, a reading of the world that constitutes both world and reader as a dynamic whole.

For Chauvet, while grace and the sacraments are not reducible to the symbolic, thinking of them in terms of the symbolic has distinct advantages over thinking of them in terms of causality. The symbolic avoids the dangers of technologizing grace, for language is most fully language when it transcends the requirements of object mastery—i.e., in poetry.[108] The symbolic also emphasizes the humanity of the sacraments, for it examines them precisely as human rites, rituals, and culture. This is important for Chauvet because "the metaphysical" elides the human in search of a reality untainted by history and culture. *Sacrament and Symbol* thus represents a sacramentology "from below."[109] Finally, examining the sacraments in the register of the symbolic is a project in the overcoming of all the ravages of metaphysics, especially the corrosive dualism of subject and object. In his symbolic account, the sacramental object and the sacramental subject are mutually constitutive, so that neither a pure objectivity nor a pure subjectivity is possible.[110] Rather, objects and subjects only are in their relations to one another. Thus, the eucharist is the presence of Christ only in its relation to the church, so that the threefold body of Christ is once again reunited.

This can be summed up in the nature of language as poetry. For Chauvet, following Heidegger, "Poetry is the human vocation."[111] He quotes G. Bachelard: "Poetry casts language into a state of emergence."[112] What he means by this is the priority of symbolic presence—the way a poem can summon, say, a wheelbarrow or a rose garden—as more fundamental than physical presence or presence by production. Poetry opens the possibility for presence as absence, for presence as what is fleeting, playing in the margins of language and life. The wheelbarrow is present but not "available," not objectively there for inspection and use. This, Chauvet and Heidegger think, is the propaedeutic for the glimpsing of Being, indeed, it is the "clearest" instance of Being in time. Being is only present as an absence, it can never be captured and dissected, for this would be to turn the transcendent into a cadaver. Poetry shows the play of Being in time, glimpsing the real in its very absence. It is, moreover, the forgetfulness of Being's transcendence that reduces language to technology for accomplishing tasks, a forgetfulness that only further guarantees the impossibility of overcoming metaphysics. In terms of Christian theology, this forgetfulness reduces the presence of Christ to a quasi-physical presence, something to be manipulated, owned, and bartered. Chauvet sees this forgetfulness at work in Christian tradition, especially scholasticism.

---

108. Chauvet, *Symbol*, 58–63.
109. This is Liam Walsh's interpretation. Walsh, "Sacraments," 329–30.
110. This is also Laurence Hemming's concern in "Henri de Lubac: Reading Corpus Mysticum," *New Blackfriars* 90, no. 1029 (September 2009).
111. Chauvet, Symbol, 57.
112. Chauvet, *Symbol*, 57; quoting Gaston Bachelard, *La poétique de l'espace* (Paris: PUF, 1957), 10.

Much of Chauvet's account resonates with my own; his attention to the mediation of symbols, the dangers of naturalizing the transcendent, and the centrality of the sacraments to the Christian life. But we should query his allergy to the language of cause, especially as found in Thomas Aquinas. This is not because cause is a better analogy than sign, but because to abandon the question of causes is to fail to fully "overcome" ontotheology. While Thomas's account certainly benefits from Chauvet's exploration of cultural anthropology, Thomas in the end subordinates the language of cause to that of sign, rendering *even causes* as symbols of God. In contrast, by studiously avoiding the language of cause, Chauvet abandons such discourse to its ontotheological fate. Thomas maintains a more radical symbolic theology by turning even the most technical into symbols, into poetry.

While for Chauvet grace and the sacraments are not reducible to the symbol, since this would reduce grace to a secular anthropology, Chauvet never indicates *in what way* this reduction is impossible. What is it about grace that is more than the anthropological dynamics of rites, rituals and community formation? Chauvet is suspicious about talk of God, presumably because of the ontotheological risks such talk involves. A contrast with Rahner will serve as an example. Rahner, himself a kind of Heideggerian, says that grace is the gift of God's own self, the abiding nearness of the mystery.[113] Chauvet, in contrast, says that grace is the gift of *ourselves* from God, on the model of Augustine's "become what you are," and that the mechanism for this reception is the otherwise normal processes of human ritual identity formation.[114] Now both are certainly true, but Chauvet has placed the emphasis entirely on human reception. This is not a pure immanentism, rather, it is the conviction that because God is not a thing in the world, God's gift of grace must work in and through creaturely realities. Too much attention to God as giver of grace risks the ontotheological picture of God as the cause of grace, as a carpenter is the cause of a bed. Chauvet therefore focuses on its human aspect. But still, what is it that separates this account of grace and the sacraments from a secular anthropology of the symbol?

For Chauvet, the answer is faith. He is admirably attentive to this dynamic of sacramental life.[115] If the sacraments were more than human ritual in any register other than faith, they would be an ontotheological reduction of divine action to a manageable and therefore manipulatable ontic force. The language of faith marks them off as something of a completely different order. This is not to say that the sacraments are run-of-the-mill human rituals that Christians have *decided* to

---

113. Karl Rahner, "Nature and Grace," in *Theological Investigations*, Vol. 4 (London: Darton, Longman & Todd, 1966), 175. For a comparison of Rahner and Chauvet, see Conor Sweeney, *Sacramental Presence after Heidegger* (Eugene, OR: Cascade, 2015), 57: "Thomas-Rahner-Chauvet reflects a progressive shift away from causal categories to a symbolic discourse." This is because Rahner does not fully jettison Aquinas's sacramental theology. My argument below shows that Rahner was right to retain Thomas.

114. Chauvet, *Symbol*, 442.

115. Chauvet, *Symbol*, 154–5, and elsewhere.

form their faith around, as though in a marketplace of ritual options. Rather, the sacraments by their very enactment create the community whose unity of life *is* the faith formed by their ritual instantiation. The content of this faith, for Chauvet, is that in Christ—especially in his passion—we see God.[116] But this answer itself risks severe ontotheological reduction if God is seen to "act" in Christ as one cause among others, as though God were some particular portion of Jesus's identity as a human.[117] To avoid this, Chauvet turns to Moltmann's crucified God—the crucifixion reveals the humanity of God and becomes an event in the life of God. To avoid turning God into the perfect being of ontotheology, Chauvet turns God into a being who *becomes*. The Passion is thus a supreme moment of Freud's Oedipus complex: the Father and Son become most fully themselves in being "crossed out by the Other."[118] While we might be tempted to put this language down to analogy, so that the Oedipus complex becomes something like the Augustine's psychological analogy, this is not an option; Chauvet has rejected analogy as merely erasing the tensions of language.[119] But if analogy is not an option, it is hard to see how this is not just pure projection—a Freudian gnostic myth of intra-divine abandonment— and as such the most ontotheological solution imaginable. God is conceived entirely along the lines of the identity formation of ontic individuals, sustained by a violent severing of self from the other. His Freudian Trinity is a pure projection of the ontic onto an infinite expanse. Has Chauvet not himself fallen prey to his critique of ontotheology: "God's sublime majesty is only the idealized projection of our own megalomania"?[120] If Thomas's theology "from above" risks degenerating into an ontotheological domestication of God (a risk that history shows to be real), Chauvet's theology "from below" risks an ontotheological projection of creaturely reality onto God.

A better theological starting point would be the doctrine of creation, as John Webster saw.[121] Under the discipline of the doctrine of creation, even causes become symbols of God. In his relentless rejection of the language of cause, Chauvet effectively writes off causation as carrying the possibility of the symbolic. Aquinas, by contrast, subsumes the movements of the created order under the logic of symbols. This is clearest in Thomas's understanding of the literal sense of scripture. Unlike human authors, God "writes" through the processes of material life.[122] The doctrine of creation allows Thomas to say that all created processes— far from being prelinguistic ontotheological foundations for knowledge of God— are in fact divine symbols, the *subjects* sustained by divine speech, and therefore

---

116. Chauvet, *Symbol*, 492–509.
117. Cf. Kathryn Tanner, *Jesus, Humanity and the Trinity* (Minneapolis, MN: Fortress Press, 2001), 16.
118. Chauvet, *Symbol*, 503.
119. Chauvet, *Symbol*, 41.
120. Chauvet, *Symbol*, 501.
121. Among many others, most notably, David Burrell, *Aquinas: God and Action*, 3rd ed. (Eugene, OR: Wipf and Stock, 2016).
122. *ST* 1a.1.10.

always-already enmeshed in the "linguistic culture" of the Trinity. In other words, divine causality *is* divine speech; it *is* symbolic. Coming to know God in the created order is a matter of learning to receive creation as an address from God, the paradigmatic instance of which is the move from the literal to the spiritual sense of scripture. It is not the case that "causes" supplant "signs" in Thomas's theology of the sacraments, rather, causes become signs under the discipline of the doctrine of creation.

This is immensely important for the sacraments. When Thomas speaks of the substances of bread and wine, for instance, he is not speaking of "the *ultimate reality* of entities," as Chauvet interprets it.[123] Thomas's notion of substance is a fundamentally relational one—a real but asymmetrical relation to God.[124] The ultimate reality of any given thing is not its substance as a self-standing thing over-against God, but a relation to God who gives substance itself.[125] Moreover, "things" do not exist simply in themselves as static realities. They exist with both forms and ends, which is another way of saying that God's action in creation is the gift of matter in motion (form) in a particular direction (*telos*). Form is the gift of motion proper to each thing and *telos* is the direction proper to each thing, a movement and an orientation by which creatures themselves act as causes. Divine causality works "most internally" to creatures, making *all* causality a fundamentally relational phenomenon. Any instance of causality in creation is a symbol of, which is to say a revelatory relation to, this original and abiding first cause. As in the Johannine phrase, "we love because he first loved us," so we cause because he first caused us. Just like Johannine love, this causality is both authentically our own and received as a free gift; just like Johannine love, our causality is an expression of our fundamental relatedness to God. Indeed, *we cause because he first loved us*. Thomas has given us a way of reading any creaturely cause as a symbol of this original divine love.

A miracle, then, is when God does not work through the regular motion of secondary causes, but acts as a primary cause. Yet this is not a subversion of the created order. It is rather the *emergence* of what is truest and most central to the created order, namely, its relation to God. A miracle, then, as poetry to language, casts creation "in state of emergence," revealing its deepest logic and highest reality, which at the same time is never discursively available. Chauvet speaks of his Heideggerian theological project as the "stripping away of a language always on the point of self-destructing [so that] the *trace* of 'the liberating presence of the very thing we sought' is disclosed."[126] A miracle, on Thomas's terms, is precisely

---

123. Chauvet, *Symbol*, 389.

124. *ST* 1a.28.1. A real relation to God, a logical relation from God—this is, contra Chauvet, the only way to maintain relationality without falling into an ontotheological conflation of divine and human registers of speech.

125. See discussion in Chapter 2 the exemplar causality in the divine ideas.

126. Chauvet, *Symbol*, 71, quoting S. Breton, *Le verbe et la croix* (Paris: Desclée, 1981), 114.

the stripping away of a created order of causes always on the verge of the *nihil* so that the trace of the liberating presence of the very thing every creature seeks is disclosed. A miracle is the poetry of creation.

Nowhere is this more evident than in transubstantiation. The accidents of bread and wine are "orphaned," since they lose their proper substances but do not modify the substance of Christ. For Aristotelian metaphysics this is impossible, since an accident must modify its substance or else cease to be. But the accidents of bread and wine do not modify Christ. They are thus radically suspended over the *nihil*—against every requirement Aristotelian metaphysics—sustained only by their original relation to God as primary cause. The accidents are sustained entirely on the power of God as first cause—as is all creation—and yet they effect the highest form of communion with God. In transubstantiation, the very logic of creation is laid bare: creation is entirely a gift, sustained above the *nihil* by the presence of God, and yet raised up into communion with God's very life. Transubstantiation is precisely the poetic *emergence* of creation's mysterious depths.

This does not reduce God to a cause among causes. Between first and second causes is an infinite qualitative difference, so that a divine cause is the kind of cause that can only be glimpsed in faith. A miracle does not make God "available for inspection," as though God left fingerprints at the scene of the crime. The body of Christ remains under the accidents of bread and wine but does not become the substance of those accidents precisely because the presence of Christ is a symbolic presence (which in no way diminishes it as the *real* presence), not a quasi-physical presence. When the accidents of bread and wine are suspended without a substance to modify, they become, in Joseph Ratzinger's words "pure signs,"[127] that is, symbols without remainder, creation in total transparency. But this transparency is only transparent to faith. That faith is given shape by the community that receives and interprets these "pure signs," the community without which the signs would not be at all. So Chauvet is not at all wrong to attend to the community-forming dynamics of symbols and symbol-making, but he short-circuits the possibilities of this reflection by failing to subordinate causes to symbols.[128]

In the sacraments we find ourselves grasped by a trinitarian movement in the very movement of creation in its highest and truest state. The language of sacramental causes allows us to see that communion with God is the poetry of creation, a poetry that reveals the presence of the absence of the risen one—the one who is definitively here, whose presence is (most) real, and yet whose presence

---

127. Benedict XVI, "The Problem of Transubstantiation and the Question about the Meaning of the Eucharist," in *Collected Works of Joseph Ratzinger*, trans. John Saward et al. (San Francisco, CA: Ignatius Press, 2013), 237; quoted in Salkeld, *Transubstantiation*, 118.

128. Moreover, the sacraments "cause" grace as ecclesially constituted and constituting symbols, and that grace causes recipients to themselves become symbols, "likenesses of God," who in turn sustain the sacraments as the community of their reception. The "hermeneutical circle" of symbols—beloved of Chauvet—thus enfolds a causal circle: what causes is in turn caused by what it caused!

is not for that discursively available. Sacramental causality allows us to see that all causes, no matter how deeply enmeshed in *techne*, are symbols, and this finally renders the sacraments as the poetry of creation, the emergence of creation's inscrutable depths. Indeed, in a world whose defining hubris is an all-powerful *techne*, the revelation that all causes are entirely dependent on the movement of the Trinity and are therefore only contingently suspended above the *nihil* is a salutary and prophetic word. Our ambitions to technocratic control falter at the table, where causality itself is seen as pure gift, its powers and pretense outflanked by the logic of gift, of grace, of *mannah*. Only thus may we actually discover how to subordinate our technology—with its many clear benefits—to poetry.

The sacramental causality of the church is thus, *contra* Barthianism, not semi-pelagian. God's perfection establishes the perfection of others. There is no need to contrast created agency with divine agency. The eucharistic church in union with its head thus effects what it signifies, it participates in God's redemption of the world; it *is* God's redemption of the world. This does not imply any diminution in either the glory or agency of God, who stands as the first cause of all creaturely causality. *Contra* Chauvet, this is not ontotheological, since it renders causality itself symbolic. The sacraments reveal all creation, even causality, to be radically suspended above the *nihil*, and like the accidents of bread and wine, the site of highest communion. Under the discipline of the doctrine of creation, the sacraments are the poetry of creation. They "cause" grace inasmuch as they reveal from within entirely human rites and rituals the action and intention of God, the poet.[129] The One Body, then, is the sacrament of God and creation precisely in its humanity and divinity. Another way of saying that the *totus Christus* is symbolism is to say that the church is poetry: creation as it emerges before the God hidden within and beyond. God as symbolized. Creation as symbol. Body of Christ as symbolism. Speaker, language, poetry.

Conclusion

This chapter has advanced two reflections on the church. Both concern the triad Symbolized–Symbol–Symbolism. The first is that the threefold body of Christ corresponds to Christ–church–eucharist. The church is the symbol of Christ, his true presence in the world, and the eucharist is symbolism, the movement of unity between church and Christ. Switching the terms so that the eucharist became the symbol of Christ and the church the guarantor of unity between symbolized and symbol, tended to technologize the eucharist, objectifying the host and turning the church into a juridical structure for ensuring a valid sacrament. I have suggested that a return to a theology of One Body helps sustain a sense of the dynamic reality of the church as a movement across time, as the reception of grace as a gift. With this theology of the One Body in place, I turned to my second concern, the relation

---

129. *ST* 3a.62.1.

of this One Body to God and the world. Creation is a symbol of God, and the Body is symbolism, the dynamic unity of God and world. This implies that the Body is a sacrament, an affirmation that is neither semi-Pelagian nor ontotheological. The doctrine of creation ensures that the church cannot compete with God's work *and* that *techne* is itself enfolded in poetry. The One Body is the world in a state of emergence, and what emerges is the presence—beyond all manipulation and control—of God's own self.

Thus the inner logic of this systematic theology. Reflection on the Trinity leads to reflection on creation. This requires an anthropology, as humanity is the microcosm of the created order. From the Trinity, through creation, emanates the church. The theological progress of this theology thus follows the divine *taxis*. To Father–Son–Spirit correlates God–creation–church. Just as the Spirit is "retroactively causal" in the generation of the Son, so the church is retroactively causal in the creation of the world. Just as the Spirit is mutually internal to Father and Son, so the church is mutually internal to God and world. I have sought to allow theological content to dictate the form of theological inquiry. It remains, then, to make as clear as possible a why this systematic theology is worth adopting. I turn then to a final appeal for symbolism.

Chapter 5

TOWARD MYSTICAL REASON

Introduction

I have been developing a paradigm advocated but insufficiently elaborated by Henri de Lubac, and to my knowledge never systematically unfolded by his interpreters in the way I have done here. I have sought to create a dogmatic outline for a systematic theology of the symbol. A symbol is a sign that mediates the presence of the symbolized, and symbolism is the dynamic movement of unity between symbolized and symbol. This leads to the triad symbolized–symbol–symbolism, which will not be found in de Lubac, or any of my sources, but which provides a helpful framework for accomplishing his aims. I have sought to ground this in the Trinity: the Father is the hidden source of divinity, the Son the replete symbol of the Father, the fullness of the Father's being expressed in another, and the Spirit is symbolism, the fully personal movement of love and unity between Father and Son. I have then argued that creatures participate in these relations analogically, so that symbolized–symbol–symbolism corresponds to God–creation–church. God is the hidden source of creation, creation the symbol of God, bearing within it the ontological trace of its maker, and the church is symbolism, the dynamic movement of love and unity between God and creation. That is, in a compact form, what a systematic theology of the symbol might include. In this chapter, I want to reflect in light of this outline on the nature of theological thought.

In *Corpus Mysticum*, de Lubac articulates the modern perplexity with Augustinian symbolism: "What, then, is this 'understanding' which in our eyes is neither reason, nor mysticism but which aspires to being both at the same time?"[1] Symbolism, according to de Lubac, is characterized by its "mystical reason," and a key test for this systematic theology of the symbol will be whether it recovers such an outlook. The burden of this chapter is to show how symbolism reclaims such mystical reason by incorporating mystery at every level of reflection. The symbolized is eternally hidden, the one mystery anterior to everything that is. The ontological trace of this mysterious source is then present in creation,

---

1. Henri De Lubac, *Corpus Mysticum*, 2nd ed., trans. Gemma Simmonds et al. (London: SCM Press, 2006), 235.

rendering all creation inherently mystical; creation points beyond itself, always-already more than itself. To *read* the mystical symbol of creation, then, is an act of mystical reason: reading the *Logos* dispersed through creation by the power and inspiration of the *Pneuma* who eternally joins symbolized to symbol. Theology is the discipline of reasoning in the Spirit, joining all creation to its mystical source in God. This finally unites not only the content of theological inquiry, but also the theologian's own rationality to the life of the Trinity, so that theological thought itself approximates a mode of prayer. This is because to "read" a symbol is to encounter the ontological trace of the symbolized. Creation "is radiant with a secret intelligibility," and to discover this secret is to encounter its radiant source, ascending to God in thought always on its way to prayer. Thus, symbolism moves from the one mystery of God to the mysticism of creation to the mystical reason of theological inquiry.

But why would such a return to mystical reason be desirable? What would it help us achieve? This movement from mystery to mysticism to mystical reason addresses several pressing concerns in contemporary theology. Addressing these concerns will be among the key contributions of this brief systematic theology. I will argue that when rightly understood, in its parts and as a whole, symbolism (1) avoids an ontotheological reduction of God, (2) avoids *both* a "Barthian" flattening of nature and a neo-Scholastic reification of pure nature, and (3) regains theology as intrinsically mystical, that is, as intrinsically linked to desire and love. Moreover, I will argue that all three must be maintained together if they are to be maintained at all. This chapter thus constitutes a final appeal for both the form and content of this systematic theology of the symbol.

First, to understand God as "the symbolized" is to avoid an "ontotheological" reduction of God. The word "ontotheological" is most famously developed by Martin Heidegger, and while its meaning is complex both philosophically and theologically, I use it here in a theological sense as a forgetfulness of the radical difference between God and creatures.[2] It is an inappropriate ratiocination about God, as though God were an object available for inspection and dissection. I take this to be a perennial temptation in theology.

The triad I have developed, however, resists such a temptation. God can only ever be known *as the symbolized*, that is, revealed precisely as hidden in and beyond created symbols. As the Father is the eternal source and hidden fount of divinity, so

---

2. The word itself originates with Kant but is significantly modified and redeployed by Heidegger. For Heidegger, it derives from a threefold understanding of metaphysics: 1) as *ratio* or truth (*logos*); 2) as reason that grounds being *as such* (onto-logic); 3) as reason that grounds being as a whole (theo-logic). Martin Heidegger, "The Onto-Theo-Logical Constitution of Metaphysics," in *Identity and Difference*, trans. Joan Stambaugh (Chicago, IL: University of Chicago Press, 2002), 57–60. See a brief summary in Andrew Prevot, *Thinking Prayer* (Notre Dame, IN: Notre Dame University Press, 2015), 48–9. See also, Judith Wolfe, *Heidegger and Theology* (London: Bloomsbury T&T Clark, 2014), 138–43, and the theological reception of Heidegger in chs. 7–8.

God is the eternal source and hidden fount of all creation. This relation of creation to God is analogical—since God is not constituted by God's relation to the world, as the Father is constituted by relation to the Son in the Spirit—nonetheless, the former relation is grounded in the latter. Symbolism thus preserves the mystery of God *as a mystery* by maintaining God's complete anteriority to everything that is. I argue this on the basis of an essay by Karl Rahner on the nature of mystery. There is only one mystery, the horizon of all human thought and desire. Theology does not make this mystery less mysterious by conquering its rational territory: God is a mystery to be entered into, not a puzzle to be solved. Knowledge is ordered to this mystery, which positively surpasses its capabilities, and as Rahner argues, this constrains knowledge to become love if it is to fulfill its nature as knowledge. God is ever the symbolized and is thus the inscrutable mystery anterior to all that is and must be loved to be known. Thus symbolism resists theology's ontotheological temptation by maintaining the transcendent mystery of God.

Second, to see creation as a mystical symbol avoids *both* a "Barthian" temptation to flatten nature in favor of a wholly determinative "God from outside," *and* an apparently settled, independent, and autonomous *natura pura* as advocated by Garrigou-Lagrange.[3] Following de Lubac, I argue that creation is a symbol because it is the temporal unfolding of the Logos, destined to be returned to God in the Logos incarnate. This twofold ministry of Christ sustains creation in a twofold mysticism: created with an ontological desire for union with the Word in which it was spoken but requiring the grace of Christ to fulfill that desire. Creation is therefore a *christological* mystery, from creation to redemption, Christ to Christ. Created nature is thus not a mere "vacuole," a placeholder for grace, a wholly passive onlooker to divine revelation as is discernable in some strands of Barthianism. But neither is it "pure" in natural self-sufficiency.[4] By its inclusion in Christ, creation is the moving image of the eternal mystery, a mystical symbol spoken by God. I will compare this account of mysticism to both Barth and Reginald Garrigou-Lagrange to argue that only the paradox of a natural desire for the supernatural does justice to both the integrous and mystical nature of creation.

---

3. I place scare quotes around "Barthian" advisedly. The issues surrounding Barth's view of created nature are complex and controverted. My point is that this trend is detectible in some strands of Barthianism. For an in-depth account of some of the issues at play, see Tyler Wittman, *God and Creation in the Theology of Thomas Aquinas and Karl Barth* (Cambridge: Cambridge University Press, 2018).

4. The use of the term "pure-nature" is not always deployed the same way by neo-Thomists. I use it to indicate the reality of nature abstracted from the actual economy of salvation. On this view, nature constitutes a perfection in itself, to which a second supernatural end can then be superadded. De Lubac does not deny a natural end for human nature, only that it can be so separated from its supernatural end. See discussion in Nicholas J. Healy Jr., "The Christian Mystery of Nature and Grace," in Jordan Hillebert, (ed.), *The T&T Clark Companion to Henri de Lubac* (London: Bloomsbury T&T Clark, 2017), 181–204.

Third, and finally, if God is a mystery as the symbolized, and creation a mystical symbol, then theology is the reading of that symbol by mystical reason. In Chapter 3 I expounded de Lubac's view of the spiritual interpretation of scripture as an all-encompassing theological program. Here I fill out this insight: theology is more like the spiritual interpretation of scripture than an exclusively rational exposition of Christian teaching: the theologian reads the spiritual sense embedded within and beyond the literal sense of creation. Theology seeks to unite the diverse aspects of the symbol of creation to the symbolized: faith seeking understanding of God and all things in relation to God. But the absolute anteriority of God sustains a certain circularity to this seeking. We can only know the Trinity through created symbols, but our symbols must be shaped and reshaped by the Trinity. This is not a weakness; it is entirely traditional, as a reading of Augustine's *De trinitate* will show. This circularity produces a perpetual process of seeking and finding and seeking again, as we ascend through a reading of symbols into God. It is finally intended to shape the image of God within us as we learn to think and speak words worthy of God in love. In symbolism, theological thought begins to approximate prayer, as the theologian encounters the *presence* of God in the symbols of God. This systematic theology of the symbol thus takes significant steps toward accomplishing de Lubac's vision of regaining theology as a discipline of mystical reason: a mysterious God speaks a mystical creation to be understood by an act of mystical reason.

One final note. These three levels must be held together; the three points of the triad cannot be understood singularly. Because the triad symbolized–symbol–symbolism is an analogy for the Trinity, a trinitarian logic governs its use: they must be grasped together or not at all. To avoid resolving one problem only to raise another, all three must be held together in a single theological vision. Thus, where a particular theology might preserve one pole exceptionally well, it risks losing the others. For example, I will argue that "Barthianism" has a strong sense of the transcendent mystery of God, but it fails to understand creation as a mystical symbol, and so fails to understand theology as mystical reason, which in turn threatens even the transcendence of God it intended to secure. That is why this brief dogmatic outline for a theology of the symbol, however lightly sketched, needs to be articulated *as a whole*. What is needed is a systematic theology of the symbol trinitarian in its parts and as a whole.

From Mysteries to Mystery

To regain mystical reason, I begin first with the nature of mystery itself. Only with a clear idea of what mystery is can we hope to regain mystical reason. I will develop this through Karl Rahner's theology of mystery. Rahner perceptively diagnoses the dominant and deficient concept of mystery in modern theology and offers instead a notion of mystery as unified, foundational, and abiding. This one abiding mystery both makes knowledge possible and requires knowledge to become love if it is to fulfill itself as knowledge. This, I am arguing, is what it means to understand

God as "the symbolized": the one mystery that is the horizon of all existence who must be loved to be known and who can never be reduced ontotheologically to one being among beings.

On the One Mystery

Karl Rahner asks, "Can [mystery] be regarded as a defective type of another and better knowledge which is still to come?"[5] Is a mystery simply something we do not *yet* understand, that is, something that otherwise should be available to reason but currently is not? His essay, "The Concept of Mystery in Catholic Theology" diagnoses this as the "average concept [of mystery] as proposed in the schools."[6] Rahner notes three remarkable traits of this conception. First, that mystery is "the property of a statement."[7] Because truth is in the domain of statements, there are statements we must make (because by faith we accept them as true) for which we do not have sufficient reason. A statement we must make in faith, which surpasses reason, is a mystery—God's triunity, for example. Second, because a truth's natural abode is in statements, and there are many statements we make in faith without sufficient reason, it follows that there are many mysteries. There is quite obviously a great deal which we affirm but do not understand, and so "mysteries" multiply. Thirdly, these mysteries are *"provisionally* incomprehensible,"[8] that is, they are only unknowable before beatitude. For Rahner, the average notion of mystery is a statement among many such statements for which we temporarily lack sufficient reason.[9]

Each of these traits, the focus on statements, their plurality, and their provisionality, all follow from a conviction that a mystery is "oriented from the start to the '*ratio*'".[10] What is mysterious is mysterious *to reason*. This is not surprising; it is the language of Vatican I.[11] As reason makes progress by degrees, mysteries decrease proportionally. As *Dei Filius* states:

---

5. Karl Rahner, "The Concept of Mystery in Catholic Theology," in *Theological Investigations*, Vol. 4 (New York: Crossroad Publishing, 1973), 42.
6. Rahner, "Mystery," 38.
7. Rahner, "Mystery," 38.
8. Rahner, "Mystery," 38.
9. This understanding of mystery is alive and well. In Thomist circles it continues to be standard. W. Norris Clarke, who is more attentive to mystery and paradox than many, affirms that there are many "mysteries, things which I, or even the human race as a whole on this earth cannot yet understand, whose sufficient reason we cannot yet crack." W. Norris Clarke, *The One and the Many: A Contemporary Thomist Metaphysics* (Notre Dame, IN: Notre Dame University Press, 2001), 22. From a previous generation, Reginald Garrigou-Lagrange follows these contours quite precisely in *The Sense of Mystery: Clarity and Obscurity in the Intellectual Life* (Steubenville, OH: Emmaus Academic, 2017). See analysis of this text below. Analytic theology tends to treat mystery similarly. Cf. Oliver D. Crisp, *Analyzing Doctrine* (Waco, TX: Baylor University Press, 2019), ch. 4.
10. Rahner, "Mystery," 38.

> And reason, indeed, enlightened by faith—when it seeks earnestly, piously and somberly—attains by a gift from God *some* understanding of the mysteries, even a very fruitful one ... But ... the Divine Mysteries by their own nature so far transcend the created intelligence that, even when delivered by revelation and received by faith, they remain covered with the veil of faith itself, and shrouded *in a certain degree* of darkness, so long as we are pilgrims in this mortal life, not yet with God.[12]

Reason can attain some knowledge subject to certain degrees of abiding darkness. I might not know everything about God, but I can know some things with confidence. Further, my lack of knowledge is only provisional, for I am "not yet with God."

As Rahner interprets Vatican I:

> The silent presupposition throughout is that we are dealing with truths which should strictly speaking have come within the scope of reason with its power to see and *comprehend*, but in this case do not meet its demands.[13]

Rahner is frank in his assessment of the average notion of mystery. A mystery understood as "one of many statements provisionally unknown to reason" is not necessarily wrong, but it fails to take seriously the unique nature of the *divine* mystery and the corresponding human orientation toward this mystery. He questions the conceptual and spiritual adequacy of the concept of "mystery" and the *ratio* to which it is addressed. What if mystery corresponds to the unity of the human spirit prior to its division into faculties? What if unknowing is not just the absence of knowledge "but a positive characteristic of a relationship between one subject and another?"[14] What if, in other words, mystery is foundational and abiding?

Rather than many statements that are unknowable to reason, Rahner proposes *one* mystery that corresponds to the deepest unity of the human spirit precisely *as* mystery. The mystery of God is irreducible, for it is the foundation of all human knowing, willing, and being. It is the "horizon" within which every finite experience is experienced, every thought thought, every desire desired.[15] Mystery

---

11. Dogmatic Constitution on the Catholic Faith, IV, available at http://inters.org/Vatican-Council-I-Dei-Filius. For an excellent account on the relation of reason and God at Vatican I, see Fergus Kerr, "Knowing God by Reason Alone: What Vatican I Never Said," *New Blackfriars* 91, no. 1033 (May 2010), 215–28.
12. Dogmatic Constitution on the Catholic Faith, IV.
13. Rahner, "Mystery," 39. Emphasis original.
14. Rahner, "Mystery," 41.
15. This is obviously indebted to the thought of Martin Heidegger. Rahner is here seeking to avoid an "onto-theological" reduction of God to one being among beings.

cannot in any way be provisional, since its abiding reality is the foundation of creaturely existence. Solve the mystery, Rahner would say, and you dissolve the creature. God is the one mystery, the entire context of all creaturely existence, and the abiding mystery of eternity.

On this picture, *ratio* should be considered "a spiritual entity of absolute transcendence," by which Rahner means that reason is the faculty that propels humans beyond themselves and into communion with God. Knowledge only "comes into being" in "self-transcendence," that is, only as it becomes love:

> Knowledge, though prior to love and freedom, can only be realized in its *true* sense when and in so far as the subject is more than knowledge, when in fact it is a freely given love. This is only possible if knowledge is ultimately a faculty ordained to an object attainable only because the object is greater than the faculty. And what but the incomprehensibility of mystery can be such an object of knowledge, since it forces knowledge to surpass itself in a more comprehensive act, that of love?[16]

Rahner has here touched on the recurring paradox of this book. In trinitarian terms, I have argued the Spirit is "retroactively causal" in the generation of the Son, for the Son only *is* inasmuch as he receives the Spirit from the Father, and yet the Son *precedes* the Spirit. This plays out in Rahner's anthropology, where knowledge precedes love and freedom, but only becomes knowledge *in love and freedom*. The Son is the Son in the Spirit. Just like trinitarian theology, a Thomist intellectualism must also acknowledge the fundamental unity of the human person, the extent to which intellect and will are mutually constitutive.

For this reason, Rahner rejects a merely elicited desire for the supernatural: "Merely to say that love is aroused when the intellect discloses the goodness and appetibility of the object, would be to fail to establish a true perichoresis and to leave the two faculties without any fundamental unity."[17] Rahner rejects the idea that desire is merely aroused, for this would divide love and desire from knowledge as two dis-integrated steps in a process.[18] In Thomist terms, knowledge is ordered to truth, the will to the good. But then how can the intellect recognize the goodness of a thing in order to propose it to the will if not formally ordered to goodness? There must be something in the nature of truth that constrains knowledge to become love. That is the abiding mystery. *Because* knowledge is ordered to a truth it cannot positively possess, it is forced "either to consume itself in protest or to transform itself in the self-surrender by which it accepts the mystery as such, that is, in love, and so to attain its proper perfection."[19] Knowledge is thus ordered

---

16. Rahner, "Mystery," 43.
17. Rahner, "Mystery," 44.
18. Rahner, "Mystery," 44.
19. Rahner, "Mystery," 44. Rahner is not arguing against Thomism on this point—he offers this as a right interpretation of Thomist intellectualism.

to the mystery, and this constrains knowledge to become love if it is to be true knowledge. In this way, the intellect and will coinhere in a unified whole—i.e., a human spirit. Knowledge must become love in the face of the eternal mystery, and because the eternal mystery is always present to the intellect as that which it cannot master, love is intrinsic to knowledge. This is true of God and creatures, for mystery is "a positive characteristic of a relationship between one subject and another."[20] Unmastery is the precondition of love, indeed, the precondition of any relationship whatsoever. Rahner therefore rejects a purely elicited desire for the supernatural, suggesting that the intellect's orientation to the mystery sustains a primordial natural dynamism toward the divine without which nature and natural knowledge cannot function at all. We desire God because we know God as that which is beyond all knowledge. Therefore if we are to truly know God, we must love God.

But this ordering to the mystery does not make the creature a mystery, strictly speaking: "Only God as such can be truly a mystery."[21] Creatures might be called mysterious, since they have the eternal mystery as both source and end, but in created reality there "can be no absolute mysteries."[22] So Rahner is not proposing something like John Milbank's interpretation of de Lubac's *desiderium naturale*, for whom the natural desire for the supernatural is a wholly natural and wholly supernatural constituent component of human nature.[23] For Rahner, "It is simply contradictory that something should belong completely to the order of creation, by being created, and still belong to the strictly divine order, by being strictly supernatural."[24] The mystery is God and God alone.

For Rahner, the incarnation and grace, however, can be called mysteries in a highly qualified sense. They are only mysteries inasmuch as they involve God's own being. In the incarnation and grace, "God communicates himself in his own person to the creature, as absolute proximity and as absolute holy mystery."[25] These two mysteries (incarnation and grace) are the mysteries of the communication of the divine to the creature, not anything in the creature as such. Therefore, "the *possibility* of such self-communication of God to the creature is what constitutes the theological mystery in these two mysteries."[26] Since only God is mystery, within the finite world the mystery can only be the *possibility* of God's presence. I will contest this point below.

---

20. Rahner, "Mystery," 41.
21. Rahner, "Mystery," 63.
22. Rahner, "Mystery," 62.
23. Cf. John Milbank, *The Suspended Middle: Henri de Lubac and the Renewed Split in Modern Catholic Theology*, 2nd ed. (Cambridge: Eerdmans, 2005), 44.
24. Rahner, "Mystery," 67.
25. Rahner, "Mystery," 67. Rahner sees incarnation and grace as the communication of God's own self because of his insistence that the economic trinity is the immanent trinity. What God does in time (i.e., become incarnate and give grace) is who God is eternally.
26. Rahner, "Mystery," 67. Emphasis original.

By maintaining the mystery as exclusively within the purview of divinity, Rahner seeks to guard the unspeakable as unspeakable. The mystery is the ground of the possibility of all categorical knowledge but is not itself a proper object of that knowledge. We cannot name God: "We could call him (if we wished to give such a title to what is meant) the nameless, that which is other than all finite things, the infinite: but we should not have thereby given him a name, merely said that he has none."[27] The mystery that is God is the horizon within which all else is grasped, and which never itself becomes something we could positively capture or express. Indeed, knowledge of finite things and knowledge of the infinite that underlies all finitude produce, for the Rahnerian subject, "two essentially different types of data for the spirit."[28] The "data" of divinity is known only as that which cannot be known, even while it makes possible the knowledge of every finite thing. The eternally unknowable mystery, then, is that which illuminates all finite knowledge; as grace it is the possibility of God's proximity; eternally, it is the content of the beatific vision. In every modulation it remains a mystery. This one mystery is the one context in which all of human existence is experienced and understood; in its light we see light. All other "mysteries" are but derivates from this one, the mystery *stricte dicta*.

Mystery and the Symbolized

This concept of mystery, I want to suggest, fills out what it means to say that God is "the symbolized." God is absolutely anterior to everything that is, the ground of all being who is not a being. God stands as the source of creation, and never as an object within it. As such, God is the horizon in which creation is intelligible: only in the light of the symbolized can we see symbols. Moreover, just as we only see symbols in the light of the symbolized, so we only glimpse the symbolized through its symbols. God cannot be circumscribed in the world of symbols, yet symbols bear the ontological trace of God, and so it is in and through symbols that we must meet God. We cannot step outside our status as creatures to gain direct access to God. There is thus a circularity to this dynamic: only against the horizon of the symbolized can we see symbols, and only through symbols can we come to know the symbolized. If it were otherwise, God would be some kind of object: if we could recognize symbols without the horizon of the symbolized or the symbolized without symbols, we would have achieved a God's-eye-view, a universal vision of all things. And this would make us God's equal, making both God and creation objects for our mastery. Rather, God can never be objectified in creation, only symbolized.

If Heidegger is right that Western theology and philosophy is perennially tempted to forget the ontological difference between being itself and finite being, symbolism resists this forgetfulness.[29] Indeed, where Heidegger took his

---

27. Rahner, "Mystery," 51.
28. Rahner, "Mystery," 62.
29. Wolfe, *Heidegger*, ch. 3.

critique of ontotheology from theological sources and then attempted to strip it of theological context, symbolism undercuts ontotheology on firmly theological grounds, namely, a theology of the Trinity.[30] The hiddenness of God in the world is a temporal participation in the hiddenness of the Father in the Son by the Spirit. The Father is the ungenerated source, the hidden fount of divinity, eternally the symbolized.[31] This eternal hiddenness of the Father is echoed in the hiddenness of God in time, who is never available to us as a *thing* that we might possess.

But does this *Deus absconditus* not make theology itself impossible? Surely, to account for God, to explain God in human words is to domesticate God, to render God one being among others, now subject to human linguistic control. This is certainly a temptation, but only if we fail to recognize what the absolute mystery does to human thought: to think of the being beyond all being requires that thinking transcend into love. We can only know God if we love God, and this loving preserves the integrity of the divine as wholly other, as that which is never "possessed" in my knowing. A God who can be understood apart from love is indeed an ontotheological idol, for such a God is an *object* of knowledge, no longer a living mystery into whom we are beckoned to enter.[32] As argued above, only if knowledge is constituted (paradoxically) by its consummation in love can theology avoid reducing God to a conceptual idol.

This dynamic of knowledge-becoming-love, as Andrew Prevot notes, renders theology inherently doxological.[33] Symbolism preserves the difference between God and creation by being intrinsically worshipful, opening upward toward a mysterious other that we can never positively possess, but are nonetheless drawn toward in desire and love.[34] A theology alive to the irreducible mystery of the divine thus closely approximates prayer, indeed, it is destined to become prayer.[35] Moreover, as Prevot convincingly argues, the prayerful posture of theology is a practice of giving and receiving hospitality by embracing God precisely *as the other* who is irreducible to my knowledge, a way of making room for God's unique otherness by embracing my very unknowing. This practice of hospitality toward God then sustains a practice of hospitality toward creatures. A theologian alive

---

30. Cf. Wolfe, *Heidegger,* 138.

31. This is not to deny subsistent relations in favor of a Franciscan/Scotist logical *taxis* founded on the primacy of the Father who must first "be" in order to beget. The latter retains a risk of ontotheology inasmuch as it seeks to make God yet another logically dictated sequence. Symbolism secures the Franciscan desire for the primacy of the Father, but in a logic of subsistent relations: the Father is ungenerated only in relation to the generated, symbolized only in relation to a symbol.

32. Cf. Prevot, *Thinking Prayer,* 16.

33. Prevot, *Prayer,* 4. Prevot goes on to argue that Heidegger slides into nihilism because in the end he refuses prayer (p. 43).

34. For a systematic theology that recentralizes desire, see Sarah Coakley, *God, Sexuality and the Self* (Cambridge: Cambridge University Press, 2013).

35. Prevot, *Prayer,* 67.

to mystery, Prevot argues, is a theologian practicing the habits that nurture a hospitality toward (and an openness to receive hospitality from) God's creatures. Theology is thus supremely prayerful, practicing hospitality to the irreducible mystery of God and God's creatures.[36] A theologian who has failed this hospitable love of God and creatures has failed as a theologian. This of course indicates that we are all failures, and that theology is necessarily an ongoing practice of hospitable reception of and reception by the ineffable. This underscores that just as God is not one object of knowledge among others, nor is God one object of love among others: love for God does not competitively replace love for others. Rather, it sustains such a love.

God is thus the mysterious source, always anterior to creation. God cannot be one being among beings, and therefore can only known in and through symbols: God can never be objectified in creation, only symbolized. God must therefore be loved to be known, not as one love among others, but as the all-encompassing mystery *by which* we love others. The practice of coming to love God sustains the practice of loving others. This takes us a long way toward a theology more closely linked to mysticism and prayer, but I do not think it goes far enough. For to say that God is the symbolized implies that creation is a symbol, and the nature of this symbol must be clearly understood if what has been gained in avoiding an ontotheological reduction of God is not to be lost. As will be shown, if creation is viewed as insufficiently symbolic, both the transcendence of God *and* the mystical tenor of theological reason will be lost. Symbolized–symbol–symbolism must be understood together, or not at all. But to prepare for this, we need to relocate Rahner's paradox.

Relocating Rahner's Paradox

For Rahner, the mystery can only be divinity as such, and therefore creatures can only be a mystery inasmuch as they exhibit the *possibility* of the nearness of the divine. I wish to contest this. It is true that nature is not grace; the natural is not the supernatural. But this does not entail that the mystery in regard to humanity is only the *possibility* of the nearness of the mystery. There is no reason, on Rahner's terms, that the mystery should not be the *actuality* of the nearness of the mystery. Indeed, there are good reasons to think that it is. Can a bare possibility, a pure potentiality really be the correlate of an inexhaustible mystery? Can an overflowing, superabundance really correspond to such a vacuous *a priori*? The mystery is not that I have a nature that might have existed under the pure possibility of God's

---

36. Much more could be said about this: the requirement to practice hospitality toward and receive hospitality from the cultural other, attending, among other things, to the history of racism and colonialism. We might also note that this makes theology irreducibly social, an ongoing tradition of hospitable discourse with *these people*. Even when our disagreements (whether across time or in contemporary discussion) seem to swamp our agreement, our ongoing argument is itself a sign of our commitment to moving forward together, at least ideally.

nearness. The mystery is that I have a nature that *does* exist under the actuality of God's nearness.

This is made clear in relation to the incarnation. It is in regard to this mystery that Rahner formulates his "possibility" argument. The problem is that if humanity is a mystery only in possibility, this would seem to make Christ, in the unity of his person, not a mystery, strictly speaking. His divinity would be a mystery properly speaking, while his humanity would be a mystery only inasmuch as it exhibited the *a priori* possibility of union with God. But does this not underestimate the unity of Christ's person in the incarnation? Christ is not half-mystery and half-possibility. There is only one Christ, one divine Son. If God is the mystery, *stricte dictu*, then we must say with Augustine that Christ is "the whole Mystery of God."[37] This latter formulation is precisely what Rahner's Christology consistently seeks to maintain. The God given to us in Jesus of Nazareth is the whole God—there is not some other God lurking behind the God of the economy.[38] It is the irreducible unity of the incarnation that ensures humanity itself is now eternally united to God in Christ. In short, in the incarnation humanity is revealed to be a mystery, united forever to the triune God in the one God-man, Jesus Christ. Humanity is not a mystery because God might come near, humanity is always-already made a mystery by being joined to God in Christ.

What has happened here is not necessarily a problem with Rahner's theology of the symbolized, the hidden mystery of God, but a failure to capture all three—symbolized-symbol-symbolism—in a single vision. In trinitarian terms, to say that the Father is eternal source is also to say that the Son and Spirit are eternally sourced, that is, the Father, Son and Spirit subsist as relations.[39] Hence, all three must be thought together. The same is true in an analogical way of God, creation, and redemption in the church. The relations between God, creation and church, while they participate in the relations between Father, Son and Spirit, are indeed different: God is not a subsistent relation to the world, since the world is a free overflow of the divine goodness.[40] Creation, however, is constituted by its real relation to the Trinity—to be created is to receive the gift of a relation to God.[41] And

---

37. Henri De Lubac, *Theology in History* (San Francisco: Ignatius Press, 1996), 218; quoting Augustine, *Epist.* 187, n. 34. (PL 33, 845).

38. Rahner expresses as much in his theology of the symbol: the incarnation shows humanity is "God's own proper environment," "The Theology of the Symbol" in *TI* 4, 235.

39. Thomas Aquinas, *Summa Theologiae* 1a.29.4. All quotations from Laurence Shapcote, O.P., trans., *Latin/English Edition of the Works of St. Thomas Aquinas* (Lander, WY: The Aquinas Institute for the Study of Sacred Doctrine, 2012). Hereafter, *ST*.

40. See Chapter 2 for an account of this freedom vis-à-vis the Spirit.

41. For a counter argument that substance precedes relation, see Steven A. Long, "Creation *ad imaginem Dei*: The Obediential Potency of the Human Person to Grace and Glory," *Nova et Vetera* 14, no. 4, English Edition (2016). Long's argument, however, is weak, for without the gift of a real relation to God, there could be no substance to be in relation. His argument would only seem to confirm the suspicion that neo-Scholastic theology sustains a secular vision of substances for whom relation with God is an inessential extra.

this real relation makes creation a symbol, albeit one that God freely emanates. In particular, creation is a participation in the divine ideas contained in the Logos set in living motion by the Spirit. It is, as Cusa puts it, the temporal unfolding of the eternal Word.[42] This unfolding is destined to return to God in Christ, the Logos incarnate. And because there is only one divine Son, both creation and redemption are the work of Christ, as Colossians 1 makes clear. Hence, because Christ cannot be split in two, creation cannot be thought in isolation from redemption. This work of Christ is indeed twofold—creation is not redemption—but it is the work of one Christ, God and human. Creation is, therefore, always-already christic.[43]

This always-already quality points toward the impossibility of separating symbol from symbolism, creation from its motion of return back to God in Christ. This motion itself is a finite participation in the life of the Spirit from Father to Son and Son to Father. To think of a symbol is necessarily to think of symbolism, for that movement is what constitutes the symbol as a symbol. And just like the Spirit is paradoxically pre-present in the generation of the Son, so the incarnation, as creation joined to God in Christ, is paradoxically pre-present in creation. The incarnation indeed *presupposes* creation, but like Spirit to Son, it is "retroactively causal" in creation itself.

All of this is to say, in the strongest possible terms, that there is no moment of bare "possibility" in creation's relation to God. In conceiving of a human mystery as the *possibility* of God's nearness, Rahner appears to pause and isolate one portion of the triad from the others, at least conceptually. He has attempted to think of humanity without its essential relation to God as a symbol, and without its gratuitous return to God in Christ by the movement of the Spirit. This problem is methodological: Rahner is seeking the conditions for the possibility of grace, and that requires that there first be a subject constituted prior to grace—a "remainder concept" of pure nature. But the perichoretic unity of symbol and symbolized disallows such a strategy: there is no symbol not already in a motion of symbolism toward God. We must, in other words, say the nearness of God in the incarnation presupposes creation, but that the incarnation is retroactively causal in creation, and therefore neither can be thought without the other. The human correlate of the mystery is not therefore the possibility of God's nearness, for there is no conceptual moment of bare possibility. To posit such a moment is to endanger the symbol as a symbol, for it takes away its constitutive relation to symbolism. The mystery is therefore God's always-already presence to creation in Christ. The point here is that we must catch all three terms—even while distinguishing them—to do justice to any of them.

If isolating the symbol from symbolism endangers the symbol, it also endangers the hiddenness of the symbolized. There is the risk that what Rahner

---

42. Nicholas of Cusa, *De Dato Patris Luminum* in Hopkins, (ed.), *Complete Philosophical and Theological Treatises of Nicholas of Cusa: Volume One* (Minneapolis, MN: The Arthur J. Banning Press, 2001).

43. See Rowan Williams, *Christ the Heart of Creation* (London: Bloomsbury T&T Clark, 2018).

has gained in terms of God's absolute otherness will be lost by so firmly *isolating* God's creation from God's own mystery. To fix such a hard boundary for God is to say that the mystery of God may go no further. But Kathryn Tanner is surely right that the incarnation reveals that there can be no such trade-off between divinity and humanity.[44] God is so utterly different from creation that God differs differently; that creation might share in God's mystery would not infringe on the absolute mysteriousness of God, but would rather emphasize it. As Rahner would doubtless agree, God is not a mystery diminished in its sharing. There is thus no reason so sharply to demarcate the mystery of God from the mystery of creation. Indeed, by sharing in the mystery *as a symbol*, creation displays in its own being, the mysterious otherness of God, namely, that God's mystery is not depleted by being shared.[45] Thus, any attempt to isolate one term of the triad from the others endangers all three. Even the symbolized loses its own hiddenness unless the symbol and symbolism are simultaneously maintained. We will see this again.

The obvious repost to this is that it endangers the gratuity of grace in the incarnation. If the Incarnation is "paradoxically pre-present" in creation, does this not make grace native to nature and therefore not a supernatural gift? This *would* endanger the gratuity of God's gifts if we think of God as bound by some kind of logico-temporal process—as though God must *first* create and *then* order to beatitude in Christ to avoid being bound to what God has already freely chosen! Must we really imagine that God creates without the slightest thought for our elevation in grace, and only then decides to redeem us? God's being and act are one (indeed, God creates and redeems in and for the *one* Christ), even as God's action is experienced as twofold by creatures. To read this sequence back into God is to think of God as a very large creature, to subject God to all the divisions of creaturely life. My notion of "retroactive causality" only endangers gratuity if we forget the different difference of God.

Having seen how understanding God as the symbolized avoids an ontotheological reduction of God, and how all three terms must be thought simultaneously if they are to be thought rightly, I turn now to a closer examination of the created symbol. As de Lubac argues, Christ's twofold work of creation and redemption sustains creation in a twofold mysticism. To that mysticism I now turn.

From Mystery to Mysticism

Once we have moved Rahner's mystery from the possibility to the actuality of divine nearness, we open the possibility of mysticism. Having gained a rich theology of mystery from Rahner, together with its insistence on the necessity

---

44. See Kathryn Tanner, *Jesus, Humanity and the Trinity* (Minneapolis, MN: Fortress Press, 2001).

45. On this, see John Webster, "Love Is Also a Lover of Life: *Creatio Ex Nihilo* and Creaturely Goodness," *Modern Theology* 29, no. 2 (April 2013), 156–71.

of love in all thinking, I will now re-engage Henri de Lubac's work to move from mystery to mysticism. My argument is that only the natural desire for the supernatural sufficiently secures the integrity of creation as a symbol, and thereby the transcendence of God as symbolized and the motion of creation toward God in symbolism. I will contrast de Lubac's account of the natural desire with certain trajectories in Karl Barth's thought, as well as the mysticism superadded to pure nature advocated by Reginald Garrigou-Lagrange.

Mysticism and the Natural Desire for the Supernatural

If Rahner takes us from many mysteries to one divine mystery, de Lubac clarifies how this one mystery sustains all of creation as intrinsically mystical. I have argued that a symbol is a sign that mediates the presence of the symbolized. It is the ontological trace of Christ that makes creation intrinsically mystical: creation is spoken in the eternal Word, and naturally longs to return to this source, a longing that can only be secured by the grace of Christ. In other words, I will argue that because creation is a symbol—a sign that mediates Christ's presence—it has a natural desire for the supernatural.

In an introductory essay to a volume on mysticism, de Lubac argues that the natural desire is the key to Christian mysticism. The essay is an attempt to articulate on the one hand why mysticism seems so consistent across religious traditions, and why, on the other hand, Christian mysticism is distinctively Christian. "Human nature is basically the same everywhere," de Lubac argues; "God has made man in his image with the idea of bringing man to resemble him—a resemblance that must be consummated in the 'beatific vision.'"[46] Citing the traditional distinction between the image and likeness of God, de Lubac argues that "in each person's creation, the image is the gift received along with his very being."[47] There is thus a "mysticism of essence" common to all humans, who, as image-bearers by nature, have an inner impulse toward their source in God. The divine likeness, however, "is something to be realized, through the action of the Holy Spirit, by man's dependence on the redeeming Incarnation."[48] The mysticism of essence requires a further "nuptial mysticism" that gratuitously joins humanity to God in Christ.

This leads to the following formulation of the natural desire for the supernatural:

> The aspiration [of the image to become the likeness] is inherent in human nature, since man is made for this union. In other words, there must be in our nature a certain capacity for the appropriation of the mystery that is both given

---

46. Henri De Lubac, *Theological Fragments*, trans. Rebeccah Howell Balinski (San Francisco, CA: Ignatius, 1989), 51–2.
47. De Lubac, *Fragments*, 51.
48. De Lubac, *Fragments*, 52.

and revealed in Jesus Christ. It is a capacity that is naturally accompanied by desire, a desire that must be described as ontological.[49]

This ontological desire, however, is liable to become an idolatrous fixation, a nameless and pernicious mysticism, "if its aim is to generate its own object, fulfilling itself alone."[50] To focus wholly on this élan in itself would indeed be "a most profound kind of atheism," celebrating the transcendence of human nature while refusing to see that unto which it longs to transcend. The natural desire for the supernatural cannot fulfill itself, nor can it generate its own object. It can only be fulfilled by grace, and this requires God's loving and entirely gratuitous gift of God's own self in Christ.

Christian mysticism, then, is the convergence of two mystical modes. The Christian mystic, according to de Lubac, shares with mystics of all faiths and none a certain sense of interiority, an experience of the depths of the self as compelled toward transcendence. This "mysticism of essence" arises from the depths of human nature itself as the image of God in time. But *Christian* mysticism has a more determinative outward dimension, a "nuptial mysticism," where the mystic experiences communion with the other, with what is outside herself, namely, with God in Christ. What makes the Christian mystic unique is the extent to which this mysticism of essence is circumscribed and subordinated to the nuptial mystery. It is the one mystery of God, now come near in Christ, that determines the inward mysticism of essence: "In Christian mysticism, the mystery is first and last."[51] A pure mysticism of essence, exclusively internal, abandons its outward religious structures once mystical experience takes hold; the wholly interiorized mystic leaves behind the concrete structures of its existence in mystical rapture. For the Christian mystic, on the other hand, there is no question of ever severing ties, ever leaving or surpassing the one mystery. Mystical ascent never climbs beyond its source in the revelation of God in Christ.

Nonetheless, neither is the interior dimension of mysticism squelched in favor of a wholly determinative "God from outside." "Rooted in the Image," de Lubac argues, "the sacred part of our being that naturally touches God, it is apt to produce a secret echo in each person."[52] Because humanity is a symbol of God, created in the Son and Spirit for communion with God, to look inward is to look outward, to seek God. This is not because nature is vacuous, so that in the end the only thing to be discovered by interiority is God, but rather because humanity is *the image of the mystery*, and this means that a proper interiority

---

49. De Lubac, *Fragments*, 52. It should be pointed out that de Lubac is critical of attempts to equate the distinction between image and likeness with a distinction between Aristotelian nature and Christian grace. Aristotelian natures exist far too autonomously to be compatible with the Christian patristic and biblical concept of the image.
50. De Lubac, *Fragments*, 52.
51. De Lubac, *Fragments*, 68.
52. De Lubac, *Fragments*, 69.

will always require a turn outward, a search for that which is symbolized in this symbol. To interiorize the mystery is to be drawn outward to God. What makes Christian mysticism distinctively Christian, according to de Lubac, is the preservation of these two poles, the interiority proper to the human person, and the harkening outward that this interiority requires; it is both essential and nuptial, something intrinsic to human nature, and yet something that must be found beyond nature.

This entire structure is anchored christologically. De Lubac argues, "If the articles of faith are numbered, the Object of Faith is marvelously one."[53] This one object of faith is none other than Christ: "Christ is not *a* mystery: he is *the* mystery—there is no other."[54] There is only one mystery, and Christ is, de Lubac quotes Augustine, "the whole mystery of God."[55] As the incarnate Son, Christ reveals the Father, not by being indistinguishable from the Father, but by being the Father's symbol, the "exact imprint" of the Father's nature.[56] Moreover, Christ is not without the Spirit. Even though Christ's ministry precedes that of the Spirit, Christ's own life and ministry are established by the Spirit: Mary is overshadowed by the Spirit and Christ is anointed by the Spirit for ministry at his baptism.[57] The Spirit is thus paradoxically pre-present, or retroactively causal in both the generation and the mission of the Son. Christ is the Son, the Realsymbol of the Father in the Spirit. We must therefore say with Augustine that Christ is the whole mystery of God.

If Christ is the whole mystery of God he is also the whole mystery of creation. To see this, we have to understand the identity of Christ as the eternal Son. Following Cyril of Alexandria and Aquinas, we must say that there are not two sons—an eternal divine Son and temporal creaturely Son.[58] Rather, Christ's human nature is entirely constituted by the person of the eternal Word. The unity of Christ's person means that everything predicated of the divine nature is predicated of the human. Hence, Christ does divine things humanly and human things divinely. Only in light of such a Cyriline Christology of unity can we understand Paul's insistence that all things are created by *Christ*—not the eternal Logos conceived independently

---

53. De Lubac, *History*, 217.

54. De Lubac, *The Church—Paradox and Mystery*, trans. James R. Dunne (Shannon, Ireland: Ecclesia Press, 1969), 14. This accords with the general shape of Rahner's Christology, even if not his essay on mystery.

55. De Lubac, *History*, 218, quoting Augustine, *Epist.* 187, n. 34. (PL 33, 845).

56. Heb 1:3, NRSV.

57. Lk 1:35; 3:22; 4:14.

58. On the import of a cyriline Christology, see Aaron Riches, *Ecce Homo: On the Divine Unity of Christ* (Grand Rapids, MI: Eerdmans, 2016); On the Cyriline shape of Thomas's Christology, see Joseph Wawrykow, "Hypostatic Union," in Rik Van Niewenhove and Joseph Warwykow (eds.), *The Theology of Thomas Aquinas* (Notre Dame, IN: Notre Dame University Press, 2005). Kathryn Tanner also develops a Christology along similar terms in *Jesus, Humanity and the Trinity*.

of Christ. Christ is the one in whom creation is spoken, for whom creation was made, and into whose image creation is being remade. In Christ, moreover, all of creation is included. By assuming a human nature, Christ assumes the entirety of creation. Thus, in the unity of Christ's person, all of creation is joined to all of God, deep unto deep. Christ is the whole mystery of God; he is also the whole mystery of creation.[59] This is why it is fitting that the *Son* become incarnate, for creation already participates in the Son as a symbol of God. In Christ, the eternal symbol becomes the temporal symbol, that all symbols might be united to God in the Spirit.

De Lubac points to what this means for human nature:

> In Jesus Christ we have had the perfect and definitive revelation of the human being as a personal being. God's revelation to man was at the same time the revelation of a relationship between man and God. What applies to one revelation, however, applies to the other: as God reveals himself in his tripersonal Being, intervening in our humanity, he also reveals us to ourselves as personal beings capable through grace of responding to him in love. What the Catholic Church calls mysticism is only the conscious actualization of this gift of God.[60]

Christ reveals God to humanity and humanity to itself. And what Christ reveals is not a nature replete within itself, but creation made *in* and *for* Christ, set in motion toward Christ in the Spirit. The twofold mysticism of human nature (essential and nuptial) thus corresponds to this twofold work of the Son in creation and redemption. Made *in* Christ, we desire to return to our source; made *for* Christ, that return is only possible because of the gratuitous gift of salvation. This is, in brief, what it means to be a symbol. To be a created symbol is to be made in Christ and for Christ, suspended in motion toward the Father in the Spirit.

But it is not humanity alone that is a symbol of God. For De Lubac, all creation is a "vast and diverse symbol across which the Face of God is mysteriously reflected. A man is religious to the very degree that he recognizes everywhere these reflections of the divine face, that is, that he lives in a sacred atmosphere."[61] De Lubac continues, "This world is for man like a first and immense sacrament, the great natural sacrament."[62] The created world is a vast symbol, and the theological

---

59. Theologies of pure nature are therefore severely christologically deficient, since they conceive of creation as constituted and intelligible in itself apart from Christ. But as Thomas says, the knowledge of the processions of Persons is necessary for a right knowledge of creatures, and as his Christology shows, Christ is nothing other than the single *esse* of the Son in two natures. See *ST* 1a.32.1.ad. 3.; 3.2. See also Wawrykow, "Hypostatic Union," 239.

60. De Lubac, *Fragments*, 63. See discussion of this passage in Bryan C. Hollon, "Mysticism and Mystical Theology," in Jordan Hillebert (ed.), *T&T Clark Companion to Henri de Lubac* (London: Bloomsbury T&T Clark, 2017), 309.

61. De Lubac, "Internal Causes of the Weakening and Disappearance of the Sense of the Sacred" in *History*, 231.

62. De Lubac, *History*, 232.

vocation is to learn to read this symbol. But this is not some general nature theology. It too has its concrete center in the person of Jesus Christ: now that sin has corrupted the natural sacrament, it "is to rediscover all its meaning and all its sacral value thanks to another great sacrament, more mysterious still and more intimate ... the wholly divine mystery in which all the others are summed up: *Sacramentum Christi, Mysterium Christi*."[63] In the *sacramentum Christi*, the "natural sacrament" of creation is restored to its sacral character, it becomes what it is: a symbol of God. Christ, the great Christian mystery, thus inflects everything with an inherent mysticism. There is no nature untouched by Christ, as John 1 and Colossians 1 make abundantly clear. Creation has an essential mysticism inasmuch as creation itself is created in Christ, and that mystical symbol is elevated into a living likeness in Christ.

Even here, Christ is not without the Spirit. Creation is spoken in Christ, but its living motion is the life of the Spirit. The eternal Word is united to creatures in Christ *by the Spirit*, and people are joined to Christ's body by the Spirit. As argued above, the Spirit is paradoxically pre-present in both the generation and the mission of the Son, and therefore a centralized Christology need not be a christomonism. If Christ reveals humanity to itself, then Christ reveals the human to be a living *spirit*, that is, always-already in a motion of love and desire by the Spirit. That is to say that in humanity all creation is a symbol, always-already in a motion of symbolism back toward God.

To sum up, creation is a symbol by being suspended in a twofold mysticism. Creation is spoken in the eternal Word and has a natural longing to return to this source. Yet that natural longing can only be fulfilled by the grace of Christ. This account of a mystical creation is countered by two modern concepts of nature. Karl Barth and Garrigou-Lagrange, in their own very different ways, call into question this twofold mysticism. While in-depth engagement with these two prolific and subtle thinkers is obviously not possible here, I will try to indicate why the view of symbols I have expounded here is superior to either a "Barthian" flattening of nature and a neo-Thomist reification of pure nature.[64]

Between Barth and Garrigou-Lagrange

This mysticism of natural desire stands in contrast to a "Barthian" construal of creation.[65] Karl Barth seeks to undermine a modern prioritization of the self

---

63. De Lubac, *History*, 232–3.

64. I use "nature" and "creation" interchangeably on purpose, for it underscores that nature (human or otherwise) is created by God, and therefore always in a narrative of procession and return.

65. I use scare quotes advisedly. Barth's thought is complex and controverted, and interpretations are vast and varied. For an overview of key themes, see John Webster, ed., *The Cambridge Companion to Karl Barth* (Cambridge: Cambridge University Press, 2000).

by appeal to a radically God-centered theology. To do this, he theologically reinterprets Kant's epistemological restriction that we cannot know God.[66] Barth embraces this alleged inability as an assault on the pretensions of modernity in its Protestant liberal and neo-Scholastic varieties. If we are to know God at all, it will have nothing to do with human ability or experience: humans "have no organ or capacity for God."[67] Therefore, if God is to be known, it must be by an absolute miracle of "self-revelation."[68] This term itself is quite modern—traceable to Hegel's own solution to the Kantian problematic[69]—but here it is placed more firmly on theological grounds, namely, the conviction that creation is sustained in existence over the *nihil* by God's gracious and free election. The absolute dependence of creation on God renders God unknowable as another subject within creation. Thus, knowledge of God can only come from divine self-disclosure. This miracle is so absolute that its closest analogues are resurrection from the dead and, indeed, creation ex nihilo.[70] Thus, Barth's most famous triad, revealer–revelation–revealedness, is specifically designed to occlude creatures: God reveals God through God.[71] Anything else would be to "speak of God by speaking of man in a loud voice."[72] Self-revelation is thus a way of allowing *God* to break the strictures of a Kantian epistemological problem, while allowing the problem itself to remain in the strongest possible terms.[73]

Of course, Kant is surely right that God is unknowable, and my own account of mystery in the previous section is but a theological variant on this same theme. But the texture of this unknowing needs clarification. Johannes Hoff has pointed to a premodern vision of unknowing exemplified by Nicholas of Cusa.[74] For Cusa, as for much premodern thought, an encounter with the infinite is not the absolute end of knowledge, rather, it transforms knowledge from a discursive to a doxological

---

66. This is not to say that Kant's philosophy is entirely untheological. See Chris Insole, *Kant and the Creation of Freedom* (Oxford: Oxford University Press, 2013).
67. Karl Barth, *Church Dogmatics* I/1 (Edinburgh: T&T Clark, 1956), 168. Hereafter, CD.
68. CD I/1, 238.
69. Georg Wilhelm Friedrich Hegel, *Lectures on the Philosophy of Religion*, ed. Peter C. Hodgson, trans. R. F. Brown, P. C. Hodgson et al. (Berkeley: University of California Press, 1988), 129–61. See discussion and citation in Johannes Hoff, "The Rise and Fall of the Kantian Paradigm of Modern Theology," in Peter Candler (ed.), *The Grandeur of Reason: Religion, Tradition and Universalism* (London: SCM Press, 2010), 187.
70. Trevor Hart, "Revelation," in *The Cambridge Companion to Karl Barth* (Cambridge: Cambridge University Press, 2000), 43–4.
71. CD I/1, 363.
72. Karl Barth, *The Word of God and the Word of Man* (London: Hodder, 1928), 195.
73. This is not to say that Barth's central *concern* is a Kantian epistemological problem. His thought remains committed to the Lordship of God. But in framing his trinitarian theology around self-revelation, Barth has given this a decidedly epistemological texture.
74. Hoff, *Kantian*, 175, citing Nicholas of Cusa, *Epistula ad Nicolaum Abergatum*, n. 9, 5–10, 1.

mode.⁷⁵ The unknowability of God does not fix a chasm between creator and creature, so much as lure the creature into a relationship of exaltation and praise. In a variant on de Lubac's twofold mysticism of human nature, revelation is seen as a dynamic movement from desire to love along a doxological continuum: praise for a mystery desired becomes ever more fervent praise for a mystery now known in love.

This twofold mystical unknowing secures the benefits and avoids the weaknesses of Barth's Kantian chasm. God remains ineffable; creation remains utterly dependent on God and entirely aporetic without reference to God; and the transcendence of the creature into loving praise of God is an *ecstatic* response, not an inward function of an isolated cartesian *ego*. But it also avoids a consistent Barthian temptation to reestablish a duality between God and creation. This is only ever a temptation, more pronounced in Barth's early work than his late, and Barth has significant internal resources for resisting it, most importantly covenant and Christology.⁷⁶ But it remains a discernable tendency. By allowing his theology to be framed by an absolute epistemological break between God and creation, Barth at times indicates a competitive contrast between God and creatures in which divine fullness and self-sufficiency *correspond to and require* creaturely lack and insufficiency.⁷⁷ Self-revelation can too easily be seen as something done *to* creation by a God who stands over and against it.

This tendency was inherited by Barthians. As I argued in Chapter 4, before his turn to Aquinas, John Webster maintained an inverse proportionality between God and creatures, a contrast in which God-in-Christ stands over-and-against creation, and even the church.⁷⁸ It is Kathryn Tanner who is perhaps most successful in avoiding this temptation, which she accomplishes by drawing out the Cyriline shape of Barth's Christology, along the lines of the Christology I developed above.⁷⁹ Thus, while Barth gestures toward a modern dualism of God–creation, this is potentially overcome christologically. But a twofold mystical unknowing avoids this temptation altogether. Rather than allowing a characteristically modern preoccupation with epistemology to frame the question, a twofold mysticism adverts to the doxological *telos* of knowledge in the unknowable goodness of God.⁸⁰ To embrace this would be to recognize that nature is not marked by an absolute

---

75. Cusa calls this the "wisdom of unknowing." Cf. Nicholas of Cusa, *De Docta Ignorantia*, trans. Jasper Hopkins (Minneapolis, MN: Banning Press, 1990), https://jasper-hopkins.info.

76. See Kathryn Tanner, "Creation and Providence" in Webster, *Companion*, 111–26.

77. This can be seen, for instance, in Barth's relatively early treatment of Mary's virginity, which for Barth indicates only the absolute human lack vis-à-vis God. CD Vol. I. 2, 143.

78. John Webster, "On Evangelical Ecclesiology," in *Essays on Christian Dogmatics II* (London: Bloomsbury, 2016), 173. See also Eberhardt Jüngel, "The Church as Sacrament?" in *Theological Essays*, trans. John Webster (Edinburgh: T&T Clark, 1989), 191.

79. Tanner, *Jesus, Humanity and the Trinity*, passim.

80. Alan Torrance has criticized Barth extensively on this score in *Persons in Communion: An Essay on Trinitarian Description and Human Participation* (Edinburgh: T&T Clark, 1996).

limit: that it has a natural impulse toward transcendence which can nonetheless only be fulfilled by grace. In other words, the Barthian temptation to contrast God and world can be overcome by the natural desire for the supernatural.

This would of course give more to nature than Barth is willing to give, but there are perfectly Barthian reasons for embracing it. In the first instance, it better guards the sovereignty of God, whose fullness cannot be diminished by its sharing. For creation to have an inner impulse toward transcendence is not a loss to God's sovereignty, but itself expressive of the very abundance of that sovereignty, as John Webster's later work makes clear.[81] If God is understood as hidden *because* creation is a symbol, then both the transcendent goodness of God and the received goodness of creation are guarded without threat to either. Moreover, it moves the center of gravity away from an epistemological problematic and toward a doxological destiny, which is to say that it secures symbolism, the intrinsic movement of desire and love between symbol and symbolized. Inasmuch as Barth's theology threatens a contrast between God and creatures, it threatens the symbolic value of creation, losing the symbolized and symbolism as well. The triad I have developed is a more fitting analogy than self-revelation: it secures everything the latter searches for, without its concomitant temptations. God reveals God by sharing God in and through symbols.

Of course, Barth's concept of self-revelation was aimed at dethroning a view of creation as autonomous within its own sphere, capable of discovering God (or the absence of God) under the power of its own lights. The Catholic theory of pure nature was at least one of Barth's targets, and Barth was right to contest such a theory, for to leave nature untouched in natural purity is neither scriptural nor traditional. Nonetheless, it too seeks to guard the transcendence of God, the value of creation and, especially in the work of Reginald Garrigou-Lagrange, the superiority of mystical wisdom. It could be argued that the theory of pure nature, as presented by Lagrange, better captures all three than my own triad. He guards divine transcendence by ensuring the utter gratuity of grace; he maintains the value of creation by giving it its own natural sphere of perfection; and he maintains the movement of symbolism between creation and God by appeal to mysticism as the highest wisdom available to humans. While space does not permit an exhaustive engagement, I will briefly indicate why this is not the case.

Lagrange's work, *The Sense of Mystery: Clarity and Obscurity in the Intellectual Life* is a series of meditations on the contrast of light and dark, the *clair-obscur* or "chiaroscuro" effect of the limits and possibilities of the human intellect.[82] His

---

81. See Webster, "Love," *passim*.

82. Because of the Coronavirus lockdown in England, I was unable to obtain a physical copy of this book and was forced to use an electronic Kindle edition. In addition to the Kindle location, I will cite the chapter number to aid in locating the reference. Reginald Garrigou Lagrange, *The Sense of Mystery: Clarity and Obscurity in the Intellectual Life*, trans. Matthew K. Minerd (Steubenville, OH: Emmaus Academic, 2017). Contemporary neo-Thomists would do well to follow Lagrange's recognition for the fundamental requirement for paradox.

account is structured by a theory of pure nature,[83] moving from what is purely natural to what is supernatural and thus represents an alternative to de Lubac's mysticism of the natural desire.[84] The combination of that which is knowable and that which is unknowable drives the human soul toward mysticism and love. The human intellect is ordered to a particular range of being; that which is too high and profound or too low and profane are incomprehensible for the human mind. Lagrange traces these kinds of obscurities through their permutations in nature and in grace to help the reader gain the "sense of mystery," by which he means a clear grasp of the "data" which is entirely available to natural reason, the supernatural "data" on the other side of the epistemic divide, and the further truth that will only be known in the beatific vision. That sense leads, finally, to mysticism, where the intellectual search is fulfilled in silent, direct contemplation of the divine essence. Gaining a sense of mystery, for Lagrange, requires an exhaustive mapping of the epistemological terrain.

Lagrange envisions a three-tiered hierarchy of wisdom. The first is the discipline of metaphysics, which "abstracts from all matter," studying being *qua* being, which is God inasmuch as God is the one creator and first cause (not yet the trinitarian God of Christianity).[85] When the metaphysician comes to know created effects, a desire is elicited to know the causes of these effects. By tracing the sequences of causes, the metaphysician can arrive at knowledge of God as first cause and can even wish to know the essence of this First Cause, but that desire remains entirely conditional on first coming to know created effects and, to avoid Pelagianism, is wholly inefficacious.

Theology is the second wisdom and provides even greater epistemic surety than the significant epistemic confidence afforded by metaphysics.[86] Infused faith has more confidence than metaphysics because it comes from God, not natural human knowledge, and this gracious gift of revelation provides new data for the intellect to analyze. Theology is, then, the rational analysis of the data of revelation.[87] It is indeed a human work, but it is rooted in the grace of faith, and so it is more reliable than metaphysics. That extra data moves the theologian beyond considering God only as creator and first cause, to God's own inner life: the divine essence, the

---

83. The concept of pure nature itself varies among neo-Thomists. I use the term here to refer to what is possible by the natural human intellect apart from grace or a calling to beatitude.

84. *The Sense of Mystery* was written before *Surnaturel*, and so it does not deal directly with de Lubac's natural desire for the supernatural. Lagrange does take aim at Maurice Blondel's philosophy of action—an influential text for de Lubac—for confusing the natural and supernatural (ch. 3, loc. 2848). He also takes aim at Suarez's active obediential potency (ch. 5, loc. 5535), but this is not to be identified with de Lubac's position. Nonetheless, the outline of Lagrange's later response to de Lubac is readily apparent in this text.

85. Lagrange, Sense, ch. 1, loc. 1169.

86. Lagrange, Sense, ch. 1, loc. 1249.

87. Lagrange, Sense, ch. 1, loc. 1253.

attributes, the Persons, etc. It thus concerns information knowable only if God chooses to reveal it.

The third wisdom beyond theology is infused wisdom from the Holy Spirit, a *quasi*-experiential knowledge of God, i.e., mysticism.[88] Theology is a rational analysis of revealed data by the intellect, mysticism arises from the infusion of charity into the will. The infusion of charity from the Holy Spirit produces a "relation of conformity" between the data of revelation and "our inner dispositions," inspiring in us not just knowledge that revealed mysteries are believable, but that they are supremely loveable.[89] This wisdom is an intuitive knowledge, a wisdom available to all regardless of their theological or philosophical training, though it presupposes a certain amount of theological knowledge, namely, the necessary dogmatic formulae of the creeds. This is a higher and surer knowledge than theology, for theology is a human work, while mystical wisdom is an infused gift. If theology analyzes the data of revelation, mysticism interiorizes that data: in mysticism, theology becomes us, affording the highest epistemic confidence.

This three-stage sequence from natural metaphysics to faith and theology to charity and mysticism is based on the *taxis* of intellect and will. Because the will necessarily follows the intellect, the metaphysician can only desire the God she knows. Her desire for God is therefore wholly elicited from her prior knowledge of God's effects. Faith then provides the metaphysician with newly revealed data, showing the First Cause to be the Trinity. In rationally analyzing that new data, the metaphysician can become a theologian. Then the Spirit can infuse the will with charity to love the newly revealed facts, and the theologian can become a mystic. The will thus follows the intellect from pure nature to grace and beyond to glory.

Thus, natural metaphysics can become theology, and theology can become mysticism, but because of the unidirectional nature of the sequence, theology is in no way intrinsic to metaphysics, and mysticism intrinsic to neither. Metaphysics has no inner drive toward theology or mysticism, for it lacks theological knowledge. The theologian will undoubtedly want to love God by the effects of grace, but such a love is not intrinsic to the theological task, defined only as "the conceptual analysis of revealed truths."[90] The mystic, of course, need not be a

---

88. Lagrane, Sense, ch. 1, loc. 1343.
89. Lagrange, Sense, ch. 1, loc. 1372.
90. Lagrange, Sense, ch. 1, loc. 1257: "Theology has for its ends: 1) the conceptual analysis of revealed truths ... 2) the deduction of other truths that are virtually contained in revealed truths." Lagrange elaborates: "The work of conceptual analysis (which is the most important part of the theological treatises on the Trinity, the Incarnation, the Sacraments, grace, etc.) and that of deducing theological conclusions is a human work undertaken on the data of revelation" [ch. 1, loc. 1262]. Thus, while mysticism is knowledge "through connaturality or sympathy, [theology] is ... according to a perfect use of reason" [ch. 1, loc. 1361].

trained metaphysician and theologian, but charity presupposes faith, which, for Lagrange, is expressed in the body of dogmatic formulae, and so some minimal measure of rational knowledge is necessary for mysticism to proceed. To put it bluntly, the mystic must have some basic measure of theological knowledge, but neither the theologian nor the metaphysician need have love.[91]

But there are trinitarian reasons to question the rigid *taxis* of intellect and will, faith and charity, theology and mysticism established by Lagrange. As Thomas makes clear, faith requires from the outset a decision of the will: faith is the *assent* to revealed dogma.[92] The intellect cannot "see" the truth of Christian teaching *en se*, since it would then no longer be faith. So faith requires for its operation an act of the will. But this act of the will that precedes faith cannot be an act of charity, since Thomas is clear that charity follows faith as the will follows the intellect. This act of the will is, Thomas cryptically says, "a certain desire for the promised good."[93] In other words, here the will precedes the intellect under the operation of grace, even though it must follow *from* the intellect. Bruce Marshall identifies the trinitarian dynamics of this paradox:

> That our assent to Christian teaching has to stem from love for the God of whom it speaks … follows from who the triune God is … Since knowledge of the Trinity is beyond our natural capacity, it requires a definite action of the triune God himself, in particular the *instinctus interior* by which the Son moves us to know him … The Father's eternal Son, however, "is not just any sort of Word, but one who brings forth Love," that is the Spirit ….Therefore, the Trinity cannot be known save by being in some way loved.[94]

The Logos cannot be separated from the Spirit, so the infused knowledge of faith cannot be separated from infused love. This love is not the love of charity, but

---

91. See Lagrange, Sense, ch. 4, loc. 3315: Love tends toward another "like a mysterious impulse that is difficult to define … thus, things of love are known by experience." And later, "the light that illuminates theological science is not experience, but instead, is virtual revelation—that is, revelation inasmuch as it virtually contains the conclusions deduced by the aid of a rational premise" [ch. 5, loc. 5704].

92. *ST* 2a–2ae.1.4. See Hoff, Self-Revelation, 177, where he argues that it is in Suarez that "the assent of faith is no longer coincident with a pre-theoretical judgment or an 'excess' of worship." It is only with Suarez that our intellectual recognition of truth is separated from our spontaneous loving reception of it.

93. Thomas Aquinas, *Quaestiones disputatae de veritate*, trans. J. V. McGlynn (Chicago, IL: Henry Regnery, 1952-4), Q.14 a.2 ad10; quoted in Bruce Marshal, "*Quod Scit Una Uetula*: Aquinas on the Nature of Theology" in Rik Van Nieuwenhove and Joseph Wawrykow (eds.), *The Theology of Thomas Aquinas* (Notre Dame, IN: Notre Dame University Press, 2005), 33, n. 70.

94. Marshall, *Uetula*, 32, n. 69.

"some desire for the promised good."[95] It is a kind of inchoate charity that makes faith possible, a paradoxical pre-presence of charity in the act of believing.[96] Faith is thus always-already love, even as it must yet become love.

This always-already quality of faith and love has its precursor in the natural desire for the supernatural. Our knowledge of created effects is always marked by desire. The reason for this, again, is trinitarian. Everything that *is* only is because spoken in the eternal Logos, and the Logos is never without the Spirit: facts are only factual because their existence is a participation in the movement of desire and love between Father and Son. To come to know anything is to be drawn into this movement of divine desire; in this sense, truth is erotic.[97] There are no pure facts that we might come to know before a desire for God is elicited, because there is no pure Son separated from the Spirit. Indeed, to imagine something like pure facts untainted by desire, or indeed, theology untainted by mysticism, would require imagining a moment of pure paternity-filiation, in which the Father and Son have a complete relation to one another, to which the relation of the Spirit could only be a superadded extra. The result would be the much-stereotyped denigration of the Spirit in Western theology. But if we insist that the Trinity condition the psychological analogy more thoroughly, then we will have to say that all knowledge is already love, even if it must still then become what it is. There is no eliding this paradoxical unity.

The strictness of this *taxis* is Lagrange's way of guarding divine supremacy (by maintaining the gratuity of grace), creaturely integrity, and mystical consummation. God, in absolute freedom, creates nature within its own complete sphere, in which it can function in perfect happiness. Then, in a second act of absolutely unconditioned freedom, God super-adds a new realm of grace by which the creature might come to know God in mystical communion. But does this actually accomplish its goals? It seems to conceive of grace as something that *threatens* nature's integrity, and so contrasts divine gift and human action. Why should we assume that a nature never without grace is somehow less robustly natural, unless we think of a tradeoff between divinity and humanity? This threatens to reduce God to one actor among actors, another creature competing for limited space. Moreover, this threatened reduction of God makes creation a symbol in only the

---

95. *De Ver.* Q.14 a.2 ad10. The question of desire, as Sarah Coakley has pointed out, is important in answering the objections of postmodernity against systematic theology: a totalizing theological system can indeed conceal an idolatrous *desire* "for mastery: a complete understanding of God, a regnant position in society, or a domination of the gendered 'other.'" Coakley, *Sexuality*, 51.

96. Lagrange avoids this paradox by urging that exterior miracles are sufficient to provide surety to the intellect, grounding faith's confidence "materially and extrinsically." Lagrange, Sense, loc. 1289. This is not without textual evidence in Thomas but is also highly problematic for the trinitarian reasons provided above. See discussion in Marshall, *Uetula*.

97. See Coakley, *Sexuality*, ch. 7.

barest sense. Creation is perfectly intelligible within its own sphere, adverting only to God-as-first-cause to plug a metaphysical gap (crudely, God becomes nothing more than the answer to the question, "how did this get here?"). But aside from knowing that something called God must have created the world, there is no inner disposition that might compel me to come to know this God. Why should I, if I can build my house and raise my family quite apart from any ongoing interface with this first cause? It becomes possible to think of creation apart from its nature as a divine word, a word to be responded to in love: creation is no longer a symbol. Long before Lagrange wrote *The Sense of Mystery*, secularism became a live option under the theory of pure nature, a danger Lagrange's account of mystery does not overcome. And this finally imperils symbolism, since creation is conceivable without any motion of desire or love back to God. There is a moment of pure intellectual encounter with the world that precedes all love and desire, from which alone curiosity about causes arises. This is even true in the discipline of theology, where it is perfectly possible to conduct theology without love, since theology comes entirely before mysticism.

It is precisely this last failure that de Lubac identifies in the shift from the theological style he calls "symbolism" to "dialectics."[98] Mysticism and reason are prized apart, if not opposed to one another, then as two separate steps in a series. But the triad I have developed does not so prize them apart. Certainly, a distinction remains. There are insightful theologians who fail as lovers of God and creatures, and there are extraordinary mystics with poor theology. But at their root, thinking and loving are joined in one perichoretic unity, and thus cannot be prized apart. That unity is itself expressive of a prior divine unity, so that symbolized is hidden in the symbol which ever moves toward it in a motion of rational love: a reasonable act of worship.[99] Losing the symbol as a twofold mysticism results in the loss of God's transcendence as the symbolized and the intrinsic movement of the symbol as symbolism. Both Barth and Lagrange in their own ways risk such losses. A return to symbolism will not only help return us to a God we might sing and dance before, but it restores humanity as singers and dancers, and recovers a song worth singing and dancing to.

The Symbol and Symbolism

We are now in a position to understand more deeply what it means for creation to be a symbol of God, and just why a symbol is an intrinsically mystical reality. The eternal Logos is the symbol of the Father, and creation is the unfolding of this eternal symbol in time.[100] Christ is the eternal symbol incarnate in created symbol; in Christ creation is gratuitously elevated and returned to its divine source. The unity of the incarnate Christ is such that Paul can say that *Christ* is the image of the

---

98. De Lubac, *Corpus Mysticum*, 221–48.
99. Romans 12:1.
100. See discussion in Chapter 2.

invisible God, firstborn over all creation, that in Christ all things were created and in Christ all things are redeemed. All of creation is thus suspended from Christ to Christ.

This suspension sustains a natural desire for the supernatural: human nature has an ontological desire for the vision of God by virtue of its creation in Christ. But that "mysticism of essence" is circumscribed by and subordinated to a nuptial mysticism: the natural desire can only be fulfilled by the grace of Christ. This means, in the first instance, that human nature is always marked by its desire to know God—there is never a moment of pure intellectual apprehension of finite sense phenomena not already marked by an ontological desire for God. And yet that desire can only be fulfilled by the gift of grace. Faith, likewise, is never without some inchoate charity, some "desire for the promised good." Theology, in turn, is never without mysticism: it is born in the mystical desire of the human soul to be united to God.

This is ultimately due to the trinitarian dynamics of human nature. The Son is never without the Spirit, and we can even say that the Spirit is "retroactively causal" in the generation of the Son, paradoxically pre-present in filiation. In the language I have developed, this indicates that the symbol is only the symbol as it is in motion toward the symbolized. Thus, even though we must distinguish nature from grace, as we must distinguish Son from Spirit, we cannot isolate one from the other in a moment of pure nature, just as we cannot isolate a moment of pure filiation. We must say that nature is not a mere "vacuole for grace," but also that nature can only be understood as always in motion toward its source and end.[101] Thus, contra certain Barthian tendencies, nature is a "thick reality," but contra Lagrange, nature's substantial reality is aboriginally in motion back toward God. My triad, symbolized–symbol–symbolism describes this paradox, avoiding the pitfalls of minimal-nature and pure-nature.

This indelible link between symbol and symbolism extends to all creation. Creation is summed in humanity, which as intellectual and material is the microcosm of a universe in which angelic and material creatures express each in their own ways the divine life of God. In humanity all creation naturally desires God, and in Christ all creation is restored. Creation is a symbol, a sign that mediates God's presence: created in Christ by the Spirit, elevated and returned to the Father in Christ by the Spirit.

Moreover, this always-already quality is an expression of God's absolute anteriority as the symbolized. There is no "me" before the twofold gift of my being and destiny, I cannot unearth some pure identity, untainted by my creation in Son and Spirit and calling to redemption in Son and Spirit. The quest for this "pure" identity is an attempt to gain a total vision of myself. To have such a total view of myself would be to step out of the process of symbolization, it would be to assume a God's-eye-view of things, assuming a perspective that can only belong to God. I can never assume the perspective of the symbolized because I am always a symbol

---

101. Steven A. Long, *natura pura* (New York: Fordham University Press, 2010), ch. 2.

in motion. To insist on the fundamental nature of this motion is to insist on the fundamental hiddenness of God's perspective, that there is no pure nature that is not always circumscribed by the infinite mystery of God: my life is indeed hidden with Christ in God.[102] This inseparability of symbol and symbolism safeguards the hiddenness of the symbolized.

The previous section argued that God-as-symbolized helps avoid an ontotheological reduction of God to one being among beings. This section has argued that understanding creation as a symbol avoids both a Barthian flattening of nature and a neo-Thomist reification of pure nature. This is only possible if all three terms of the triad are held together. In the next section, I will turn to the third term of the triad, symbolism, with specific reference to the discipline of theology as one mode of symbolism, of joining the symbol to the symbolized in an act of mystical reason. I will do this by a reading of Augustine.

From Mysticism to Mystical Reason

If we are to return to something like mystical reason, the arguments from the preceding two sections will need to be taken into account. Rahner helps us see that we are ever faced with the symbolized, the God who is mysteriously present within all things, and yet always beyond. As beyond, God is the absolute horizon within which all created things are intelligible; God is the sustaining ground of the "radiant intelligibility" flowing from all things. This is to settle reason *within* mystery. Reason functions by constant reference to the abiding mystery of God. Moreover, because reason cannot attain this primordial mystery, it is constrained to become love if it is be truly reasonable. Thus we have moved from many mysteries, as statements provisionally inaccessible to reason, to one mystery that sustains all reason as reasonable and oriented toward fulfillment in love. I then moved from one mystery to mysticism, showing that all creation lives by participation in a movement of desire and love between Father and Son. There is thus a twofold mysticism in the heart of creation. That twofold mysticism links theology explicitly to mysticism in a way that makes them mutually internal to one another. Taken together, these two commitments—that God is the symbolized, creation the symbol—open the possibility of mystical reason. God speaks creation in the speaking of the Word, and creation is therefore shot through with "mystical reasons," ontological traces of its creator. The theological task, then, is the uncovering and reading of those mystical reasons, joining them to the symbolized. It can do so because it knows by faith that God is symbolized in creation, and it also knows that creation is always-already in motion toward God. Mystical reason is the attention necessary to catch these symbols on their way back to God and to join with them, ascending to God in praise. Thus, the one mystery sustains creation in a twofold mysticism which can be "read" in an act of mystical reason.

---

102. Colossians 3:3.

This way of framing the theological task makes it very similar to, if not simply the extension of the spiritual interpretation of scripture. This is, in fact, Augustine's practice. When Augustine conducts the spiritual interpretation of scripture, he is searching for "mystical reasons" latent within the literal sense.[103] These mystical reasons are correspondences between "levels" of discourse. The literal sense, say, a number in an obscure Old Testament passage, opens upward to a corresponding spiritual sense.[104] That correlation is always subordinate to the Christian gospel, and so is not a wild flight of exegetical fancy. But neither is it a logical entailment. It is entirely reasonable because scripture (or creation) is spoken in the Logos, and so always related to Christ; Christ is the rationale of all things. But it is also mystical because it is a search for a reason hidden within the literal sense that is only disclosed by the Spirit in grace. This mysticism, moreover, is a mysticism of desire, since the dynamics of hiddenness and revelation correspond to desire and delight.[105] To move "beyond" the letter to the spirit is to move through the letter toward God in desire and love. Mystical reason is this movement between levels of discourse.

Augustine employs this logic from the spiritual interpretation of scripture in his reading of the human soul as an analogy for the Trinity. The literal sense of the human soul opens upward to the spiritual sense of God's own trinitarian life, both in the economy in Christ, and eternally in generation and procession. In a crucial moment in *De trin.*, Augustine argues on the basis of 1 Cor 13:12 that understanding the mind in a trinitarian manner requires the interpretation of an enigma.[106] An enigma, Augustine explains, is an acutely obscure allegory, and Augustine appeals to the spiritual interpretation of scripture as an analogue for the kind of interpretation of the mind he is attempting. Like scripture, the mind has a literal sense that opens onto a spiritual sense. This movement from the "literal" to the spiritual, from the production of inner words in love to the eternal generation of the Word in the Spirit, is governed by the rule of faith. The entire construct of Christian faith from creation, sin, and death to redemption and glory, and especially the trinitarian life of God thus control the analogy used to understand the Trinity.

This is quite circular. Augustine offers analogies by which to understand the Trinity, but then urges that the analogies themselves can only be understood rightly when conformed to the doctrine of the Trinity. Thus, the various triads Augustine offers all eventually fail: they do not live up to the promise of delivering us to contemplation of God and must be revised again. John Cavadini has argued

---

103. For example, in Augustine, *The Trinity* 4.10, trans. Edmund Hill (New York: New City Press, 1991), 160.
104. Cf. Henri de Lubac, *Medieval Exegesis*, 3 vols., trans. Mark Sebanc (Grand Rapids, MI: Eerdmans, 1998).
105. See, for instance, Augustine, *On Christian Teaching*, 2.10-15, trans. R. P. H. Green (Oxford: Oxford University Press, 1997), 32–3.
106. *De trin.* 15.8.15 (Hill: 406).

that Augustine leads the reader through the various triads not as merely heuristic exercises to discover whether or not a particular analogy "works." Rather, Augustine uses the doctrine of the Trinity to show how all analogies and all human efforts finally fail in their image-bearing potential.[107] The result is that the analogies used to understand the Trinity must undergo transformation by Christ into a more complete trinitarian pattern.

For Augustine, this transformative process takes place principally in the production of inner words in rightly ordered love. An inner word is not a particular word in any language. It is a pre-reflexive self-expression and is wholly equal to the mind itself. The pre-linguistic quality of the inner word has been argued to be problematic, since all experience is linguistic and cultural. Language is not, it has been argued, the translation of a pure inner experience prior to all language and expression.[108] Rather, our language shapes experience itself, and is so bound up with it that experience can never be divorced from its cultural–linguistic context. Yet Augustine is not unaware of the irreducibly linguistic and cultural nature of human experience.[109] Augustine locates the inner word as a pre-linguistic moment in the mind because, as a constituent component of the image of God, it cannot be tied to any particular linguistic expression; God's native language is not Greek or Latin. The inner word is "an eternally valid precultural reality focused on a capacity for self-awareness and self-expression which is a product of culture—of signs and sign systems—but not reducible to any particular cultural expression."[110] An inner word is something like the capacity for culture. It is a way of saying that the human mind is symbolic, that is, that it comes into being by expression in a symbol, but without prescribing the content of that symbol.

To get a grip on this admittedly obscure notion, Augustine leads the reader through a number of triads focused on the moment the inner word is "incarnated" in an outer word. These outer trinities represent the ways an inner word is actualized in signs and signification, how the *imago Dei* is manifested in culture. It is the quality of this incarnation that occupies Augustine precisely *because* he is aware that all human experience is linguistic and cultural. Any inadequacy of our language and culture to incarnate the divine image is a direct result of the corruption of the mind itself, the mind's inability to image God. And this corruption is self-replicating, since it produces corrupt cultures that in turn form minds.

In Cavadini's words, the "'boxed set' of trinities, described in books 9–15" can thus be seen as a "phenomenology of culture production," or perhaps more

---

107. John Cavadini, *Visioning Augustine* (Oxford: Wiley Blackwell, 2019), 1–22. The context of *De trin.* is Augustine's argument against the viability of Porphyrian ascent independent of Christ.

108. See, for example, the criticism in Robert Markus, "St. Augustine on Signs," *Phronesis* 2, no. 1 (Brill: 1957), 60–83.

109. Cf. Cavadini, *Augustine*, 48.

110. Cavadini, *Augustine*, 47.

accurately, a phenomenology of human corporate corruption.[111] A corrupt culture is the incarnation of a shared corrupt inner word, a corruption which that culture nurtures and passes on from one generation to another. The point of the inner word is not that the human mind experiences the world in pre-linguistic raw encounter, but that at the root of the cultures which pervade and constitute our experience lies a failure to image God by failing to know God and ourselves rightly. The inner word is the capacity of the mind to image God by symbolizing itself. And the failure of this symbol is the root of the failure of society to love justice and mercy. To say that the inner word is pre-linguistic is to say that some opaque mixture of image-bearing and sin structures from the outset all our experience.

It would seem, then, that our hopes of contemplating God in God's image are bound to fail. Both the image and the seer are impaired. Here the ideal of Porphyrian ascent that has structured *De trin.* is shipwrecked. Porphyrian ascent moves from matter to the immaterial via the human soul, but Augustine has shown this ascent to be entirely impossible. We need another image and another vision. Augustine seeks to break this introspective circuit by returning to the blood of Christ in all its contingency, temporality, and materiality.[112] The failure of our own inner words and their incarnation in broken cultures is met by the incarnation of the eternal Word, the very Word of God spoken in the language of creation. When Augustine moves from the literal sense to the spiritual, he exposes the failure of the soul to live up to this spiritual potential. In turning the soul toward Christ, Augustine aims to help the reader move toward that spiritual fullness.

This search for the mystical reasons of the soul is as much about the formation of the will as of the intellect: only an inner word begotten in right love is worthy of God. In the first instance, the spiritual sense is *hidden* within the literal to entice desire to know what is hidden.[113] In the second, attention to Christ as *revealed* is intended to shape our loves—by showing us the shape of a life ordered by right love, and by giving us a living image of God on which to fix our love. In both hiddenness and manifestation, Augustinian theology is intended to help heal the human will. Augustine thus leads his readers through a pedagogy of both intellect and will that starts from the Trinity, moves through various analogies, then reformulates those analogies in light of the Trinity known in and through Christ, in order to return again to God.

What is remarkable about this process is how successfully it integrates multiple levels of discourse. God's inner life, God's action in time, human society, the human mind, and finally the thinker herself are all enfolded in a single theological

---

111. Cavadini, *Augustine*, 49.
112. On the centrality of Christ in Augustinian contemplation, see Rowan Williams, "The Soul in Paraphrase: Augustine as Interpreter of the Psalms," in *On Augustine* (London: Bloomsbury, 2016), 25–40.
113. Augustine, *On Christian Teaching*, 2.10-15 (Green: 32–3).

vision. That vision is unfolded in the making and remaking of triads, an attempt to unite all things to God. Augustine does not conceive of these multiple levels of discourse sequentially, but as a kind of perpetual spiral. The relationship between the human mind and the Trinity is not a stepwise sequence, but a circling through multiple senses of reality, each one opening onto the next, with the Trinity finally shaping and reshaping the whole.

De Lubac rightly called these multiple levels "symbolic inclusions."[114] The mind is symbolically included in the Trinity, so that reflection on the Trinity—always necessarily in and through Christ—shapes reflection on the mind, and ultimately forms the trinitarian shape of the theologian herself. To ascend through symbolic inclusions is to find oneself also symbolically included, where thinking emerges into prayer. To search for such symbolic inclusions is to look for integration at every possible level: to find God in all things, and to bring all things to God in praise. It is a spiritual interpretation of creation, moving from its literal sense to the spiritual sense embedded within and beyond it, before returning again to creation in a never-ending movement of desire and love.

These inclusions between levels of discourse are governed by the Christian gospel, and reading them is more a matter of aesthetic discernment than logical deduction. A human inner word and love are participations in the eternal Word and Spirit, but Son and Spirit are not straightforwardly an inner word and love.[115] They are certainly not quasi-mechanical effusions of the divine intellect and will, as for Scotus.[116] This is to enforce an inappropriate logical entailment between levels of discourse—to reify the analogy. Once reified, analogies become brittle, ceasing to be responsive to the transformative process of thinking our analogies into the Trinity. One can see this not only in the Franciscan tendency to reify the psychological analogy, but also in the intellectualism of baroque Thomism, where the *taxis* of intellect and will ceases to be disciplined by perichoretic unity. Beyond fixing an airtight logical framework for the Trinity, then, developing triads is a search for resonances and correspondences by which the Trinity may be better understood and loved, but never circumscribed. Lewis Ayres has described this dynamic:

> One of the constitutive tasks of our journey down the path towards understanding of faith is, then, to grow in the ability to hone these correspondences, identifying and applying the principles that allow us to "look" beyond the created categories within which scripture speaks.[117]

---

114. De Lubac, *Corpus*, 226.
115. *De trin.* 15.42 (Hill, 428). Thomas expresses something similar in the language of appropriation. See Gilles Emery, O.P., *Trinity in Aquinas* (Naples, FL: Sapientia Press, 2003), ch. 4.
116. See discussion in Chapter 2.
117. Lewis Ayres, *Augustine and the Trinity* (Cambridge: Cambridge University Press, 2010), 152.

The honing of these correspondences is a matter of "attention," of attending to resonances between the eternal life of God, and the material structures of life in time under the discipline of scripture.

Because of the doctrine of creation, i.e., creation by the Father's speaking of the Word in the Spirit, everything is foundationally related to the triune life of God. But this relation remains obscure and ineffective unless creation itself is elevated by Christ. And Christ is only received in his body, the eucharistic church. Thus, what sustains and structures this kind of movement between levels of discourse is first the relations of Father–Son–Spirit, and then the relations of God–creation–church, where church is understood as the *totus Christus*. These are something like the doctrinal conditions for the possibility of symbolic theology. And coming to read the symbols of life in time is a matter of judging the fittingness of analogies, their appropriateness to the shape of this whole. It is a process of discerning correlations and resonances that is never fully finished, and the very act of pursuing it shapes the quality of our own inner analogy, the image of God.

We will have to become comfortable with the circularity of this: we know God through symbols, but we interpret symbols through our knowledge of God. Hence, I have proposed a trinitarian theology of the symbol and also argued that we only understand the Trinity through symbols. But this circularity is necessary if we are to do justice to the hiddenness of God as the symbolized, to the sacral value of creation as a symbol of God, and the mystic quality of theological thought as an act of symbolism. There is only one mystery, and that mystery is the context of all we know and love; it is the ultimate horizon of creaturely existence. It thus remains, strictly speaking, unknowable in any *objective* sense; we are never subjects standing over and against God as an object. But this eternal mystery has in fact come near in Christ, revealing all of creation to have an inner dynamism toward gratuitous consummation in grace. But even here, we have not escaped the mystery. We have been given symbols—all of which gain their essential orientation in Christ the Realsymbol—and we must learn to read them if *we* too are to become true symbols. But we can never step outside this process of symbolism to gain an objective grasp on the mystery we represent in our persons. The mystery thus founds and ends our quest. Therefore, theology must keep returning to Christ in whom its language and loves are perpetually reformed on the road to glory. Any understanding we obtain from perpetual return must become again a seeking. This is why, Augustine explains, the psalmist says to seek his face forevermore,[118] for to find God is to seek God, whose inexhaustible plenitude compels us to seek again.

This indicates that the psychological analogy is not a literal account of the processions. Rather, as Lewis Ayres argues, "Augustine seems to see this way of exploring the divine life as a way of bringing together a variety of scriptural (and philosophical) resources and dynamics, not as a 'model' which can simply carry the field."[119] Augustine's trinitarian theology combines numerous motifs and sources

---

118. *De trin.* 15.2.2.
119. Ayres, *Trinity*, 325.

as a fruitful synthesis through which to enter into the mystery of God. That attempt is only ever provisional, and "progress" is determined by the reformation of our own minds and hearts, and the cultures they shape and are shaped by—there is therefore a political aspect to all theological thought. As Cavadini describes it:

> In the *trin.*, we have a theology which is, strictly speaking, neither apophatic nor kataphatic, but specifically trinitarian in its call neither to renounce language nor to accept its limitations as received, but to present the image of God ever more clearly in a transformed and transforming begetting of words.[120]

My argument is that to reclaim such a theological style requires something like the systematic theology of the symbol I have developed. If we are, as theologians, to search for mystical reasons in loving regard for God, then creation itself must be a symbol that can be "read" in grace, and thereby returned in praise to the God who remains symbolized within and beyond it. Anything less risks reducing God to an ontic thing, flattening nature or reifying an autonomous pure nature, and severing theology from mysticism, knowledge from love.

It must be emphasized that if my triad, symbolized–symbol–symbolism, represents the doctrinal conditions for the possibility of reclaiming an ancient theological practice, it carries the same inadequacy as Augustine's. Inasmuch as symbolized–symbol–symbolism represents some kind of logico-temporal process, God is not like this. To use this kind of language at all is to acknowledge my own creaturely limitation, since it is language taken from the experience of temporal existence. But I have argued that temporal existence opens beyond itself, and the theological task is to find ways to go one speaking of God in light of our inescapable finitude, never allowing its limits to go unheeded or its transcendent destiny unexplored. If the modern era was marked by a loss of faith in transcendence, an evacuation of the sacral value of creation, and a severing of knowledge from love, the postmodern era has seen numerous clumsy attempts at their rediscovery and reintegration: "spiritual but not religious" names a longing for the transcendent, sacred and loveable, *and* a commensurate ambivalence about how or where to find them. One urgent requirement then is a new illuminative synthesis, one that unites all things to God in a single theological vision. I propose a trinitarian theology of the symbol as such a vision. This vision is not actually new, as the scope of this account has shown. It is, however, newly articulated, an attempt to giving living voice to a living tradition toward the knowledge and love of the living God.

---

120. Cavadini, *Augustine*, 52.

CONCLUSION

Symbolism: A Reprise

Henri de Lubac sought to recover a form of theology that he called "symbolism," a patristic mode of thought that assumed a real unity-in-distinction between symbolized and symbol, sustaining a thoroughly sacramental vision. Yet de Lubac never developed this systematically. While numerous theologians have engaged and developed de Lubac's work in various ways,[1] none have integrated symbolism consistently into trinitarian theology, and thus into a systematic whole. There remains, then, a need for a systematic theology of the symbol.

The word "symbolism" comes from a patristic theology deeply engaged with Neoplatonism. As we have seen, a symbol is a sign that mediates the presence of the symbolized. Symbolism was the theological discipline of searching for these symbols in scripture and creation, and through them encountering the "ontological trace" of the symbolized. As Peter Struck summarizes Dionysius, contemplation of symbols has "the anagogic power to lift us up" to the symbolized itself.[2] Thus, there is the symbolized, the symbol and the reading of the symbol that de Lubac calls symbolism. This, I argued in the first chapter, is an apt analogy for the Trinity. In dialogue with Augustine, Rahner, and de Lubac, I argued that the Father is "the symbolized," the hidden source and eternal fount of divinity. The Son is the eternal symbol, the fullness of the Father's being expressed in another. The Spirit is symbolism, the wholly personal agent of love and unity between symbol and symbolized. This network of relations must be understood together. The symbol is only a symbol in relation to symbolism, the movement of unity between symbol and symbolized. This was expressed in the trinitarian

---

1. To pick two of many, Hans Boersma, *A Return to Mystery: Nouvelle Theologie and Sacramental Ontology* (Oxford: Oxford University Press, 2013); John Milbank, *The Suspended Middle: Henri de Lubac and the Renewed Split in Modern Catholic Theology*, 2nd ed. (Cambridge: Eerdmans, 2014). See below for an analysis of Hans Urs von Balthasar.

2. Peter Struck, *Birth of the Symbol: Ancient Readers and the Limits of Their Texts* (Princeton, NJ: Princeton University Press, 2004), 262.

paradox of the Spirit. The Spirit proceeds from the Father by the Son, but is also the gift given by the Father to the Son in generation, and thus is paradoxically "pre-present" or "retroactively causal" in the generation of the son. Thus, the divine *taxis* also expresses a perichoretic unity. Trinitarian theology points toward the triad symbolized–symbol–symbolism.

God's being and God's act are one, and so God's action in time is undertaken according to a trinitarian pattern. To express this reality I formulated a second triad, God–creation–church. God is the symbolized, the hidden source and fount of creation. Creation is a symbol, a sign that contains the "ontological trace" of God. The church, understood as the *totus Christus*, is the movement of love and unity between creation and God; it is the world reconciled. The rest of the work seeks to explain this pattern. The doctrine of the Trinity thus opens onto a *trinitarian* doctrine of creation. The Father speaks creation in the speaking of the Logos: creation is thus the Logos "unfolded" through time, in the words of Nicholas of Cusa, while the Logos does not depend on or require this unfolding.[3] Moreover, creation is set in motion back toward the Father by the life of Spirit. This motion is symbolism, a dynamic movement toward the God who is its source and significance. Thus, creation is enacted according the trinitarian processions. This makes creation a symbol of God—truly mediating the divine life, although not necessary to the divine life. I also argued that a poor trinitarian theology leads to an impoverished account of creation, as was seen with Duns Scotus. For Scotus, I argued, because the productive powers of the divine essence are prior to the Persons, creation is a symbol primarily of productive power, not trinitarian persons. As the distinction between God's absolute and ordained power was centralized in later centuries, it became less apparent that divine power was needed to sustain creation, eventually occluding God altogether. I argued that a "symbolic" Trinity better accounts for the sacral value of creation and the fundamental importance of its relation to God than does a Trinity founded on essential productive power. Creation is a symbol, created in, by and for the trinitarian persons.

Creation culminates in humanity, the creature par excellence. To approach this immense topic, I expounded an isomorphism between human nature and the division of scripture between Old and New Testaments. Just as Christ is only intelligible as *Israel*'s messiah, that is, the life and ministry of Christ presupposes and fulfils the promises and expectations of the Old Testament, so grace presupposes and fulfills without destroying nature. Nonetheless, just as there is never a moment that the Old Testament is without Christ, who is mystically present within it, so nature is never without grace. Moreover, just as Christ came in a way that was entirely unanticipated, so grace only ever comes as a gratuitous gift. The natural desire for the supernatural, then, mirrors the structure of scripture: humans naturally desire the triune God, but that desire can only be fulfilled by

---

3. Nicholas of Cusa, *De Dato Patris Luminum* 4.110, in Jasper Hopkins, *Complete Philosophical and Theological Treatises of Nicholas of Cusa*, Vol. 1 (Minneapolis, MN: Arthur J. Banning Press, 2001), 381.

grace. Between scripture and human nature there is a symbolic resonance, so that understanding one can open onto an understanding of the other. Moreover, only this anthropology makes sense of the reading practice of spiritual exegesis. Only if every literal sense—every nature—opens onto a spiritual sense can spiritual exegesis not be merely an arbitrary addition to a literal history to which it does not otherwise belong. The shape of the human is the shape of scripture: the literal sense is the symbol of the spiritual hidden within and beyond it; the movement from literal to spiritual (whether of scripture or nature) can only be enacted by grace.

Such a movement is only possible within a community formed by the Realsymbol. Following Augustine's principle that the church is the world reconciled, I argued that the eucharistic church in communion with its head is symbolism, the dynamic unity of creation the symbol and God the symbolized. This means the church is pneumatologically constituted. It also means that the church is not reducible to an ontic space to be defended; the church is the redemption of time, the *movement* of creation back toward God, and God toward creation in Christ. To say that the church is symbolism is to join de Lubac in saying the church is a sacrament: it effects what it signifies, namely, the union of God with creation. I defended this view against a Barthian concern that this is Pelagian, and a Heideggerian concern that it is ontotheological. The latter led to the conclusion that if poetry is language in a state of emergence, the church is the poetry of creation: creation in emergence before God, God emerging within creation.

If the church is symbolism, then theology is one particular mode of symbolism. Specifically, it is the discipline of mystical reason. This argument unfolded in three steps, from one mystery to mysticism to mystical reason. First, God, as "the symbolized" is an abiding *mystery* that can never be possessed by creaturely knowledge. God is wholly anterior to all that is and coming to know God requires coming to love God. This was seen to guard against the threat of any ontotheological reduction of God. God, the abiding mystery, then speaks creation in the speaking of the Word with a view to elevation in Christ. Creation is thus a symbol by having a twofold *mysticism*: desirous by nature for the vision of God, but requiring grace for the fulfillment of that desire. This was seen to guard against a Barthian flattening of nature and a neo-Thomist reification of pure nature. And this finally renders theology a discipline of *mystical reason*. Because creation is spoken by God, it is shot through with "mystical reasons" to be read in the Spirit. That reading, like the spiritual interpretation of scripture—of which it is an extension—is intended to form the character of the theologian. To "read" a mystical symbol is to encounter the symbolized in and through it, so that theological thought approximates a mode of prayer. Symbolism is thus reasonable and mystical, mystical reason.

Thus, the trinitarian logic of Father–Son–Spirit leads to the triad symbolized–symbol–symbolism. Because creatures exist by participation in the Trinity, this triad can be correlated to God–creation–church. Creation is a symbol of God, the church is symbolism, the union of God with the world. The breadth of this account has been necessary, for the three terms must be held together if they are to be held at all. Thus, I have attempted a dogmatic outline, however lightly sketched, of a systematic theology of the symbol. This theology of the symbol is my own contribution—it does not exist in this form in Augustine, Aquinas, Rahner, or even de Lubac. I have sought to think with and beyond these lights, in the hope that God might be more clearly known and more dearly loved.

There remain, however, a number of serious questions about this presentation. This account might strike the Protestant as a studious avoiding of the issue of sin. Where might sin and evil fit in this account? And where, then does the cross fit? What of resurrection? In what remains I want to briefly sketch these themes from within a perspective of symbolism. Doing so will enable an engagement with the work of Hans Urs von Balthasar, arguing both for and against his project. I do so here, as a conclusion, not to relegate the work of Christ on the cross to a footnote, but as a culminating reflection on the work of Christ in whom alone every symbol shines truly.

Evil, the Symbol, and the Cross

privatio boni

What, then, of evil? What of the cross? Evil is, I will argue, the privation of the symbol and the fracturing of the possibility of symbolism. But to ascertain what a privation of the symbol might mean, I must first look at what is good about symbols.

In the *Summa*, Thomas says:

> Everything is therefore called good from the divine goodness, as from the first exemplary, effective, and final principle of all goodness. Nevertheless, everything is called good by reason of the similitude of the divine goodness belonging to it, which is formally its own goodness, whereby it is denominated good. And so of all things there is one goodness, and yet many goodnesses.[4]

God is the exemplar, efficient, and final cause of goodness. Creatures are good inasmuch as they are similitudes of this original goodness—inasmuch as they symbolize God. The goodness of a thing depends upon its quality as a symbol, the extent to which it images the goodness of God appropriate to it. To take up Rahner's terminology, to be is to be a symbol; to be a symbol is to be good.

Moreover, goodness is appropriated to the Spirit because it indicates the object of love and desire. It thus implies the work of the Spirit between Father and Son as well as governing and drawing creation toward God.[5] Whereas a creature's very existence is good inasmuch as it is a symbol, its *movement* through time is good

---

4. St. Thomas Aquinas, *Summa Theologiae* 1a.6.4. All quotations from Laurence Shapcote, O.P., trans., *Latin/English Edition of the Works of St. Thomas Aquinas* (Lander, WY: The Aquinas Institute for the Study of Sacred Doctrine, 2012). Hereafter, *ST*.

5. *ST* 1a.39.8.

because it is symbolism, a symbol in motion toward the Father. This movement is effected in humans as they ascend through the chain of symbols to know God through signs and things, now definitively centered on the life of Christ.

Thomas follows Augustine in arguing that evil is the privation of this goodness.[6] Evil is not a thing, a reified opposite to the good, but a pure lack, an unspeakable contradiction. This is because the divine nature is goodness itself, and to reify evil would either establish a dualism in which God has an eternal opposite or would fracture the divine unity by establishing both evil *and* good in the divine nature. Both options are unacceptable, and so Thomas and Augustine maintain that evil is nothing but the lack of the good, like darkness to light or cold to heat. For creatures whose goodness is their symbolic quality, this means that evil is the degradation of the quality of the symbol. When a symbol does not symbolize as it should, when it distorts the picture it is meant to re-present, when the symbolized is no longer visible in the symbol, or is less visible in the symbol, privation has occurred. Evil, then, in its most general sense, is distortion between symbolized and symbol, between God and creature, and concomitantly the fracturing of the possibility of symbolism. When such distortion intervenes between symbol and symbolized, it becomes difficult if not impossible "read" the symbol. In evil, the clarity of the symbol is diminished, and the capacity for symbolism, for uniting the symbol to the symbolized is also damaged.

This points toward the intuitive power of the *privatio boni* tradition. It has often been argued that *privatio boni* grossly undervalues the phenomenon of sin, whose effects are experienced as all-too-real.[7] Is it not a terrible moral failure to deny the reality of anyone's suffering? On a logic of symbols, however, *privatio boni* does far better justice to the experience of evil: it does not explain sin, for sin is the deprivation of explicability itself. The symbol has been robbed of its intrinsic symbolic value and meaning. Evil is this degradation of symbolic meaning, and because we are made for knowledge and love, the absurdity of evil can only be felt as pain and loss. The *absence* of God is felt most acutely in sin, evil, and its resultant suffering, precisely because it is the "nature" of sin and evil to obscure the presence of God by distorting the symbol–symbolized relation. This is why sin and evil are experienced as a darkness, an oblique confusion, a loss. Every attempt,

---

6. *ST* 1a.48.1; Augustine, *De civitate Dei* 11.9. For an account of Thomas's view, see Rudi A. te Velde, "Evil, Sin, and Death: Thomas Aquinas on Original Sin," in Rik Van Nieuwenhove and Joseph Wawrykow (eds.), *The Theology of Thomas Aquinas* (Notre Dame, IN: University of Notre Dame Press, 2005), 143–66. For Augustine, see G.R. Evans, *Augustine on Evil* (Cambridge: Cambridge University Press, 1982). The literature on evil is immense. See Kenneth Surin, *Theology and the Problem of Evil* (Oxford: Basil Blackwell, 1986). I will, do little more than state my position here. I will, moreover, assume a tight connection between sin and evil, even though they are not to be conflated.

7. Todd Calder, "Is the Privation Theory of Evil Dead?" *American Philosophical Quarterly* 44, no. 4 (2007), 371–81. Calder views the *privatio boni* tradition as phenomenologically disproved.

then, to make sin or evil intelligible as some meaningful or potentially meaningful substance in the created order is ultimately a metaphysical and theological disaster. In the final analysis it colludes in the distortion of God, looking *through* the prism of the ugly to obtain an account of God's beauty.[8] Sin and evil are, rather, the inability to see God in creation, the frustration of the human desire to know goodness and beauty itself. It is the experience of the loss of the availability of God in the mediating symbols of the world.

This is why the criticism of *privatio boni* as minimizing the very real effects of evil misses the mark. *Privatio boni* ensures that the effects of sin and evil are seen for the ugliness and barrenness they are; it is a refusal to decorate the darkness with unwarranted speculation about goods attained elsewhere.[9] It is the only logic that makes sin and evil truly *lamentable,* for it affords a lamentation not short-circuited by some calculus of greater goods. It recognizes that where sin and evil have their way, God cannot be found, for sin and evil are the erosion of the "findability" of God. This is not because God is now absent or inattentive, but that the *symbol* has become deformed. Sin and evil are the privation of the symbol, the distortion of representation of the symbolized, and the ensuing impossibility of symbolism. It is the drying up of reason and the death of mysticism.

Death

This is why death is the last and greatest enemy, for it is, for the human, the most immanent sundering of symbol and symbolized. Karl Rahner argues that the body is the symbol of the soul. The body–soul union is essential to human nature, for the soul comes into being by expression in its bodily symbol. Death, then, is the utter separation of symbol from symbolized. It makes symbolism impossible, both for the dead and for the living. For the dead, the *union* of their bodily symbol with their soul is no longer attainable, and so the symbolism of body and soul is lost. For the living, symbolism is likewise lost, for the symbol of the deceased is no longer available. Their living, symbolic presence no longer presents itself to be known and loved.

This loss, this apparently final privation of symbol from symbolized, is the paradigmatic instance of *privatio boni*. If sin is the failure to symbolize God, death is the failure to symbolize self, and the latter is but the immanent expression of the former. Death is "the wages of sin" because it is the perverse consummation of the "logic" of privation. It is thus a loss, a darkness, wholly and entirely lamentable. But Paul will indeed speak of longing to depart and be with the Lord, and so there

---

8. See Rowan Williams, "Insubstantial Evil," in *On Augustine* (London: Bloomsbury, 2016), 79–106 for a navigation of these themes in relation to Augustine.

9. On the importance of refusing a rationalization of evil, see Karen Kilby, "Evil and the Limits of Theology," *New Blackfriars* 84, no. 983 (January 2003), 13–29; on the relation of this to suffering, see Kilby's "Julian of Norwich, Hans Urs von Balthasar, and the Status of Suffering in Christian Theology," *New Blackfriars* 99, no. 1081 (May 2018), 298–311.

is happiness in death.¹⁰ Yet the happiness of death, for Paul, is funded by the *bodily* resurrection of Christ. And so to understand how death might be the last and greatest enemy and yet contain joy for the Christian, we need to turn to the death, repose, and resurrection and Christ.

Mysterium Paschale: *For and Against Balthasar*

Hans Urs von Balthasar's articulates a powerful and probing theology of the death of Christ. For Balthasar, the death and resurrection of Christ is the temporal dramatization of the eternal relation of Father, Son, and Spirit. The cross shows not only the depth of the darkness of human sin, but also the depths of difference between the persons of the godhead.¹¹ Balthasar's Trinity is marked by a complete internal *kenosis* in which each person pours itself out into the others.¹² This self-emptying is a true emptying—it represents an eternal "loss" of self, an eternal self-destitution: "We shall never know how to express the abyss-like depths of the Father's self-giving, that Father who, in an eternal 'super-Kenosis,' makes himself 'destitute' of all that he is and can be so as to bring forth a consubstantial divinity, the Son."¹³ It is thus that between Father and Son there is an infinite distance, an "abyss" which is only spanned by the return gift of self in the Holy Spirit. It is this difference between Father and Son that founds the possibility of creation—only an eternal difference between divine persons can fund a temporal difference between God and creation.¹⁴ Moreover, this eternal abyssal distance grounds the possibility of sin.¹⁵ The reason for the latter is that generation and spiration are the gift of another in absolute and unlimited freedom. In Rowan Williams' summary: "The Father does not determine the Son, but rather gives the Son infinite space to be

---

10. Phil. 1:23; 1 Thess. 4:13-18.

11. Cf. Rowan Williams, "Balthasar and the Trinity," in *The Cambridge Companion to Hans Urs von Balthasar* (Cambridge: Cambridge University Press, 2004), 40: "A conception of [intra]divine difference has opened up so radically that it effects everything that can be said of God's relation to what is not God."

12. Hans Urs von Balthasar, *Mysterium Paschale* (San Francisco, CA: Ignatius, 1990), 35, and elsewhere. Hereafter, *MP*. Due to Coronavirus restrictions, I was not able to obtain a physical copy of this book, and have relied on the Kindle edition. I have cited the chapter number and Kindle location to aid referencing.

13. *MP*, preface, Loc. 66. Williams, "Balthasar," 38.

14. For a fruitful deployment of this theme, free from the negative tendencies of Balthasar's treatment, see Simon Oliver, "Analogy, Creation and Descent in Cusa and Aquinas," in Isabelle Moulin (ed.), *Participation et Vision de Dieu Chez Nicolas de Cues* (Paris: Librairie Philosophique J. Vrin, 2017), 125–41. Oliver clarifies that Kenosis as self-giving is not a giving-away. This is on the basis of a strong and salutary theology of super-abundance coming from Cusa's Neoplatonism.

15. Theodrama 4, 323: the generation of the Son "is the positing of an absolute, infinite difference, within which all possible other differences, as they emerge within the finite world, including even sin, are encircled and embraced."

who he is."[16] This gift of absolute freedom to the other then sustains an account of creation in which creatures are granted a share of this absolute freedom. And this includes the freedom to refuse to return the gift of love.

Of course, creatures do refuse the gift, and are plunged into the abyss, as it were, between the divine persons. If they are to be rescued, God will have to come to them. Hence, the incarnation. In the Incarnation, Christ receives the divine gift perfectly and constantly as a human and returns the gift completely. Because the gift is given kenotically, it must be returned kenotically. Thus Christ empties himself entirely on the cross, descending to the deepest depths of darkness possible. Holy Saturday, then, is not a victorious descent in which Christ kicks down the doors of Hell, but is victorious inasmuch as Christ abides in total and absolute abandonment in what is not God. In freely giving himself to this depth, Christ accomplishes the return gift required for the *kenotic* circle to be completed. The Father receives Christ's offering, and in turn offers himself again in fellowship and communion. Thus, the infinite distance has once again been spanned: God has descended to the depths of darkness and distance and joined it all to godself in Christ.

This account is powerful and provocative and captures a great number of scriptural and patristic themes. Space does not permit a full survey of all that Balthasar's theodramatic account of the mystery of the Passion successfully accomplishes. I will highlight just a few. It is profoundly Anselmic, properly understanding that atonement is an intra-trinitarian affair, not as a meek Son appeasing an angry Father, but as a temporal expression of the gift of love eternally offered from God to God. Moreover, Balthasar has rightly drawn attention to the difference a doctrine of the Trinity makes for a doctrine of creation: only an eternal difference between persons can sustain a temporal difference between God and creation.[17] He has, moreover, sought to do all of this a way that takes seriously the "drama" of revelation as unfolded in scripture. And perhaps most impressively, he has integrated an enormous amount of theological themes to trinitarian theology, as I have also sought to do throughout this book.

Yet I want to indicate several ways that symbolism accomplishes what Balthasar wishes to, without some of the weaknesses of his account. A number of significant problems have been pointed out by commentators. Balthasar has a tendency to assume an enormous amount of knowledge about the inner divine life: there is a concern that Balthasar's theodrama reads too deeply into the luminous darkness, assuming a very clear picture of the interpersonal dynamics of the divine.[18] This in turn funds an "epic" resolution to dramatic tension; that is, Balthasar often assumes a God's-eye-view of things, flattening the complex and ambiguous particularities of history in favor of an exhaustive schema.[19] This "epic" resolution and exhaustive

---

16. Williams, "Balthasar," 41.
17. I have sought to elucidate a similar point in Chapter 2.
18. Cf. Karen Kilby, *Hans Urs von Balthasar: A (Very) Critical Introduction* (Grand Rapids, MI: Eerdmans, 2012), ch. 5.

schematization is perhaps manifested in his controversial approach to gender and sex.[20] There is, additionally, the question of whether or not Balthasar has slipped into tritheism, with three divine "selves" freely self-emptying into one another.[21] Rather than address each of these individually, I want to focus on one particular line of critique that I believe to be at or near the core of them all, namely, the role that emptiness plays in Balthasar's Trinity, for it is here that my account differs most markedly from his.

For Balthasar, inner trinitarian life is marked by an absolute kenosis between the persons: the Father completely empties himself into the Son. While Balthasar will dialectically maintain that the Father "does not lose himself … he does not extinguish himself by self-giving," this is set against the statement that the Father's *ur-kenosis* is a "destitution," an "absolute" self-emptying.[22] There is a *sense* here of risk, of vulnerability in the begetting of the Son.[23] The reason for the latter is that the Father begets the Son in absolute freedom, bestowing on the Son something like an infinite indeterminacy: "the Father does not determine the Son," rather, the Son is given "infinite space to be who he is."[24] The utter self-emptying of the Father "risks" that the Son, in infinite freedom, will not return the gift, leaving nothing but the empty abyss of kenotic love poured into a broken cistern. While this "risk" is never realized in the divine life, it is precisely this risk that funds the possibility of sin. When creatures do indeed refuse the gift, *they* are plunged into the void, and Christ must descend into that abyss (the abyss wholly within God) to complete the kenotic circle. Williams is frank about what this entails: "There is a kind of 'nothingness' within the divine life, Balthasar suggests, a groundlessness of freedom in the generation of such total otherness."[25] This "nothingness," this "abyss" is, on Balthasar's terms, the distance that distinguishes the persons, the nothingness that allows the Father to be the Father to the Son. It is difficult to avoid the conclusion that this entirely unconditioned freedom, this "nothingness" at the very least *risks* a kind of "trinitarian nihilism" in which the persons are dependent on an infinitely expansive *nihil* in order to be freely personal. Trinitarian difference, and so trinitarian life, *requires* something like nothingness. To put it as simply as possible, if the abyss is in God, the abyss *is* God.

This intra-divine *nihil* then risks a logic of scarcity, a quasi-agonistic view of the persons in which "selfhood" is received at the price of another. The whole process

---

19. Ben Quash, *Theology and the Drama of History* (Cambridge: Cambridge University Press, 2005), ch. 3.

20. For an overview of Balthasar's thought on the sexes, see Corinne Crammer, "One Sex or Two? Balthasar's Theology of the Sexes" in *Companion*, ch. 8. For a more critical appraisal, see Kilby, *Critical*, ch. 6.

21. See, for instance, the critique in Kevin Duffy, "Change, Suffering and Surprise in God: Von Balthasar's Use of Metaphor," *Irish Theological Quarterly* 76, no. 4 (2011), 378.

22. *Theo-Drama* IV, 325; *MP*, Preface.

23. Cf. Kilby, "Hans Urs von Balthasar on the Trinity," in *Companion*, 211.

24. Williams, "Balthasar," 41.

25. Williams, "Balthasar," 42.

could in fact be narrated as an *exchange*: the Son's life is purchased at the price of the Father's, received only as the destitution of the other. This is in fact what Holy Saturday reveals. Christ so fully destitutes himself as to descend to the very depths of the abyss, gazing not on the beatific vision, but a vision of "sheer sin as such ... contemplated in its bare reality as such (for sin *is* a reality)."[26] Here, in contemplating sin itself—treated as a substantial *res*—Christ accomplishes his own utter self-destitution, restoring kenotic return precisely in the darkest emptiness possible.[27] Christ's damned vision is therefore the vision of his own victory, for obediential loss just is eternal communion. While certainly overstated, John Milbank is not entirely wrong in accusing Balthasar of "an abandonment of the metaphysics of cosmic harmony in favor of a gnostic hypostasization of the violence of the cross."[28] I would add that this is because the violence of the cross does not annihilate the abyss, but enfolds it in deity itself, revealing it to have been always latent in the infinite distance between the persons eternally. This much, at the very least, is risked by Balthasar's kenotic Trinity.

Symbolism, however, does not conceive of difference in these terms, and in fact points to ways that Balthasar's own speculation renders the intra-divine abyss superfluous. From paternal plentitude flows the Son, a perfect and replete symbol whose union-in-distinction with the Father has nothing to do with an infinite indeterminacy, distance or abyss, but is a distinguished unity wholly hypostasized in the person of the *Holy Spirit*. The difference in the godhead is not a gap, but a person. Balthasar indeed accounts for the union-in-distinction of Father and Son by the Spirit, while also urging the Spirit as a second difference, an interpretation of the Word of the Father in ever-increasing glory. Indeed, the Spirit is seen to be the divine freedom itself in hypostatic form.[29] But if this is the case, one wonders why Balthasar has need of "infinite distance," "abyss," and "nothingness" at all. There is in fact a strange isomorphism between the role of the Spirit and role of the abyss in Balthasar's Trinity. If the Spirit is both the love *between* Father and Son and the ecstatic outpouring of love "beyond," what is the relation of this same Spirit to the abyss *between* the Father and Son, and the *nothingness* that grounds the divine freedom spiraling outward and "beyond"? Is the Spirit in a dialectical relationship with this *nihil*? Surely not. Is the *nihil* another name for the Spirit? Again, surely not. It would seem, then, that if the Holy Spirit is the fully personal agent of unity and love and the hypostatic person of divine freedom itself, there

---

26. Balthasar, *MP*, ch. 4, loc. 2589.

27. It is tempting to put down much of the distortion of Balthasar's account to a partial reifying of sin as a substance. Because sin is some kind of *thing*, it requires an eternal ground. For a discussion of Balthasar on sin, and the ways he partially reifies sin, before subsuming it into the divine drama, see Les Oglesby, *C.G. Jung and Hans Urs von Balthasar: God and Evil, a Critical Comparison* (New York: Routledge, 2014), 123–4.

28. Milbank, *Suspended*, 80.

29. John R. Sachs, "Deus Semper Major—Ad Dei Gloriam: The Pneumatology and Spirituality of Hans Urs von Balthasar," *Gregorianum* 74, no. 4 (1993), 639.

is no need to posit any darkness or abyss whatsoever in the divine. And once the *nihil* is banished in favor of what we might term the necessary surplus of the Spirit, then the specter of an eternal scarcity is finally put to rest as well. If we have the Spirit—and Balthasar surely does—we need nothing, not even "nothing."

Holy Saturday, then, will take on a different texture in a theology of the symbol. Balthasar is absolutely correct that the difference between Father and Son grounds the difference between God and creation. On my terms, because the Father is symbolized in the Son, God may be symbolized in creation. But it is not the distance between Father and Son that grounds creation, it is their likeness which is at once a difference which is not a distance. This likeness between God and creation, however, is ruptured by sin: distortion enters the symbolized–symbol relation, and this in turn hinders symbolism: humanity can no longer "read" the symbols rightly. In becoming human, Christ the eternal symbol takes on the conditions of the temporal symbol. But whereas in Adam, the rupture between the human symbol and God is echoed in the rupture between the human body and soul, Christ had no rupture with God. Christ, as a human, lived as a replete human symbol, fully "transparent" to the symbolized, even as the symbolized remained hidden within him. Thus, every moment lived by the incarnate Logos is redeemed: birth now symbolizes God again because the eternal symbol has been born. Adolescence now symbolizes God because the eternal symbol grew in wisdom and stature, etc.

However, death itself does *not* symbolize God, because death is not a thing. Death is the privation of the symbol and the impossibility of symbolism, and as such has no antecedent condition in the God who is pure actuality. Christ's descent to the dead is therefore a descent into utter meaninglessness, where symbols no longer symbolize, and where symbolism is impossible. This is true of Christ, whose soul once separated from its body cannot symbolize itself; it is true of Christ's community who cannot encounter his soul in and through his physical body. Thus, Christ descended to the depths of human sin, disfigured beyond recognition, a soul without its symbol into the darkness of the grave. Unable to symbolize God in a holistic way, unable to symbolize himself, unable to be embraced and "read" by the symbolism of his community. Christ does not descend to kick over the all the tables of Hell; he descends to be forsaken. In the silence of Holy Saturday, the eternal Word experienced in the humanity of Jesus the deepest rending of symbolized from symbol possible for the human; the lowest possible point, the dissolution of the symbol.

And yet because this depth is experienced by the eternal symbol, the dissolution is a triumph. The dissolution itself is not enfolded in God, for dissolution is not a thing to be enfolded. Rather, in descending, the eternal word gathers to himself all fragmented symbols, the scattered pieces of humanity, hardly even vestiges of themselves, and in his own person restores their symbolic value. Where it seemed symbols could no longer symbolize God in death, now that the eternal Word died a human death even dead symbols can symbolize God. This is not because the eternal Word is cut off from the Father. Rather, because the eternal Word *remains* the Word of the Father, in perfect union with the Father in the Spirit, human symbols in death are joined to this unity: even a dead symbol can now symbolize God because God has undergone creaturely dissolution. What unites Christ in the grave with the Father in heaven continues to be the Holy Spirit, whose wholly personal love sustains the union-in-difference between Father and Son. The Spirit is expansive enough to encompass both Christ in the grave and Father in heaven, for "love is as strong as death, passion fierce as the grave."[30] And because the Spirit maintains the union of Father and Son even in human death, all humans in death can once again symbolize God, for God has joined them in their death.

Easter Sunday, then, constitutes two restitutions. In rising, Christ brings those fragmented symbols with him, now united in the reunion of his own body and soul. His resurrection becomes the hope of theirs, and their fragmented persons are held vouchsafe in his united person: they are held in security until the resurrection. Even in death symbols are united to Christ, and thus symbolize God even in their dissolute state, awaiting the fullness of restitution of body with soul in the resurrection. This is why Paul can expect to depart the body and be with the Lord *and* expect the resurrection of the dead as the fullness of God's purposes for the earth. Paul is confident that he will meet Christ in death, for Christ has raised the souls of the dead with himself, and because Paul's confidence is founded on Christ's resurrection, he looks forward as well to his own resurrection.

If the first restitution of the resurrection is the human ability to symbolize God, even in death, the second is the restitution of symbolism. This, in turn, has two dimensions. First, human symbols are indeed *united* to God in death. The same Spirit that united Father to Son in Christ's death and that raised Christ from the dead now dwells in us, and in our own deaths unites us to God.[31] Symbolism, as the unity of symbolized and symbol, is thus restored between the dead and God by the Spirit. The second dimension is horizontal. Recall that death, as a communal reality, ends the community's ability to "read" the symbol of their loved one and so come to know God in and through them. The resurrection of Christ restores this ability, albeit in an attenuated way. For because the dead are alive in Christ, we remain with them in one body—the church, the *totus Christus*. That unity is established and sustained at the eucharist, whose work of unity spans time and space. Symbolism now entails prayers offered on behalf of one another, as well as ongoing reflection on the lives all the dead in Christ, and especially of the saints, whose lives are not just memories of events long-since gone but living witnesses to God's goodness.[32]

I have argued that symbolized–symbol–symbolism corresponds to God–creation–church, and it is the death and resurrection of Christ that establishes and sustains this correspondence. Creation can symbolize God in spite of the distortion

---

30. Song of Solomon 8:6, NRSV.
31. Rom. 8:11.
32. Much more could be said about the nature of judgment, the possibilities of various post-mortem states, but space simply does not permit an examination of those important questions.

of sin because the eternal symbol was made incarnate and descended to the depths of dissolution. In his rising, he joins in his body—the church—the living and the dead, restoring the unity of love between symbol and symbolized, and between the community of symbols. This unity, secured by Christ, is effected by the Spirit who *is* the personal love stronger than the grave. If death is the privation of the symbol and the impossibility of symbolism, the reunion of symbolized and symbol in a living union is the essence of salvation. Salvation is the reunion of humanity with the God it has consistently failed to symbolize, and this reunion is coextensive with the reunion of body and soul, and the embodied soul with community. And because symbolism corresponds to the church, salvation is found in the union of Christ's body, the *totus Christus*.[33] There is no salvation outside the church because the church just is this living unity.[34]

This union is the eternal work of the Spirit: Christ is raised in the Spirit, and the community now sees Christ in the Spirit. While we await the eschatological fullness of unity, we are joined to Christ's own body, the church, in the eucharist *by the Spirit*. As we groan in estrangements of every conceivable kind—our malfunctioning bodies, our disordered communities, our sins and the sins of our societies—the Spirit groans in us in a language too deep even for words, that is, in the eternal desire of Father for Son and Son for Father, now distended through time as the pilgrim church. That desire will only be fulfilled when every symbol shines purely with the radiant intelligibility of the symbolized, and God is all in all. Truly, the Spirit and the Bride say "come."

---

33. It is in this way that we should understand the phrase "no salvation outside the church."

34. Of course, as Augustine makes clear, this means the boundaries of the institutional church are not coextensive with the Kingdom of God.

BIBLIOGRAPHY

Aquinas, Thomas. *Quaestiones disputatae de veritate*. Translated by J. V. McGlynn. Chicago, IL: Henry Regnery, 1952–4.
Aquinas, Thomas. *Summa Contra Gentiles*. Notre Dame, IN: University of Notre Dame Press, 1975.
Aquinas, Thomas. *Summa Theologiae*. Translated by Laurence Shapcote. *Latin/English Edition of the Works of St. Thomas Aquinas*. Lander, WY: The Aquinas Institute for the Study of Sacred Doctrine, 2012.
Athanasius. *On the Incarnation*. In *Nicene and Post-Nicene Fathers*, Second Series, Vol. 4. Available at http://www.newadvent.org/fathers/2802.htm
Augustine. "Homilies on 1 John," Homily 1. *The Nicene and Post Nicene Fathers*. Edited by Philip Schaff. New York: The Christian Literature Company, 1888.
Augustine. *On Christian Teaching*. Translated by R. P. H. Green. Oxford: Oxford University Press, 1997.
Augustine. *The Literal Meaning of Genesis*. Translated by John Hammond Taylor. *Ancient Christian Writers* 41. New York: Newman Press, 1982.
Augustine. *The Teacher* in *The Teacher; The Free Choice of the Will; Grace and Free Will*. Translated by Russel P. Robert. Washington, DC: Catholic University of America Press, 1968.
Ayres, Lewis. "The Soul and the Reading of Scripture." *Scottish Journal of Theology* 61, no. 2 (2008), 173–90.
Ayres, Lewis. *Augustine and the Trinity*. Cambridge: Cambridge University Press, 2010.
Ayres, Lewis. *Nicea and Its Legacy*. Oxford: Oxford University Press, 2004.
Badcock, Gary. *The House Where God Lives*. Cambridge: Eerdmans, 2009.
Balthasar, Hans Urs von. *Mysterium Paschale*. San Francisco, CA: Ignatius, 1990.
Balthasar, Hans Urs von. *The Glory of the Lord: A Theological Aesthetics*, 7 vols. San Fancisco, CA: Ignatius Press, 1982–9.
Balthasar, Hans Urs von. *The Theology of Henri de Lubac: An Overview*. Translated by Joseph Fressio and Michael Waldstein. San Francisco, CA: Ignatius, 1991.
Balthasar, Hans Urs von. *Theo-Drama: Theological Dramatic Theory*, 5 vols. San Francisco, CA: Ignatius Press, 1988–98.
Balthasar, Hans Urs von. *Theo-Logic*, 4 vols. San Francisco: Ignatius Press, 2000–5.
Barth, Karl. *Church Dogmatics* I/1. Edinburgh: T&T Clark, 1956.
Barth, Karl. *Church Dogmatics* I/2. Edinburgh: T&T Clark, 1956.
Barth, Karl. *The Word of God and the Word of Man*. London: Hodder, 1928.
Benson, Joshua. "Review of *The Unintended Reformation: How a Religious Revolution Secularized Society* by Brad S. Gregory." *The Catholic Historical Review* 98, no. 3 (July 2012), 503–16.
Blankenhorn, Bernhard. "Review of Boersma's *Heavenly Participation: The Weaving of a Sacramental Tapestry*." *The Thomist* 78, no. 3 (July 2014).
Boersma, Hans. *Heavenly Participation: The Weaving of a Sacramental Tapestry*. Grand Rapids, MI: Eerdmans, 2011.

Boersma, Hans. *Nouvelle Théologie and Sacramental Ontology: A Return to Mystery*. Oxford: Oxford University Press, 2009.
Boeve, Lieven. "Theology in a Postmodern Context and the Hermeneutical Project of Louis-Marie Chauvet." In *Sacraments: Revelation of the Humanity of God*. Edited by Philippe Bordeyne and Bruce T. Morrill. Collegeville, MN: Pueblo, 2008. 5–24.
Bonino, Serge-Thomas, editor. *Surnaturel: A Controversy at the Heart of Twentieth-Century Catholic Thomistic Thought*. Ave Maria, FL: Sapientia Press, 2009.
Bossy, John. "The Mass as a Social Institution 1200–1700." *Past and Present* 100 (1983), 29–61.
Boulnois, Olivier. "La théologie symbolique face à la théologie comme science." *Revue des sciences philosophiques et théologiques* 95 (2011–12), 217–50.
Boulnois, Olivier. "Quand Commence L'Ontothéologie? Aristote, Thomas D'Aquin et Duns Scot." *Revue Thomiste* XCV, no. 1 (January–March 1995), 84–108.
Bouyer, Louis. *La vie de la liturgie*. Paris: Editions du Cerf, 1957.
Broadie, Alexander. "Scotist Metaphysics and Creation ex Nihilo." In *Creation and the God of Abraham*. Edited by David Burrell, et al. Cambridge: Cambridge University Press, 2010.
Buckley, Michael J. *Denying and Disclosing God: The Ambiguous Progress of Modern Atheism*. New Haven, CT: Yale University Press, 2004.
Burrell, David. *Aquinas: God and Action*, 3rd Edition. Eugene, OR: Wipf and Stock, 2016.
Calder, Todd. "Is the Privation Theory of Evil Dead?" *American Philosophical Quarterly* 44, no. 4 (2007), 371–81.
Callahan, Annice. "Karl Rahner's Theology of the Symbol." *Irish Theological Quarterly* 49, no. 3 (September 1982).
Candler, Peter. *Theology, Rhetoric and Manuduction*. Grand Rapids, MI: Eerdmans, 2006.
Cavadini, John C. *Visioning Augustine*. Oxford: Wiley Blackwell, 2019.
Chauvet, Louis Marie. *Symbol and Sacrament*. Translated by Patrick Madigan and Madeleine Beaumont. Collegeville, MN: Pueblo, 1995.
Clarke, W. Norris. *Creative Retrieval of St. Thomas Aquinas*. New York: Fordham University Press, 2009.
Clarke, W. Norris. *The One and the Many: A Contemporary Thomist Metaphysics*. Notre Dame, IN: Notre Dame University Press, 2001.
Coakley, Sarah. *God, Sexuality and the Self*. Cambridge: Cambridge University Press, 2013.
Congar, Yves. *I Believe in the Holy Spirit*. Translated by David Smith. New York: Crossroad, 1997.
Conzelmann, Hans. *The Theology of Saint Luke*. Translated by G. London Buswell: Faber and Faber, 1961.
Crammer, Corinne. "One Sex or Two? Balthasar's Theology of the Sexes." In *The Cambridge Companion to Hans Urs von Balthasar*. Edited by Edward T. Oakes SJ and David Moss. Cambridge: Cambridge University Press, 2004. Chap. 8.
Crisp, Oliver D. *Analyzing Doctrine*. Waco, TX: Baylor University Press, 2019.
Cross, Richard. *Duns Scotus*. Oxford: Oxford University Press, 1999.
Cross, Richard. *Duns Scotus on God*. Aldershot: Ashgate, 2005.
Cross, Richard. "Nicaea and Its Legacy." *Reviews in Religion and Theology* 13, no. 1 (January. 2006), 16–18.
Cross, Richard. "Where Angels Fear to Tread: Duns Scotus and Radical Orthodoxy." *Antonianum* Annus LXXVI Fasc. I (January–March, 2001).
Cunningham, Conor. *Genealogy of Nihilism: Philosophies of Nothing and the Difference of Theology*. London: Routledge, 2002.

Deely, John. *Basics of Semiotics*. Bloomington: Indiana University Press, 1990.
Deely, John. *Four Ages of Understanding*. Toronto: University of Toronto Press, 2001.
Dogmatic Constitution on the Catholic Faith. Available at http://inters.org/Vatican-Council-I-Dei-Filius
Dogmatic Constitution on the Church: Lumen Gentium. Available at https://www.vatican.va/archive/hist_councils/ii_vatican_council/documents/vat-ii_const_19641121_lumen-gentium_en.html
Dolezal, James. *God without Parts: Divine Simplicity and the Metaphysics of God's Absoluteness*. Eugene, OR: Pickwick, 2011.
Doolan, Gregory. "Aquinas on the Divine Ideas and the Really Real." In *Nova et Vetera* 13, no. 4 (2015), 1059–91.
Doolan, Gregory. *Aquinas on the Divine Ideas as Exemplar Causes*. Washington, DC: The Catholic University of America Press, 2008.
Doyle, Dennis M. *Communion Ecclesiology*. Maryknoll, NY: Orbis Books, 2000.
Duffy, Eamon. *The Stripping of the Altars*. New Haven, CT: Yale University Press, 1992.
Duffy, Kevin. "Change, Suffering and Surprise in God: Von Balthasar's Use of Metaphor." *Irish Theological Quarterly* 76, no. 4 (2011), 370–87.
Emery, Gilles. "The Ecclesial Fruit of the Eucharist in St. Thomas Aquinas." In *Trinity, Church and the Human Person*. Naples, FL: Sapientia Press, 2007.
Emery, Gilles. *Trinity, Church and the Human Person*. Naples, FL: Sapientia Press, 2007.
Emery, Gilles, O.P. *Trinity in Aquinas*. Naples, FL: Sapientia Press, 2003.
Feingold, Lawrence. *The Natural Desire to See God According to St Thomas Aquinas and His Interpreters*. Naples, FL: Sapientia Press, 2010.
Fields, Stephen. *Being as Symbol*. Washington, DC: Georgetown University Press, 2007.
Fitzmyer, Joseph. *The Gospel According to Luke (I–IX)*. New Haven, CT: Yale University Press, 2009.
Flynn, Gabriel and Murray, Paul D., editors. *Ressourcement: A Movement for Renewal in Twentieth-Century Catholic Theology*. Oxford: Oxford University Press, 2012.
Frei, Hans. *The Eclipse of the Biblical Narrative: A Study of Eighteenth and Nineteenth Century Hermeneutics*. New Haven, CT: Yale University Press, 1974.
Friedman, Russell. "Medieval Trinitarian Theology from the Late Thirteenth to the Fifteenth Centuries." In *The Oxford Handbook of the Trinity*. Edited by Gilles Emery and Matthew Levering. Oxford: Oxford University Press, 2011. 197–209.
Friedman, Russell. *Medieval Trinitarian Thought from Aquinas to Ockham*. Cambridge: Cambridge University Press, 2010.
Funkenstein, Amos. *Theology and the Scientific Imagination*, 2nd edition. Princeton, NJ: Princeton University Press, 1986.
Garrigou-Lagrange, Reginald. *The Sense of Mystery: Clarity and Obscurity in the Intellectual Life*. Translated by Matthew K. Minerd. Steubenville, OH: Emmaus Academic, 2017.
Gregory, Brad. *The Unintended Reformation: How a Religious Revolution Secularized Society*. Cambridge, MA: Harvard University Press, 2012.
Grumett, David. "De Lubac, Christ and the Buddha." *New Blackfriars* 89, no. 1020 (March 2008), 217–30.
Hart, David Bentley. "The Mirror of the Infinite: Gregory of Nyssa on the *Vestigia Trinitatis*." *Modern Theology* 18, no. 4 (October 2002), 541–61.
Hart, Trevor. "Revelation." In *The Cambridge Companion to Karl Barth*. Edited by John Webster. Cambridge: Cambridge University Press, 2000. 37–56.
Hays, Richard. *Echoes of Scripture in the Gospels*. Waco, TX: Baylor University Press, 2016.

Hays, Richard. *Reading Backward: Figural Christology and the Fourfold Gospel Witness.* London: SPCK, 2015.

Healy Jr., Nicholas J. "The Christian Mystery of Nature and Grace." In *The T&T Clark Companion to Henri de Lubac.* Edited by Jordan Hillebert. London: Bloomsbury T&T Clark, 2017. 181–204.

Healy, Nicholas M. *Church, World and the Christian Life: Practical-Prophetic Ecclesiology.* Cambridge: Cambridge University Press, 2000.

Hegel, Georg Wilhelm Friedrich. *Lectures on the Philosophy of Religion.* Edited by Peter C. Hodgson and Translated by R. F. Brown et al. Berkeley: University of California Press, 1988.

Heidegger, Martin. "The Onto-Theo-Logical Constitution of Metaphysics." In *Identity and Difference.* Translated by Joan Stambaugh. Chicago, IL: University of Chicago Press, 2002.

Hemming, Laurence. "Henri de Lubac: Reading Corpus Mysticum." *New Blackfriars* 90, no. 1029 (September 2009), 519–34.

Hillebert, Jordan, editor. *The T&T Clark Companion to Henri de Lubac.* London: Bloomsbury T&T Clark, 2017.

Hillebert, Jordan. "Introduction to Henri de Lubac." In *The T&T Clark Companion to Henri de Lubac.* Edited by Jordan Hillebert. London: Bloomsbury T&T Clark, 2017. 3–28.

Hoff, Johannes. "The Rise and Fall of the Kantian Paradigm of Modern Theology." In *The Grandeur of Reason: Religion, Tradition and Universalism.* Edited by Peter Candler. London: SCM Press, 2010.

Hollon, Bryan C. "Mysticism and Mystical Theology." In *T&T Clark Companion to Henri de Lubac.* Edited by Jordan Hillebert. London: Bloomsbury T&T Clark, 2017.

Hopkins, Gerard Manley. "Duns Scotus's Oxford." In *Gerard Manley Hopkins: The Major Works.* Oxford: Oxford University Press, 2002.

Horan, Daniel. *Postmodernity and Univocity: A Critical Account of Radical Orthodoxy and John Duns Scotus.* Minneapolis, MN: Fortress Press, 2014.

Hughes, Kevin. "The 'Fourfold Sense': De Lubac, Blondel and Contemporary Theology." *Heythrop Journal* XLII (2001), 451–62.

Hütter, Reinhard. *Dust Bound for Heaven.* Cambridge: Eerdmans, 2012.

Insole, Chris. *Kant and the Creation of Freedom.* Oxford: Oxford University Press, 2013.

Jordan, Mark D. "The Intelligibility of the World and the Divine Ideas in Aquinas." *The Review of Metaphysics* 38, no. 1 (September 1984), 17–32.

Jüngel, Eberhardt. "The Church as Sacrament?" In *Theological Essays.* Translated by John Webster. Edinburgh, T&T Clark, 1989.

Jüngel, Eberhardt. *Theological Essays.* Translated by John Webster. Edinburgh, T&T Clark, 1989.

Kerr, Fergus. "Knowing God by Reason Alone: What Vatican I Never Said." *New Blackfriars* 91, no. 1033 (May 2010), 215–28.

Kilby, Karen. *Balthasar: A (Very) Critical Introduction.* Grand Rapids, MI: Eerdmans, 2012, ch. 5.

Kilby, Karen. "Evil and the Limits of Theology." *New Blackfriars* 84, no. 983 (January 2003), 13–29.

Kilby, Karen. "Hans Urs von Balthasar on the Trinity." In *The Cambridge Companion to the Trinity.* Edited by Peter C. Phan. Cambridge: Cambridge University Press, 2011. 208–22.

Kilby, Karen. "Julian of Norwich, Hans Urs von Balthasar, and the Status of Suffering in Christian Theology." *New Blackfriars* 99, no. 1081 (May 2018), 298–311.

Kilby, Karen. "Perichoresis and Projection: Problems with Social Doctrines of the Trinity." *New Blackfriars* 81, no. 956 (October, 2000), 432–45.

Kilby, Karen. "Philosophy, Theology and Foundationalism in the Thought of Karl Rahner." *Scottish Journal of Theology* 55, no. 2 (2002), 127–40.

King, Peter. "Scotus on Metaphysics." In *The Cambridge Companion to Duns Scotus*. Edited by Thomas Williams. Cambridge: Cambridge University Press, 2003. 15–68.

Ledsham, Cal. "Love, Power and Consistency: Scotus' Doctrines of God's Power, Contingent Creation, Induction and Natural Law." *Sophia* 49 (2010), 557–75.

Libera, Alain de. *La philosophie médiévale*, 3rd edition. Paris: Presses Universitaires de France, 1998.

Lindbeck, George. *The Nature of Doctrine: Religion and Doctrine in a Postliberal Age*. Philadelphia, PA: Westminster Press, 1984.

Long, D. Stephen. *The Perfectly Simple Triune God*. Minneapolis, MN: Fortress Press, 2016.

Long, D. Stephen. "Thomas Aquinas' Divine Simplicity as Biblical Hermeneutic." *Modern Theology* 35, no. 3 (July 2019), 496–507.

Long, Steven A. "Creation *ad imaginem Dei*: The Obediential Potency of the Human Person to Grace and Glory." *Nova et Vetera* 14, no. 4, English Edition (2016).

Long, Steven A. *Natura Pura*. New York: Fordham University Press, 2010.

Louth, Andrew. *Discerning the Mystery*. Oxford: Clarendon Press, 1983.

Lubac, Henri de. *Aspects of Buddhism*. London: Sheed and Ward, 1954.

Lubac, Henri de. *At the Service of the Church: Henri de Lubac Reflects on the Circumstances that Occasioned His Writings*. Translated by Anne Elizabeth Englund. San Francisco, CA: Communio Books, 1993.

Lubac, Henri de. *Augustinianism and Modern Theology*. Translated by Lancelot Shepperd. New York: Crossroad, 2000.

Lubac, Henri de. *Catholicism: Christ and Common Destiny of Man*. Translated by Lancelot Sheppard and Elizabeth Englund, OCD. San Francisco, CA: Ignatius, 1988.

Lubac, Henri De. *Medieval Exegesis*, 3 vols. Grand Rapids, MI: Eerdmans, 1998–2009.

Lubac, Henri de. *Mémoire sur l'occasion de mes éctrits*. Namur, Belgium: Culture et Vérité, 1989.

Lubac, Henri de. *Pic de la Mirandole*. Paris: Aubier Montaigne, 1974.

Lubac, Henri de. *Surnaturel: Etudes Historique*. Aubier: Editions Montaigne, 1946.

Lubac, Henri de. *The Church—Paradox and Mystery*. Translated by James R. Dunne. Shannon, Ireland: Ecclesia Press, 1969.

Lubac, Henri de. *The Mystery of the Supernatural*. New York: Herder and Herder, 1967.

Lubac, Henri de. *The Splendor of the Church*. Translated by Michael Mason. San Francisco, CA: Ignatius, 1986.

Lubac, Henri de. *Theological Fragments*. Translated by Rebeccah Howell Balinski. San Francisco, CA: Ignatius, 1989.

Lubac, Henri de. *Theology in History*. San Francisco, CA: Ignatius Press, 1996.

Markus, Robert A. "St. Augustine on Signs." *Phronesis* 2, no. 1 (Brill: 1957), 60–83.

Marshal, Bruce. "*Quod Scit Una Uetula*: Aquinas on the Nature of Theology." In *The Theology of Thomas Aquinas*. Edited by Rik Van Nieuwenhove and Joseph Wawrykow. Notre Dame, IN: Notre Dame University Press, 2005.

McPartlan, Paul. *The Eucharist Makes the Church*. Edinburgh: T&T Clark, 1993.

Mettepenningen, Jürgen. *Nouvelle Theologie—New Theology*. Edinburgh: T&T Clark, 2010.

Metz, Johann Baptiste. *Faith in History and Society*. Translated by David Smith. New York: Seabury Press, 1980.

Milbank, John. "Enclaves, or Where Is the Church?" *New Blackfriars* 73, no. 861 (June 1992), 341–52.

Milbank, John. "Sacred Triads: Augustine and the Indo-European Soul." *Modern Theology* 13, no. 4 (October, 1997), 451–74.

Milbank, John. *The Suspended Middle: Henri de Lubac and the Renewed Split in Modern Catholic Theology*. 2nd edition. Cambridge: Eerdmans, 2005.

Milbank, John. *The Word Made Strange*. Oxford: Blackwell, 1997.

Milbank, John. *Theology and Social Theory*, 2nd edition. Oxford: Blackwell, 2006.

Milbank, John and Pickstock, Catherine. *Truth in Aquinas*. New York: Routledge, 2001.

Moberley, Walter. *Old Testament Theology: Reading the Hebrew Bible as Christian Scriptures*. Grand Rapids, MI: Baker Academic, 2013.

Mobley, Joshua. "Symbolism after Dialectics: de Lubac, Rahner and Symbolic Theology." *The International Journal of Systematic Theology* 20, no. 4 (October, 2018), 537–53.

Möhle, Hannes. "Scotus's Theory of Natural Law." In *The Cambridge Companion to Duns Scotus*. Edited by Thomas Williams. Cambridge: Cambridge University Press, 2003. 312–331.

Mohler, Johann Adam. *Symbolism*. Translated by James Burton Robertson. New York: Crossroad Publishing, 1997.

Monti, James. "Late Medieval Liturgy: A Celebration of Emmanuel—'God with Us.'" In *The T&T Clark Companion to Liturgy*. Edited by Alcuin Reid. London: T&T Clark, 2016. 93–107.

Morgan, Edward. *The Incarnation of the Word: The Theology of Language of Augustine of Hippo*. London: T&T Clark, 2010.

Motzko, Maria Elisabeth. "Karl Rahner's Theology: A Theology of the Symbol." PhD dissertation, Fordham University, 1976.

Narcisse, Gilbert. *Les Raisons de Dieu*. Fribourg: Éditions Universitaires Fribourg Suisse, 1997.

Nicholas of Cusa, *Complete Philosophical and Theological Treatises of Nicholas of Cusa*, Vol. 1. Translated by Jasper Hopkins. Minneapolis, MN: Arthur J. Banning Press, 2001.

Nieuwenhove, Rik van and Wawrykow, Joseph, editors. *The Theology of Thomas Aquinas*. Notre Dame, IN: University of Notre Dame Press, 2005.

Norris Jr, Richard A., editor. *The Christological Controversy*. Philadelphia, PA: Fortress Press, 1980.

Oglesby, Les. *C.G. Jung and Hans Urs von Balthasar: God and Evil, a Critical Comparison*. New York: Routledge, 2014.

Oliver, Simon. "Analogy, Creation and Descent in Cusa and Aquinas." In *Participation et Vision de Dieu Chez Nicolas de Cues*. Edited by Isabelle Moulin. Paris: Librairie Philosophique J. Vrin, 2017. 125–41.

Oliver, Simon. *Creation: A Guide for the Perplexed*. London: Bloomsbury, 2017.

Oliver, Simon. *Philosophy, God and Motion*. London: Routledge, 2005.

Oliver, Simon. "Trinity, Motion and Creation ex Nihilo." In *Creation and the God of Abraham*. Edited by David Burrell. Cambridge: Cambridge University Press, 2010. 133–51.

Pickstock, Catherine. *After Writing*. Oxford: Blackwell, 1998.

Pickstock, Catherine. "Duns Scotus: His Historical and Contemporary Significance." *Modern Theology* 12, no. 4 (October 2005), 543–74.

Pope Benedict XVI. "The Problem of Transubstantiation and the Question about the Meaning of the Eucharist." In *Collected Works of Joseph Ratzinger*. Translated by John Saward et al. San Francisco, CA: Ignatius Press, 2013. 218–242.

Pope Francis, *Amoris Laetitia*, especially §300, Available at: https://w2.vatican.va/content/dam/francesco/pdf/apost_exhortations/documents/papa-francesco_esortazione-ap_20160319_amoris-laetitia_en.pdf

Pope Pius Xii, *Humani generis*, available at http://www.vatican.va/content/pius-xii/en/encyclicals/documents/hf_p-xii_enc_12081950_humani-generis.html

Prevot, Andrew. *Thinking Prayer*. Notre Dame, IN: Notre Dame University Press, 2015.

Quash, Ben. *Theology and the Drama of History*. Cambridge: Cambridge University Press, 2005.

Radner, Ephraim. *Time and the Word*. Grand Rapids, MI: Eerdmans, 2016.

Rahner, Karl. *Foundations of Christian Faith*. Translated by Williams Dych. London: Crossroad, 1978.

Rahner, Karl. *Karl Rahner in Dialogue: Conversations and Interviews 1965–1982*. Translated and edited by H. Biallowons, et al. New York: Crossoad 1986.

Rahner, Karl. "Nature and Grace." In *Theological Investigations*, Vol. 4. London: Darton, Longman & Todd, 1966. 165–88.

Rahner, Karl. "The Concept of Mystery in Catholic Theology." In *Theological Investigations*, Vol. 4. New York: Crossroad Publishing, 1966. 36–73.

Rahner, Karl. "The Theology of the Symbol." In *Theological Investigations*, Vol. 4. New York: Seabury, 1966. 221–52.

Rahner, Karl. "Theology and Anthropology." In *The Word in History*. Edited by Patrick T. Burke. London: Collins, 1968. 1–24.

Rahner, Karl. *Theological Investigations Vol. I*. London: Longmann, Dartmon and Todd, 1963.

Ramsey, Michael. *The Gospel and the Catholic Church*. London: SPCK, 1990.

Ravens, David. *Luke and the Restoration of Israel*. Journal for Study of the New Testament Supplement Series 119. Sheffield: Sheffield Academic Press, 1995.

Reid, Alciun. *The Organic Development of the Liturgy*, 2nd edition. San Francisco, CA: Ignatius Press, 2005.

Reid, Alciun, editor. *The T&T Clark Companion to Liturgy*. London: Bloomsbury T&T Clark, 2016.

Reid, Alcuin. "In Pursuit of Participation—Liturgy and Liturgists in Early Modern and Post-Enlightenment Catholicism." In *T&T Clark Companion to Liturgy*. London: Bloomsbury T&T Clark, 2016. 133–152.

Reinburg, Virginia. "Liturgy and the Laity in Late Medieval and Reformation France." *The Sixteenth Century Journal* 23 (1992), 526–47.

Riches, Aaron. "Christology and *duplex hominis beatitudo*: Re-sketching the Supernatural Again." *International Journal of Systematic Theology* 14, no. 1 (January 2012). 44–69.

Riches, Aaron. *Ecce Homo*. Grand Rapids, MI: Eerdmans, 2016.

Rouwhorst, Gerard. "The Mystical Body Falling Apart?" *Religion and Theology* 23 (2016), 35–56.

Sachs, John R. "*Deus Semper Major—Ad Dei Gloriam*: The Pneumatology and Spirituality of Hans Urs von Balthasar." *Gregorianum* 74, no. 4 (1993).

Salkeld, Brett. *Transubstantiation*. Grand Rapids, MI: Baker Academic, 2019.

Sammon, Thomas Brendan. *The God Who Is Beauty: Beauty as a Divine Name in Thomas Aquinas and Dionysius the Areopagite*. Cambridge: James Clarke Company, 2014.

Schmutz, Jacob. "The Medieval Doctrine of Causality and the Theology of Pure Nature." In *Surnaturel: A Controversy at the Heart of Twentieth-Century Thomistic Thought*. Edited by Serge-Thomas Bonino. Ave Maria, FL: Sapientia Press, 2009. 203–50.

Scotus, John Duns. I *Ordinatio* 8.1.3, no. 82. Translated by Peter L. P. Simpson, available at https://www.aristotelophile.com/current.htm
Scotus, John Duns. *Questions on the Metaphysics*. In *Duns Scotus on the Will and Morality*. Translated by Allan B. Wolter. Washington, DC: The Catholic University of America Press, 1986.
Scotus, John Duns. *Quodlibetal Questions*. In *God and Creatures: The Quodlibetal Questions*. Translated by Felix Alluntis and Allan Wolter. Princeton, NJ: Princeton University Press, 1975.
Shepherd of Hermas. *The Fathers of the Church: The Apostolic Fathers*. Translated by Francis X. Glimm, et al. New York: Christian Heritage, 1947. 241–2.
Strauss, Mark. *The Davidic Messiah in Luke-Acts*. Edinburgh: T&T Clark, 1995.
Struck, Peter. *Birth of the Symbol: Ancient Readers and the Limits of Their Texts*. Princeton, NJ: Princeton University Press, 2004.
Surin, Kenneth. *Theology and the Problem of Evil*. Oxford: Basil Blackwell, 1986.
Sweeney, Conor. *Sacramental Presence after Heidegger*. Eugene, OR: Cascade, 2015.
Tanner, Kathryn. "Creation and Providence." In *The Cambridge Companion to Karl Barth*. Edited by John Webster. Cambridge: Cambridge University Press, 2000. 111–26.
Tanner, Kathryn. *Jesus, Humanity and the Trinity*. Minneapolis, MN: Fortress Press, 2001.
Ticciati, Susannah. *A New Apophaticism: Augustine and the Redemption of Signs*. Leiden: Brill, 2013.
Torrance, Alan. *Persons in Communion: An Essay on Trinitarian Description and Human Participation*. Edinburgh: T&T Clark, 1996.
Turner, Denys. *Faith, Reason and the Existence of God*. Cambridge: Cambridge University Press, 2004.
Turner, Denys. *Julian of Norwich Theologian*. New Haven, CT: Yale University Press, 2011.
Velde, Rudi A. te. "Evil, Sin, and Death: Thomas Aquinas on Original Sin." In *The Theology of Thomas Aquinas*. Edited by Rik van Nieuwenhove and Joseph Wawrykow. Notre Dame, IN: University of Notre Dame Press, 2005. 143–66.
Voderholzer, Rudolf. *Meet Henri de Lubac: His Life and Work*. San Francisco, CA: Ignatius Press, 2008.
Vos, Antonie. *The Theology of John Duns Scotus*. Boston, MA: Brill, 2018.
Walsh, Liam. "Sacraments." In *The Theology of Thomas Aquinas*. Edited by Rik Van Nieuwenhove and Joseph Wawrykow. Notre Dame, IN: University of Notre Dame Press, 2005. 326–64.
Watson, Francis. *Text and Truth: Redefining Biblical Theology*. Edinburgh: T&T Clark, 1997.
Watson, Gerard. "St Augustine and the Inner Word: Philosophical Background." *Irish Theological Quarterly* 54, no. 2 (1988), 81–92.
Wawrykow, Joseph. "Franciscan and Dominican Trinitarian Theology (Thirteenth Century): Bonaventure and Aquinas." In *The Oxford Handbook of the Trinity*. Edited by Gilles Emery and Matthew Levering. Oxford: Oxford University Press, 2011. 182–96.
Wawrykow, Joseph. "Hypostatic Union." In *The Theology of Thomas Aquinas*. Edited by Rik Van Niewenhove and Joseph Warwykow. Notre Dame, IN: Notre Dame University Press, 2005. 222–251.
Webster, John. *Essays on Christian Dogmatics II*. London: Bloomsbury, 2016.
Webster, John. "Love Is Also a Lover of Life: *Creatio Ex Nihilo* and Creaturely Goodness." *Modern Theology* 29, no. 2 (April, 2013), 156–71.

Webster, John, editor. *The Cambridge Companion to Karl Barth*. Cambridge: Cambridge University Press, 2000.

Webster, John. "Trinity and Creation." *International Journal of Systematic Theology* 12, no. 1 (January, 2010), 4–19.

Williams, Rowan. "A Paradoxical Humanism." In *The T&T Clark Companion to Henri de Lubac*. Edited by Jordan Hillebert. London: T&T Clark-Bloomsbury, 2017. xiv–xix.

Williams, Rowan. "Balthasar and the Trinity." In *The Cambridge Companion to Hans Urs von Balthasar*. Edited by Edward T. Oakes and David Moss. Cambridge: Cambridge University Press, 2004. 37–50.

Williams, Rowan. *Christ the Heart of Creation*. London: Bloomsbury T&T Clark, 2018.

Williams, Rowan. "Incarnation and the Renewal of Community." In *On Christian Theology*. Oxford: Blackwell, 2000. 225–38.

Williams, Rowan. "Insubstantial Evil." In *On Augustine*. London: Bloomsbury, 2016. 79–106.

Williams, Rowan. *On Augustine*. London: Bloomsbury, 2016.

Williams, Rowan. "The Literal Sense of Scripture." *Modern Theology* 7, no. 2 (January, 1991), 121–34.

Williams, Thomas. "The Doctrine of Univocity Is True and Salutary." *Modern Theology* 21, no. 4 (October 2005), 575–85.

Wippel, John. *Metaphysical Themes in Thomas Aquinas*. Washington, DC: Catholic University of America Press, 1984.

Wippel, John. "The Reality of Non-Existing Possibles According to Thomas Aquinas, Henry of Ghent, and Godfrey Fontaines." *The Review of Metaphysics* 34, no. 4 (1981), 729–40.

Wippel, John. *Thomas Aquinas on the Divine Ideas*. Toronto: Pontifical Institute of Medieval Studies, 1993.

Wippel, John. "Thomas Aquinas on the Ultimate Why Question: Why Is There Anything at All Rather than Nothing Whatsoever?" *The Review of Metaphysics* 60, no. 4 (June 2007), 731–53.

Wittman, Tyler. *God and Creation in the Theology of Thomas Aquinas and Karl Barth*. Cambridge: Cambridge University Press, 2018.

Wolfe, Judith. *Heidegger and Theology*. London: Bloomsbury T&T Clark, 2014.

Wolter, Michael. *The Gospel According to Luke*. Translated by Wayne Coppins and Christopher Heilig. Waco, TX: Baylor University Press, 2016.

Wong, Joseph. "Karl Rahner's Theology of Symbol and Three Models of Christology." *Heythrop Journal* 27, no 1 (1986), 1–25.

Wong, Joseph. *Logos-Symbol in the Christology of Karl Rahner*. Rome: Libreria Ateneo Salesiano, 1984.

Wood, Susan K. *Spiritual Exegesis and the Church in the Theology of Henri de Lubac*. Edinburgh: T&T Clark, 1998.

Wright, William M. "Patristic Exegetical Theory and Practice in de Lubac and Congar." *New Blackfriars* 96, no. 1061 (January 2015), 61–73.

Zizioulas, John D. "The Mystery of the Church in Orthodox Tradition." *One in Christ* 24 (1988).

INDEX

analogy 54, 58–9, 81–8
Aquinas, Thomas 53–72, 99–101, 113–16, 131 n.31, 146, 150–4, 181–3
Augustine 3–6, 14, 21–30, 34, 40–1, 48–51, 54, 82, 138, 160, 185–91, 197
Ayres, Lewis 14, 34, 45, 107–8, 111, 190

Balthasar, Hans Urs von 10–11, 42–3, 199–203
Barth, Karl 13, 140–2, 159, 175–78
Benedict XVI, Pope 153
Boersma, Hans 3, 9–10
Bossy, John 135

causality 84–8, 141–55
Cavadini, John 26–7, 186–91
Chauvet, Louis-Marie 136, 141, 147–55
Chenu, Marie-Dominique 4 n.13
Congar, Yves 39, 135
Cross, Richard 75, 77, 79 n.128, 84, 85
Cyril of Alexandria 32–4, 173, 177

death 131, 198–9
Deely, John 23, 40 n.73
desire
    general 12–16, 20, 27, 39–43, 49–50, 60–2, 71, 79, 83, 132, 138, 158–9, 162, 166, 182, 185–6, 188–9, 194–8, 205
    natural desire for the supernatural 3, 7, 41–2, 71, 90, 92–103, 91–103, 109–16, 122, 159, 163–4, 171–5, 182–5, 194
dialectics (including dialectical antitheses, dialectical contrasts) 5–7, 24, 26, 42, 46, 106–7, 125
divine ideas 66–72, 112, 169
Doolan, Gregory 66–8

Eros 41–2, 46
Exegesis 1–2, 6–7, 39–40, 47–8, 103–22

Feingold, Lawrence 42, 92, 94, 100, 109, 112, 114–15
filioque 15, 41, 61, 72

Garrigou-Lagrange, Reginald 178–85
grace 2–5, 7, 15–16, 36–7, 42, 71, 86–8, 90–116, 122, 136, 141, 147–50, 154, 159, 164–91

Heidegger, Martin 12, 31–2, 140, 148–52, 158, 165–6
Hoff, Johannes 176–7
Horan, Daniel 55, 72–3
Hütter, Reinhardt 92, 97, 103–6, 111 n.85, 112, 114

inner word (word of the heart) 14, 20–2, 26–9, 49–50, 56, 58–9, 72, 82, 84, 99, 186–9
intellect 23, 26, 54–84, 99, 114–15, 163–4, 178–84, 188–9

Kilby, Karen 43

Lindbeck, George 36–7
liturgical reform 134–5
liturgy 2, 115, 126, 134
Logos 12, 16, 23–4, 28, 31, 47, 51, 66, 71, 82, 93, 99, 101–3, 113, 140, 158–9, 169, 173, 181–3, 194, 203
Long, D. Stephen 63–4
Long, Stephen A. 3 n.7, 13 n.49, 92–8, 168 n.41
love 11, 13–16, 19–22, 26–31, 40–5, 47, 49–50, 53, 56, 58–72, 77–8, 82–3, 90, 99, 101–2, 109–10, 113, 115–16, 122, 127, 132, 136–8, 152–3, 157–67, 174–5, 177–91, 193–205
Lubac, Henri de 1–11, 13, 15–17, 19–20, 39–51, 92–103, 106–20, 123–35, 139, 141, 157, 158–60, 164, 170–5, 183, 186, 189, 193

Markus, R. A. 21, 23–4, 28
Marshall, Bruce 181–2
Mary 116–22
McPartlan, Paul 126–30
Metz, Johann Baptist 36–7
Milbank, John 10–11, 36–8, 43, 61–2, 98, 128, 164, 202
motion 10, 13–16, 44, 65, 72, 90, 93, 98–9, 113, 122, 124, 131, 138, 139, 145–6, 152, 169, 171, 174–5, 183–5, 194, 197
mutual inclusion 62, 68, 76, 77, 79
mystery
    God 3, 91, 124, 157–70
    humanity 103 n.43
    sacraments 20, 39–49, 125–7, 130–3, 136–7, 147, 150
mysticism 170–85

nature
    Christ, divine and human 33–5, 37, 143–4
    divine nature 61, 64–5, 67, 70–1, 97–8, 162, 170
    human nature 2, 7, 10, 13, 15–16, 91–116, 122, 158, 164, 167–8, 171–5, 178, 184, 198
    pure nature 2, 8, 13, 36–8, 54, 87, 91–116, 122, 158, 169, 178–84
neo-scholasticism/neo-thomism 2–3, 13, 16, 36, 42, 93–8, 104–5, 115, 158–9, 175–9, 185
Nestorius 32–3
Nicholas of Cusa 12, 66–7, 169, 176–7

Oliver, Simon 99 n.26, 102 n.37
ontotheology 140, 150–1, 166

paradox 3, 7, 10, 15–16, 23–4, 41–2, 45, 49, 50, 62, 64, 72, 76–7, 79, 90–1, 96–9, 102, 110, 126–7, 133, 139, 159, 161 n.9, 163, 167, 169–70, 173, 181–2, 184, 194
perichoresis 77, 80, 163, 169, 183, 189, 194
Pickstock, Catherine 68 n.73, 77 n.116
proportionality 42, 94–8, 102–4
psychological analogy 54–63, 76–81

Rahner, Karl 14, 20, 30–9, 44, 50, 101, 103, 150, 159–70, 185, 198
Ramsey, Michael 129–30
redemption 15, 26, 51, 90, 101, 109, 113, 130–1, 138–40, 147, 154, 159, 168–70, 174, 184, 186, 195
ressourcement 1, 2, 6, 8–9, 14, 17, 31, 39
resurrection 19, 25, 112, 129, 143, 176, 199, 204
Riches, Aaron 33 n.53, 173 n.58

sacraments
    baptism 129–30
    Christ 175
    church 7, 124–40
    creation 89, 174–5
    Eucharist 31, 124–37, 152–3
    general 3–4, 7, 9–10, 20, 30, 39–49, 131
    Scotus, John Duns 15, 72–90, 189.
semiotics 21–4, 49
sin 5, 25–8, 43, 86, 116, 130–1, 175, 186, 188, 196–205
spiritual interpretation of scripture 5–6, 8, 13, 15, 46–8, 92–3, 103–22, 128, 151–2, 160, 186–90
substantive relations 64–5
symbolic inclusion 5, 24, 26, 30, 42, 44–6, 48–50, 54, 60, 119, 189

Tanner, Kathryn 170, 177
time 12–13, 15–16, 112–13, 118, 121, 129, 131, 133, 137, 139–40, 154
transcendence
    divine 28, 149, 167, 172, 183
    human 36, 98, 103, 111, 115, 120, 122, 163, 177–8
Trinity
    Father 2, 9, 11–12, 14–16, 19–51, 53–63, 65–72, 76–9, 89–90, 99–100, 102, 114–15, 126, 132–3, 151, 157–9, 163, 166, 168–9, 173, 181–2, 199–205
    general 2, 11–12, 15, 29, 29, 30, 33–4, 42–3, 51, 53–90, 95, 113, 115, 140, 151–2, 155, 157–60, 166, 180–2, 186–91, 199–202
    Son 2, 11–12, 14–16, 19–51, 54, 56–72, 76–8, 82–3, 88–90, 99–100, 102,

104, 109, 112–15, 118, 126, 132–3, 151, 159, 163, 168–9, 173–5, 181–2, 184, 189, 190, 193–205

Spirit 2, 5, 9–12, 14–16, 19–51, 53–63, 65–72, 76–8, 80–1, 83, 88–90, 92, 99–100, 102, 109–11, 113, 115, 117–22, 130–3, 135–40, 144, 155, 158, 163–66, 168–9, 172–5, 180–2, 184, 186, 189–90, 196, 199, 202–5

univocity 74–7, 81–8

Webster, John 141–7, 151, 177
will 41, 55–82, 84, 87, 99–100, 163–41, 180–1, 188–9
Williams, Rowan 25, 118, 130, 137, 199, 201
Wippel, John 63 n.52, 100 n.28

Zizioulas, John 126–9

www.ingramcontent.com/pod-product-compliance
Lightning Source LLC
Chambersburg PA
CBHW062223300426
44115CB00012BA/2193